DUNCAN MACMILLAN: PLAYS ONE

T0322378

Duncan Macmillan

PLAYS ONE

methuen | drama

LONDON • NEW YORK • OXFORD • NEW DELHI • SYDNEY

METHUEN DRAMA
Bloomsbury Publishing Plc
50 Bedford Square, London, WC1B 3DP, UK
1385 Broadway, New York, NY 10018, USA
29 Earlsfort Terrace, Dublin 2, Ireland

BLOOMSBURY, METHUEN DRAMA and the Methuen Drama logo are
trademarks of Bloomsbury Publishing Plc

First published in Great Britain by Oberon Books 2016
Reprinted 2020
This edition published by Methuen Drama 2021
Reprinted 2023, (twice), 2024

A catalogue record for this book is available from the British Library.

ISBN: PB: 978-1-3502-7029-9
eBook: 978-1-7831-9338-7

Printed and bound in Great Britain

To find out more about our authors and books visit www.bloomsbury.com
and sign up for our newsletters.

Contents

Introduction

I sometimes think that theatre is the perfect art form for death. It's so easy to kill a character. Rosencrantz and Guildenstern are dead because the four words that begin this sentence are spoken aloud. And each night, the event of a play lives its full span, every last one of its words gets spoken – and then it dies. That particular performance is now impossible to revisit or reclaim or redo. It is over: decisively gone.

And these five plays all, in their different ways, think about the way life might tip over into death – try and find a way of holding life from death, of coping with the climate, with depression and suicide and addiction. Duncan, like all the greatest writers, distils whole lifetimes into single luminous evenings.

Lungs jump-cuts across two whole histories, two parallel lines which the play weaves a connecting thread between: a couple falling together, falling apart. It's like an internet history recording crucial moments, saving their lives. *Monster* too is about saving a life: carving a bright future from a dark history. And the list that forms the spine of *Every Brilliant Thing* might really be life or death for someone - perhaps someone in the audience.

But that's just one way of arranging them. Here's another:

Monster is the EP, finding the voice; *Lungs*, the breakthrough, skyrocket, platinum-selling, worldwide album; *People, Places & Things* and *Every Brilliant Thing* the first two albums from the mature artist, striking out in unusual instrumentations, new forms. There are also two collaboration records, with unexpected guest vocalists – two dates: *2071* and *1984*[1].

And here's one more:

Emma thinks 'quixotic' means 'romantic, chivalrous. Visionary'. What she doesn't seem to know is that it also means 'impractical, foolhardy, unrealistic. Likely to fail.' I don't know whether the final moments of *People, Places & Things* are pure optimism or pure capitalism. I don't know whether Duncan intends the play to endorse the 'leap of faith' that takes Emma to rehab, and I don't know whether he wants us to stop having babies – or stop living – to save the world. I'm not sure he knows the answers. But they're good questions.

They're global themes, not existential ones – and these plays think about the realities of being alive in the world right now, about the rituals of the early 21st century, about checking into rehab, starting the baby conversation, putting out the recycling or putting the family dog to sleep. And the way the success or failure of those rituals can break and change us, even as we try and break and change them.

It's rare for a new play to get a first production that does the text full justice: mostly, the rehearsal time is spent getting the engine to run the course of the evening without stalling. And none of these plays are old enough yet to have had major revivals; and I'm looking forward to seeing them as fully unpacked for their caffeinated, frustrated, funny line-by-line or for their formal and theatrical innovation as much as they have been for their socio-political anxieties.

That said, one other way of arranging these five plays would be by their deep love for the littlest details of what it means to be alive: trying to see not just broad-stroke good things, but *every* brilliant thing. A cigarette. A picnic. Good music, played on vinyl. Real coffee. Donuts (there are several donuts). These things might be small. But then small might be all that we need to make the difference between life and death.

Welcome to Duncan Macmillan's first collection of plays.

I think they're great.

Robert Icke
March 2016

---

[1] Footnote: this volume is an appendix to this collection, also published by Methuen Drama.

MONSTER

For Mum

In memory of Emma Bailey
(May 1983–May 2007)

Monster won two prizes in the inaugural Bruntwood Playwriting Competition. It was first performed at the Royal Exchange Theatre, Manchester, on 20 June 2007, with the following cast:

TOM, Andrew French

DARRYL, Mikey North

JODI, Sarah-Louise Young

RITA, Mary Jo Randle

Director Jacob Murray

Designer Louis Price

Lighting Richard Owen

Sound Claire Windsor

Voice Mark Langley

Characters

TOM

DARRYL

JODI

RITA

A table and two chairs. They remain onstage until the final scene. The action of the play takes place in 2007.

'The monster a child knows best and is most concerned with [is] the monster he feels or fears himself to be.'

– BRUNO BETTELHEIM

'You made your children what they are [...] These children that come at you with knives, they are your children. You taught them. I didn't teach them. I just tried to help them stand up [...] You can project it back at me, but I am only what lives inside each and every one of you. My father is your system [...] I am only what you made me. I am a reflection of you.'

– CHARLES MANSON

Morning. School.

The sound of children running, laughing, shouting, screaming.

TOM sits at the table. He looks at his watch and straightens his tie. He sits rigidly upright, staring at the door.

,

He glances at his shoes, then back at the door.

,

He rubs one of his shoes on the back of his trousers, then leans down to look at it.

He sits back up.

,

He leans down and rubs his shoe with his sleeve.

DARRYL enters, his hooded top hanging off one shoulder, underneath which he wears a burgundy school sweatshirt. He is chewing. He drops his bag on the floor and stares at TOM.

TOM sees him and stands.

,

TOM   Darryl.

Sit down.
Sit down Darryl.

,

Alright, let's run through some rules.
First, and most important, is that you get here on time for the lesson to begin. That means before the lesson is due to start. That way you'll be ready to go.

Second, the bag goes on the hook.

DARRYL looks at the hook.

,

Sit down please Darryl.

I'm Tom,

TOM extends his hand for DARRYL to shake. DARRYL stares at it.

I'm going to be with you for the rest of this year.

,

TOM withdraws his hand.

,

Third, there's no eating during lessons. What are you eating?

DARRYL opens his mouth and sticks out his tongue, on which is a large blue sweet.

Bin.

Bin.

In the bin please Darryl.

,

DARRYL crunches the sweet in his mouth, then chews it slowly and swallows it, without ever taking his eyes off TOM.

Silence.

Sit down please Darryl.

Silence.

We're not getting off to a good start here are we?

Am I going to have to call your Mum?

DARRYL   Don't think so.

TOM   I will.

DARRYL   She's dead init?

                '

TOM   I'm sorry.

DARRYL   Live with my Nan.

TOM   Sorry Darryl.

DARRYL   What you done?

TOM   No, really I'm

DARRYL   you ain't done nothing.

TOM   No.

DARRYL   Did it herself.

                '

DARRYL sits opposite TOM, leaving his bag where it is.

                '

TOM   Darryl, do you understand why you've been
                taken out of lessons?

                Darryl?

                '

DARRYL   Yes.

TOM   Why?

DARRYL   'Cause Head of Year's a bitch init?

TOM   No.

DARRYL   Beyatch.

TOM   No.

DARRYL	Wants a smack.
TOM	Darryl
DARRYL	Godzilla.
TOM	Now,
DARRYL	she come up in here now I'd box her down. I'd be like, 'hey, Miss, man, eat this bitch' and she'd be like 'noooo' and I'd like 'booosch!' like that thing that thing have you seen it, that thing that video mobile
TOM	Darryl,
DARRYL	that 'Happy Slappers'.
TOM	Darryl we don't refer to it as that in this school.
DARRYL	It's wicked.
TOM	What do we refer to it as?
DARRYL	Fucking excellent.
TOM	Common assault.
DARRYL	Oh yeah, yeah. Common assault yeah. Video the common assault on your mobile and send it everyone. It's slammin'.
TOM	Darryl, three students have been excluded this year for
DARRYL	there's this one, yeah, where they get this girl in a headlock, yeah, they hold her so she can't move and then 'bout ten a these guys
TOM	I don't want to hear about that Darryl. I'm not impressed by that.
DARRYL	I got Saddam. What's your number? I'll text it you.

TOM	Will you put that away?
DARRYL	You got Bluetooth?
TOM	Put your phone away.
DARRYL	Have you though?
TOM	Sit properly please Darryl.
DARRYL	Bet you got an old dinosaur phone init? Big cream-coloured brick with antennae and shit.
TOM	Sit on your chair properly please.
DARRYL	Like your crepes init?
TOM	My what?
DARRYL	Your shoes.
	,
TOM	What about my shoes?
DARRYL	They're shit. Sorry, but they is. They're wack. You gived them an ikkle bit a scrub and t'ing, polish dem up an' that. But dey still cheap init? Laces don't match. New laces. Old shoes. You had dem for *time*.
TOM	You're very observant Darryl.
DARRYL	True dat. Keep my eyes open init?
TOM	I'm impressed.
DARRYL	Can I axe you a question?
TOM	Darryl,
DARRYL	can I though?
TOM	No. Not right now.

DARRYL   Gosh man. Just want to arks a question init?

'

TOM sits down.

TOM   What do you want to know?

DARRYL   What would you do, yeah, if you were on
a plane and someone was like 'you're all
gonna die, I'm gonna fly this bitch into a
wall'?

TOM   Darryl, why don't we look at the

DARRYL   would you be scared?

TOM   Darryl, come on let's

DARRYL   would you though? I bet you would.
I bet you'd shit yourself.

TOM   Darryl, alright, listen,

DARRYL   did you go to this school?

TOM   No, I

I went to school in Surrey.

DARRYL   Is it?

TOM   Yes.

DARRYL   Why?

DARRYL has taken a lighter from his pocket.

TOM   Because that's where I lived.
Will you sit on your chair properly Darryl?

DARRYL   Well posh init?
Surrey?

TOM   Not really.

DARRYL ignites the lighter.

Darryl give me that. You know the rules.

DARRYL runs a finger through the flame.

DARRYL	Can I axe you a question?
TOM	Give that to me. Now.
DARRYL	Why?
TOM	Because of fire regulations.
DARRYL	I'm not gonna burn the school down.
TOM	Just give it to me please.

,

| DARRYL | Alright. |

DARRYL pushes the lighter across the table.

TOM reaches over, takes it and puts it in his pocket.

,

TOM	Tell me how you feel your lessons have been going. How about History?
DARRYL	Can I axe you a question?
TOM	If you do some work you can ask all the questions you want.
DARRYL	Can I?
TOM	Absolutely.
DARRYL	Can I axe you one now though?
TOM	Work first.
DARRYL	But it's important.
TOM	Is it?
DARRYL	Yeah. I really think I should be allowed to arks it.

,

TOM   Well, I'm sorry, you'll have to do a little bit
           of reading for me first. And stop picking your
           teeth.

DARRYL   But I won't be able to do anything 'til
           I've axed my question. Believe. Can't
           concentrate, you get me?

TOM   Where's your History book?

DARRYL   I'm serious.

TOM   So am I.

           ,

DARRYL   What would happen, yeah, if

TOM   Darryl, I'm not answering any questions until

DARRYL   this is about History.

TOM   Is it?

DARRYL   Yes man, Sir. 'Bout the stuff we've been
           doing in History bruv.

TOM   Darryl,

DARRYL   it's historical.
           His-tor-i-cal.

           ,

TOM   Go on.

           ,

DARRYL   What would happen, yeah, if
           I mean, what would you do, yeah

           what if you

TOM   if you don't have a question then

DARRYL	I do man, chillax. I'm phrasing it, yeah?
	Gosh.
	,
	What if, yeah if you, like, woke up one day and both your legs had been blown off what would you do?
	'Cause in History this guy was in his house and a bomb landed boom! Right on his house, yeah, and he woke up and he didn't have any legs.
	,
TOM	What's your question?
DARRYL	Are you deaf?
TOM	No.
DARRYL	Do you have a hearing problem though?
TOM	Darryl, I just didn't understand your question.
DARRYL	Didn't understand.
TOM	No.
DARRYL	Wasn't clear enough for you is it?
TOM	That's right.
DARRYL	Question was, yeah, listen up Surrey. What would you do if you woke up without legs?
	,
TOM	What would *you* do?
DARRYL	I don't know.

15

It'd be well bad.

TOM	Do you know why the war began? How it started?
DARRYL	Whose fault?
TOM	Yes.
DARRYL	Blame game.
TOM	If you like.

,

DARRYL	What would happen, yeah, if you got both your legs blowed off and your arms blowed off?

And your head blowed off?
What would you do?

TOM	Where's your History book?

,

DARRYL	History book.
TOM	Where is it Darryl?

,

DARRYL	On a shelf.
TOM	On a shelf.
DARRYL	Shelf in a room.
TOM	Darryl, I'm not impressed.
DARRYL	It's on a shelf man, in the room.
TOM	Darryl
DARRYL	in a building
TOM	Darryl

DARRYL	let me finish.
TOM	We can do without the book.
DARRYL	Can I axe you a question?
TOM	No.
DARRYL	Are you gay?
TOM	Darryl, that is really none of
DARRYL	are you though?
TOM	That's not relevant.
DARRYL	Do you love cock?
TOM	Darryl, I I don't appreciate being asked questions like that.
DARRYL	Is it?
TOM	Yes.
DARRYL	You don't appreciate it?
TOM	It's inappropriate.
DARRYL	Oh right. Don't appreciate those kind of questions is it?
TOM	That's right.
DARRYL	It's inappropriate.
TOM	Exactly.
	,
DARRYL	You are though init?
TOM	No. I'm not. Actually.

I've got a girlfriend.

DARRYL   Have you?

TOM   Yes.

DARRYL   Have you though?

TOM   Darryl, History.

DARRYL   Because Mr Winters in upper school has got kids and he's a bandit.

TOM   Well, I don't know about Mr Winters.

DARRYL   You saying he is?

TOM   No, I'm saying I don't know him.

DARRYL   I fucking knew it. Bender.

TOM   Darryl, we don't use language like that in this school.

DARRYL   Don't we?

TOM   We don't.

DARRYL   Fucking or bender?

TOM   What?

DARRYL   What words? Fucking or bender? Or fucking bender?

TOM   Where's your History book?

DARRYL   What book?

TOM   The book you've been using in History.

DARRYL   Haven't got a book.

TOM   What have you got?

DARRYL   Ain't got nuffing.

TOM   In your bag.

DARRYL	In my bag.
TOM	What have you got in your bag?
DARRYL	Ain't you listening?
TOM	Your bag's empty?
DARRYL	What did I just say?
TOM	Why do you have an empty bag?
DARRYL	Is she fit?
TOM	What? Who?
DARRYL	Your bitch. She blonde?
TOM	Darryl, that's none of your business, and please don't
DARRYL	that's you init? Down with the swirl.
TOM	Darryl,
DARRYL	she a screamer?
TOM	Darryl, why do you think you're not in lessons?

,

DARRYL	'Cause I bit Kieran.
TOM	No. Did you?
DARRYL	Bit his head.
TOM	Why?
DARRYL	Oh, you know.
TOM	No, I don't.
DARRYL	Yeah you do, you know sometimes it's like you know sometimes you kind of like
	just don't

fit.

Like you're a

no matter what you do nobody really gets you.
You get me?

TOM   Yes.

DARRYL   Which shouldn't matter because they're all
             they're all just cunts anyway. They're all
             fucking

             just want to fucking

DARRYL kicks the table.

             ,

             does my head in.

TOM   Okay.

DARRYL   It's like at Mum's funeral, yeah, bunch a
             people in this church all hushed up. No
             sound, everyone just sat there and I wanted
             to shout something, you get me?

             ,

TOM   Yes. Yes I do.

DARRYL   Just holler. Just shout some fucking, sorry,
             some bad words or some shit. Or just scream
             loud as I could. Or, like, when school took
             us to the museum and I just wanted to break
             everything.
             I didn't. Didn't touch nothing. Kept hands in
             pockets.
             It's like with Nan's special glasses, you know

DARRYL holds his hand up as if holding a glass.

             like crystal or whatever, her posh stuff I just
             want to drop it. Or her angels. The house is full

of fucking statues of bitches with wings and fat
flying naked kids. Sometimes I go a bit Mariah
Carey and dash one at a wall. A bit Barrymore.
You know fire extinguishers?

TOM   Do I know

DARRYL   I just want to let them off. I done it once with
Kieran, we nicked one from his Dad's garage
and let it off round the back a Safeway's.
Hyphy.

TOM   What else?

DARRYL   Uh?

TOM   What else do you
how else do you feel sometimes?

,

DARRYL   You know the station?

TOM   Yes.

DARRYL   Sometimes when the train's coming and I'm
stood behind someone on the platform and
they're well near the edge there's a second
when I think I'm gonna ram 'em. Shove 'em
square into the train yeah?

TOM   Right.

DARRYL   Don't you get that? Ever?
Like when you walk past a pregnant woman
don't you just want to fucking thump them in
the stomach?

TOM   No.

DARRYL   I never done it.

TOM   Darryl, that's really

21

DARRYL   and like sometimes when I'm helping Nan
in the kitchen and her back is turned, she's
got this knife in her kitchen, yeah, this fuck
off great big fuck and I'll have it in my hand
'cause I'm opening a packet or whatever and
she'll be at the sink and she's just a just a just
a

TOM   Darryl,

DARRYL   just a cardigan, like a little wall of wool and
I'm like

TOM   Darryl, have you ever talked to a

DARRYL   it's intense man, like I got
not like I've
not that I'd

TOM   because I really think you should

DARRYL   just get vexed though init? Nan says I ain't
got no feelings.

But it ain't even like that though.

You know
sometimes it gets bad yeah and

I remember what it was like before I was born.
I remember how it felt.

You know what Mr

TOM   what?

DARRYL   Your name. Mr

,

TOM   just call me Tom.

DARRYL   Ain't you a real teacher?

TOM   I

yes. Yes I am.

DARRYL   You ain't though is you? You're from an
          agency.

TOM   No.

DARRYL   Can't believe dis. Now dey be leavin'
          me with an agency. Well you can go fuck
          yourself agency. I ain't doin' shit.

TOM   I'm getting back into teaching. I trained in

DARRYL   to rass.

TOM   You're my
          the school is understaffed and
          they've brought me in to

DARRYL   rah rah rah.

TOM   You're kind of like my project.

DARRYL   Oh shit.

TOM   Darryl. Language.

DARRYL   To raatid. Fucking shit.

TOM   Darryl.

DARRYL   You know how many teachers I've had this
          year?

TOM   How many?

DARRYL   I been out of lessons four months and I've
          had nine support teachers.
          I counted.

TOM   Well, I'm sorry about that.

DARRYL   Bad init?

TOM   It is.

DARRYL	It's shit. It's fucking shit agency.
TOM	Darryl, listen, I'm here at least until the end of the year. I'm not going anywhere. I've got to be here.
DARRYL	Good for you.
TOM	I mean it.
DARRYL	For your project.
TOM	That's right.

DARRYL looks out of the window.

,

Tell me about what you've been doing in History.

DARRYL	History?
TOM	Yeah.

,

Or Geography?

English?

,

Maths?

DARRYL	Can I axe you a question?

,

TOM	Go on.
DARRYL	Did you always want to be a teacher?
TOM	Why do you ask?
DARRYL	Did you though?
TOM	What do you want to be when you grow up?

	I mean, when you leave school. What do you want to do? Eventually?
DARRYL	Because you're a bit old to be a trainee teacher.
TOM	Not really.
DARRYL	You are though init?
TOM	Not really. And I'm not exactly a
DARRYL	I'm going to be famous.

,

TOM	As what?
DARRYL	Uh?
TOM	Famous as what? Famous for doing what? You can't just be famous.
DARRYL	Can.
TOM	Alright. But you wouldn't want that.
DARRYL	I would actually.
TOM	It's not a it's not a brilliant thing to be. Everyone knowing who you are. You not knowing who they are.
DARRYL	Oh. My. Gosh.
TOM	What?
DARRYL	You're a trainee teacher.
TOM	Yes.
DARRYL	So shut up.

,

TOM	I was

and this is really none of your business, but
I used to have another job and
I decided to retrain as a teacher.

The other job was

it became

,

so, you're right. I am a bit older than most
trainee teachers.

Darryl.
Will you sit properly on your

DARRYL   drawn the short straw.

TOM   How do you mean?

DARRYL   This school.

,

TOM   I

DARRYL   you heard of Charles Manson?

,

TOM   Yes.

DARRYL   He's well famous.

TOM   How did you hear about Manson?

DARRYL   Was you fired?

TOM   When? What?

DARRYL   What job was it?

TOM   It

I worked in the city.

DARRYL   Oh right. In the city.

TOM   Yes. How did you hear about

DARRYL   big business.

TOM   Yes,
             I suppose so.

DARRYL   Bet you're well loaded.

TOM   I wasn't very high up.

DARRYL   Not high up.

TOM   Middle management.

DARRYL   In the middle yeah?

TOM   Brand management.

DARRYL   Labels.

TOM   Food, not clothing. But, yeah, that's right.
             Marketing certain foods to children. I was

             originally I trained as a
             in psychology. Educational psychology. And I
             I intended to be
             to go into
             education. But in the
             I mean, as it turns out I went into

             business.

             There's a term in psychology known as the
             educable moment when a child is at their most
             receptive and that's something that advertisers
             are very interested in and

             ,

             Darryl, how did you hear about Charles
             Manson?

DARRYL   Carl got this DVD yeah, from America. It's
             wicked.

27

TOM	Who's Carl?
DARRYL	Nan's boyfriend.
TOM	I'm not sure he should be showing you films like that.
DARRYL	You know what he did?
TOM	Carl?
DARRYL	Manson.
TOM	Yes.
DARRYL	Wicked init?
TOM	No.
DARRYL	Yes it is. It's well good. Painted the walls with blood. He's still alive init?
TOM	I don't know.
DARRYL	He is. So was you fired then?
TOM	No. No I
DARRYL	you was though, init?
TOM	I wasn't fired.
DARRYL	I bet you was though.
TOM	Who else do you admire?
DARRYL	Ad-what?
TOM	Who else is wicked?
DARRYL	Tupac.
TOM	Why?

DARRYL   He's made like a billion albums since being
          gunned down.

          *DARRYL drums loudly on the table, making the sound of a
          machine gun.*

          Plus UK hip hop is dry.

TOM   Do you talk like this to everyone?

DARRYL   Like what?

TOM   The way you speak. Do you speak that way
          with everybody or are you just trying to
          impress me?
          You think you'll impress me by talking that
          way? Because I'm black.

DARRYL   Shame. Are you being racist?

TOM   I'm just asking you whether you would talk
          like this to me if I was white like you. If you
          think that by talking like that we'll have
          some kind of connection because you think
          that's how black people talk.

DARRYL   Are you cussing me? You calling me a
          wangsta?

TOM   A what?

DARRYL   A wigga?

TOM   I'm just asking whether

DARRYL   you ain't black.

          '

TOM   Excuse me?

DARRYL   You're from Surrey.

          '

TOM   I'm not going to explain or justify my
               heritage to you Darryl.

DARRYL   You ain't black.

               ,

               TOM looks down at his hands.

               ,

               He takes a deep breath and looks back up at DARRYL.

               ,

TOM   Who else do you admire?

               ,

DARRYL   Jack the Ripper.

TOM   Okay.

DARRYL   You seen the movie?

TOM   No.

DARRYL   It's well bad.

TOM   Who else?

DARRYL   It's shit.

TOM   Did Carl show that to you?

DARRYL   Was it hard? Your middle job?

               ,

TOM   It had

               ,

               certain pressures.
               Certain pressures which made it

               it's not what I intended to use my training for
               and

,

I found it difficult to progress.

I was there for a number of years and I was never

or they'd give me jobs that I wasn't really right for and I wasn't quite equipped to

DARRYL   did you meet any celebrities?

TOM   One or two.

DARRYL   Who?

TOM   Darryl, I think you've had enough questions for now.

DARRYL   Who though?

TOM   Darryl, let's do some work.

DARRYL   Oh my gosh. Who?

TOM   Well

DARRYL   Osama Bin Laden.
            He's excellent.

TOM   No Darryl, he isn't.

DARRYL   What do you think it would be like to kill someone?

            ,

TOM   I think it would be pretty horrible.

DARRYL   Why?

TOM   It's just about the worst thing you can do.

DARRYL   Why?
            What would happen if I did? What would happen to me?

,

| TOM | Well, |
| | you'd be put in prison. |

| DARRYL | Is it? |

| TOM | For the rest of your life. |

| DARRYL | How would you do it? |

| TOM | I wouldn't. |

| DARRYL | Gun. |
| | Blat blat. |

| TOM | Darryl, you're wasting time now. Let's |

| DARRYL | AK47. When you absolutely |

| TOM | Darryl, |

| DARRYL | positively |

| TOM | please Darryl, |

| DARRYL | have to kill every motherfucker in the room |
| | accept no substitute. |

| TOM | Very good. Now let's |

| DARRYL | or just stab them. Like Manson. |

DARRYL bangs the table.

Rip 'em apart. That's what I'd do. Get close.
There's this knife in my Nan's kitchen which is

| TOM | Darryl. |

| DARRYL | It ain't even about how though, it's about |

| TOM | Darryl. |

| DARRYL | What? You're disrupting my flow man. Cha! |

| TOM | Do you want me to call senior staff? |

DARRYL	Why?
TOM	Because you're not working.
DARRYL	I haven't done anything.
TOM	You're not working.
DARRYL	Yeah, but I ain't done nothing wrong.
TOM	Sit on your chair properly.
DARRYL	You getting pissed off?
TOM	No.
DARRYL	Getting well angry.
TOM	I don't get angry.
DARRYL	Is it?
TOM	Let's just
DARRYL	not ever?
TOM	I'm not like that.
DARRYL	Like what?
TOM	Let's look at History. Alright?
DARRYL	History's *long*.
TOM	History's probably the most important subject.
DARRYL	Why?
TOM	Because well, because
DARRYL	you don't know, do you?
TOM	Yes.
DARRYL	Do you though?

TOM   Yes.

DARRYL   Except you don't though.

TOM   It's important to know.

DARRYL   Why?

TOM   Well,
              History's important to learn about so you don't
              end up repeating old mistakes.

DARRYL   Might make mistakes is it?

TOM   Exactly.

DARRYL   If I don't learn History?

TOM   That's right.

DARRYL   Like what?

              ,

TOM   Well, like

              like all the things that have gone wrong in
              the world. If we forget about all that, we'll
              inevitably end up

DARRYL   like wars and shit.

TOM   That's right. Exactly.

DARRYL   Except there's still wars init?

TOM   What, now? Now there's lots, yes.

DARRYL   England's at war init?

TOM   Well, the British government has engaged in

DARRYL   ain't they done their History though? Don't
              the government know their History?

TOM   What do you know about the world wars?

DARRYL	You seen 'Pearl Harbour'?
TOM	No.
DARRYL	You seen 'Platoon'?
TOM	Darryl, do you know when the First World War began? Will you sit properly on your chair? I'm not telling you again.

,

Listen,
if you do well today I'll

I'll give you a sticker.

,

DARRYL	Yeah?
TOM	Yes.

,

DARRYL	Your job, yeah,
TOM	you can only have a sticker if you concentrate for the rest of the lesson.

,

DARRYL	Can I pick which one?
TOM	Which what?
DARRYL	Sticker.
TOM	You haven't earned it yet.
DARRYL	But can I though?
TOM	Yes. If you work for the rest of the lesson you can choose what sticker you want.

DARRYL   Gold one?

TOM   If you want.

DARRYL   Gold ones are best init?
                Blinga blinga.

TOM   Gold ones are the best. Definitely.
                But you'll have to work really hard to earn a
                gold one.

                Silence.

DARRYL   What do you want me to do?

2

Evening. House.

TOM has taken his jacket and tie off. JODI sits on the table behind him, massaging his shoulders. She has a tea towel over her shoulder and a glass of wine by her side.

,

TOM   God help me if he ever gets bored of stickers. Then I really am screwed.

,

She kisses the top of his head.

It's almost enough to make me want to move back to the city.

JODI climbs down from the table. She drains her wine glass.

It's a joke.

JODI   It's not funny.

JODI exits to the kitchen.

TOM   I didn't mean

I'm

,

TOM stares at his shoes.

JODI enters, carrying cutlery and two tall glasses which she places on the table. TOM takes one and stares at it as JODI arranges the cutlery.

JODI   I hope you're hungry.

It's all come out of a book, so it should be good.

,

It's in the oven.
Duck.

Something a bit posh.

TOM is holding the glass in the air as if about to drop it.

,

Tom?

,

I've finished the red.
There's some champagne in the fridge.

Actually Tom, will you do me a favour and
fetch it?

JODI is watching him.

,

Tom?

,

TOM	Sorry. Yes. Yes I'll go.
	Did you say champagne?
JODI	What's wrong?
TOM	I'm sorry.
JODI	What's happening?
TOM	Nothing, I'm fine. Just tired. It's really starting to
	been a long week.
JODI	Have a lie down, I can keep dinner going.
TOM	No, I'm

JODI	do you want a glass of water? I can
TOM	stop being so jumpy.
JODI	I'm not. I'm looking after you.
TOM	I don't need to be

I'm fine.
I'm fine.

,

| JODI | Are you hungry? |
| TOM | Yes. |

Yes I think so.

JODI	Have a drink.
TOM	Alright.
JODI	It's in the kitchen.

,

| TOM | Right. |

TOM stands and puts the glass on the table. He walks to the kitchen.

| JODI | Tom. |

Look at me.

He does.

Hey.

,

Hey.

,

He's just a kid.

I love you.

Okay?

,

TOM   Okay.

JODI   Okay?

,

TOM   Yes.

,

He leaves. JODI watches him go, anxiously.

,

She hurriedly takes a candle and some matches from a drawer in the table, and lights it. She takes a small jewellery box from her pocket, opens it and looks at the ring inside. She is very nervous.

She closes the box and places it in front of where he was sitting.

She dims the lights.

She sits at the table.

She checks her appearance, touching her hair and straightening her clothes.

She sits staring at the box, biting her lip.

,

She impulsively grabs the box and hides it.

She blows out the candle and puts her head in her hands.

,

She composes herself.

,

She checks her appearance, touching her hair and straightening her clothes.

She relights the candle.

,

She slowly places the box back where it was.

She checks herself and notices the tea towel, pulls it off her shoulder and sits on it.

TOM enters with the bottle. He is oblivious to the change in lighting.

> I couldn't find the glasses.

JODI   They're right here.

TOM   Oh.

TOM smiles.

He sits and begins to unwrap the foil from the champagne.

JODI watches him nervously.

,

> Thing about Darryl is that I think he could've been quite bright, or at least, not as disruptive, if he'd been brought up better.

JODI   Darryl.

TOM   That's his name.
        I've told you that.

> This pasty little white kid who talks like he's straight outta Compton.

JODI smiles.

JODI   I still don't get it. I thought the point was you were going to be paired up with a black kid. Be a role model.

TOM	Yeah well.
	You know, on my first day he even said that I wasn't black.
	,
JODI	Well,
	,
TOM	what?
JODI	Nothing.
TOM	Go on.
JODI	No nothing.
	Just,
	you're not really are you?
TOM	Yes Jodi, I am.
JODI	Yes I know, of course you are.
	But you're from Surrey.
TOM	That's what he said, what does that mean? What difference does that
JODI	just
	you're not very
	street.
	Are you though?
TOM	What does that matter? That's got nothing to do with
JODI	all I mean is that
	how many black kids did you know growing up?
TOM	That's completely

JODI   alright. Alright, forget it.

TOM shakes his head. JODI watches him removing the foil from the bottle.

Silence.

And is it? Too late for him?

TOM   What?

JODI   You said he could have been
that he could have, had it not been for

TOM   his parents splitting up, or
you know, his Nan's
partner, he lets him watch all these films.

His mother's dead. She

TOM stops opening the champagne. He looks up at JODI very briefly.

I don't know about his father. Whether he was
ever even

JODI   a lot of kids come from broken homes.

TOM   I know.

JODI   A lot of good kids.

TOM   Of course they do, that's not
I'm not saying

JODI   a lot of kids watch nasty films.

TOM   Yes, I know but

JODI   I did.

TOM   I know that.
No. I know.

You're right.

,

JODI reaches across the table. TOM puts down the bottle and takes her hands in his.

JODI	Tom,
TOM	but I do think that he could have been alright with better parents. That's all I'm saying.
JODI	I wanted to
TOM	he's got an amazing eye for detail. He continually

he keeps saying things that amaze me.
Most of the time he's just
aggravating
but sometimes he has these flashes of

JODI	has he been seen by a specialist?

,

TOM	What do you mean?
JODI	You know a a professional

TOM looks away from JODI.

JODI takes her hands away from TOM.

is he statemented?

TOM	Yes.
JODI	Has someone done an evaluation? You know, a psychological
TOM	I'm sure someone must've
JODI	should he even be in a proper school?

,

TOM	Do you think that's what it is, that he's he's got something
JODI	I don't know.
	Maybe.
	,
TOM	No.
	No, he's alright.
	He's alright. Just disruptive. I'm sure if he grows up a bit and cuts back on the sugar he'll
	although you know,
	he mutters.
	He mumbles away to himself under his breath. He doesn't think I can hear him.
	,
	I'm sorry. Sorry. Gosh, look at me.
JODI	'Gosh'?
TOM	Look at me, have I been this distracted since I started teaching?
JODI	Who says 'gosh'?
TOM	I'm sorry if I've been out of it. It really takes it out of you. Sitting there, one-to-one, it's really
	let's have an evening.

TOM picks up the bottle.

JODI	I'm worried about you.

TOM	I'm fine.
JODI	It's not been long.
TOM	Alright.
JODI	It's only been
TOM	look, let's not do this alright?

He puts the bottle back on the table.

JODI	But I alright, I'm sorry, but I just wanted to say that just for the record, you made me a promise when we left the city that
TOM	alright.
JODI	Just let me say this. Please.

,

You made me a promise and we made lots of
changes.

TOM	I know.
JODI	I made changes.
TOM	I know that.
JODI	You seem to be you seem to be letting it get to you.

You're supposed to be taking it easy.

,

There. I've said it.

TOM	Fine.
JODI	I know everything's probably

TOM	it's fine. It's okay.
	You've said
	you've said what you needed to say and
	you're right.
	Okay?
	,
JODI	Okay.
	Good.
	,
	Thanks for letting me just
TOM	is the food alright?
	,

JODI looks towards the kitchen.

	,
JODI	We can leave it a minute.
	Tom,
TOM	I know you're looking out for me and I know
	I know you're worried about me. But I'm fine now.
	Really.
	I'm sorry if I've been boring you with it all.
JODI	Not boring,
TOM	like I don't get enough of this kid at work.
JODI	Tom, I've got something
TOM	I've been really selfish.
JODI	There's something else I need to

47

TOM   what did you say it was? Duck?

,

JODI   Yeah.

I'll go check on it.

She gets up.

TOM   Do you want a hand?

JODI   I'm alright.

JODI moves towards the kitchen.

TOM notices the jewellery box. He looks up at JODI.

TOM   Jodi?

JODI stops and turns to face him.

JODI   Yeah?

,

TOM   What's this?

She takes a deep breath.

Silence.

TOM picks up the box carefully and opens it.

JODI shifts on the spot, looking towards the kitchen, playing anxiously with her hands.

TOM stares into the box.

,

This is

I mean

is this

,

what is this?

I mean
is it

,

JODI   it is.

,

TOM   Oh.

Wow.

,

Jodi,
we said

I mean,
this is great, it is, it's fantastic, just

we said that we'd only ever get married if
well, not ever, only ever, but
the main reason we'd want to get married is if
we
if you

if you were

JODI   I am.

,

TOM   Since when?

,

JODI   Month.

Month and a half.

Nearly two months.

,

TOM   Oh.

Silence.

JODI   I haven't been able to tell you.

                 ,

                 Sorry.

TOM   No, no don't

JODI   I just wanted to

TOM   it's great, it's all

JODI   shit.

TOM   No, it's

JODI   shit.

TOM stands.

TOM   Oh, listen, no don't

JODI   I thought you'd be
                 I thought it's what you wanted, that it would

TOM   just give me a second.

JODI is trying not to cry.

JODI   I'm so scared. I'm so scared Tom.

TOM   I

                 I'm

Silence.

TOM looks at the ring.

                 ,

JODI   the
                 I'll just check on the

TOM	leave it a second.
JODI	It'll dry out, I have to
TOM	Jodi
JODI	see if it's

JODI exits.

,

TOM looks at the ring.

,

He sits down at the table.

3

Morning. School.

TOM sits at the table, rubbing his ring finger.

,

DARRYL enters, his hooded top hanging off his shoulder.

DARRYL   Wha gwan?

He drops his bag on the floor and paces around the room, looking at the walls.

TOM   Sit down please Darryl.

DARRYL   What's up wit dis place today?

TOM   Nothing. Everything's

DARRYL   dem's all wearing suits init? All the teachers got new do's.

TOM   New

DARRYL   haircuts.

You ain't.

TOM   No.

DARRYL starts jogging on the spot.

DARRYL   You got the same gear on as always init agency?
Worn the same shit for months.

TOM   Sit down please.

DARRYL   All been spruced up everywhere. Posh glasses in the canteen. Tablecloths.

I weren't supposed to be in there.

TOM   No, you were supposed to be here ten minutes

DARRYL   just wanted to try that thing that thing, you
                know that thing that pulling the tablecloth
                and letting the glasses all smash.

TOM   Actually Darryl, I think the point is to keep
                the glasses intact.

                ,

                You didn't, did you?

DARRYL   Nah man. Dey wouldn't let me near.

TOM   Now, Darryl, I've put together a list of
                attainable targets for

DARRYL   inspections init?

TOM   Not exactly.

DARRYL   Last time there was inspections I went out in
                the minibus.
                Five days, five field trips.

                DARRYL starts throwing punches into the air.

TOM   It's not exactly

DARRYL   all us trouble-makers. Ruffnicks. Stuffed in a
                minibus and shipped out of school.

                Sent the shit teachers out with us and all.

                Guess that be you now agency.

                Bowling, ice-skating.

TOM   Yes, well, it's not exactly

DARRYL   farm, glass-blowing. Fucking glass-blowing.

TOM   The school is having a visitation from

DARRYL   inspectors init?

TOM   No, it's

it's someone from the government.
They wanted to look around a school which

DARRYL stops jogging.

DARRYL	is it Tony Blair?
TOM	No Darryl.
DARRYL	It is though init?
TOM	I'm sure the Prime Minister has more important things to do than
DARRYL	oh my gosh.
TOM	Sssh.
DARRYL	Don't sssh me.
TOM	Just keep it down alright?
DARRYL	Is he coming in here?
TOM	No. There's
	as far as I understand, there's going to be a formal tour around the sports grounds and the new science block and then a gathering in the canteen.
DARRYL	A gathering.
TOM	That's right.
DARRYL	What dey looking for?
TOM	They want to see how the school is doing. What it's like.
DARRYL	'Cept they won't though.
TOM	Well, they're here.
DARRYL	Yeah, but this ain't the school. Have you been out there?

	Everyone movin' bookie, looking dodge. It's like that film, have you seen it?
TOM	No.
DARRYL	That 'Dawn of the Dead'. 'Stepford Wives' or some shit.
TOM	Well, anyway, we need to keep our voices down.
DARRYL	Is it?

Silence. They look at each other.

DARRYL starts jogging on the spot.

	Can I go on the computers later?
TOM	We'll have to do some work first.
DARRYL	But you said.
TOM	You're not going on without doing some good work.
DARRYL	Can't I go on now?
TOM	Nope.
DARRYL	Beg you do.
TOM	No Darryl.
DARRYL	Why?
TOM	Because
	because it's a privilege not a
DARRYL	you don't know do you?
TOM	I'm trying to tell you.
DARRYL	'Cept you don't though.

DARRYL throws some punches into the air.

TOM	Sit down Darryl.
DARRYL	How about if I sit down at the computers?
TOM	No.
DARRYL	Why?
TOM	Because
	alright, listen
	how about we do ten minutes concerted work now
DARRYL	on the computers.
TOM	Let me finish. Ten minutes of excellent work now and then I'll set you a project for the rest of the lesson for which you can use the Internet.

DARRYL stops boxing.

DARRYL	Project.
TOM	A project.
DARRYL	PJs.
TOM	Hmm?
DARRYL	From the PJs init? Projects? NYC. East Coast hip hop. You get me?

,

TOM	I've no idea what you just said.

DARRYL starts boxing again.

DARRYL	Do I get a sticker?
TOM	If you complete the project.
DARRYL	Gold one?
TOM	Absolutely.
DARRYL	Will you write down that I did good in my homework book?
TOM	Yes.
DARRYL	Will you tell Godzilla?
TOM	Darryl,
DARRYL	Head a Year. The beast.
TOM	I'll tell the Head of Year that you did well.
DARRYL	Can I go back into class?
TOM	I'll talk to her Darryl, but I really don't think that
DARRYL	why?
TOM	Darryl, you know why.
DARRYL	Shit agency, I mean Sir, man, Kieran don't even care anymore. Believe. We're mates init? Bredren. I never even bit him that hard. Barely left a mark, you get me?
TOM	Darryl, that's not the point.
DARRYL	Arks him brah. Axe Kieran if he's bothered.
TOM	Darryl,
DARRYL	call 'im.
TOM	Put your phone away Darryl.
DARRYL	Just give 'im a ring init. Ringadingazinga.

TOM yawns.

Am I boring you?

TOM   No, I just

DARRYL   keeping you up agency?

TOM   I just haven't had as much sleep lately as I'd

,

sorry.

DARRYL   Whatever.

TOM   Darryl, will you sit down please?

DARRYL   I'm pacing. Let a man walk.

TOM   What have you had at break? Did you have
         a fizzy drink? Sweets?
         I thought we'd decided that you shouldn't

DARRYL   was thirsty bruv. Nothing quenches a thirst
         quite like the real t'ing.

TOM   Darryl, don't you remember we had a
         conversation about

DARRYL   yeah yeah yeah, healthy greens and fruits.

TOM   And you told your Nan?

DARRYL   I tell her. Woman cooks a mean meat and
         rice.

TOM   Darryl sit down.

DARRYL   What harm am I doing?

TOM   Darryl,

DARRYL   what harm though?

TOM   Darryl,

DARRYL   what harm though?

TOM   Sit.
                      Now.

DARRYL stops pacing. He stands staring at TOM.

,

I am *not* in the mood today Darryl. Okay?

,

Sit down.

,

I'm going to count to ten.

One.
Two.

Three.

DARRYL   Gosh man why are you so dry?

TOM   Four.

DARRYL   Why you act like you got stick up your rass?

TOM   Five.

DARRYL   Is it 'cause you had a breakdown at your old job?

                      Sat in your garage with the engine running.

,

TOM   Six.

DARRYL   It is though init? You went a bit

DARRYL whistles and twirls his finger round his ear.

TOM   seven.

DARRYL   Girl in upper school's cousin used to work
            with someone who knew you and she said
            something about why you can't be a proper
            teacher just agency or whatever 'cause you
            went fruit-loops.

            Says you thumped your girl.

            Had a breakdown at work. Went schizo and
            your bird made you jack it in.

            That's what I reckon.

TOM   Sit down.

DARRYL   Insane in the membrane.

TOM   Sit.

DARRYL   Don't you know I'm loco?

TOM   Stop it.

DARRYL   Or what? You gonna smack me down?

TOM   I'm warning you.

DARRYL   Why'd you do that for? Why did you hit
            your girl for?

TOM   Shut up.

            DARRYL throws punches into the air, staring at TOM.

DARRYL   Nobody's supposed to know that is they?
            About you going Bobby Brown?
            Wouldn't a got the job otherwise.

TOM   Shut up.

            DARRYL moves closer to TOM.

DARRYL   Or what? You going to give me a smack?
            Gonna lick me in head? I'd love to see that.

            TOM stands.

TOM	Shut up.
DARRYL	You best raise your weight.
TOM	Sit down.

DARRYL is very close to TOM, arms outstretched.

DARRYL	Step up pussy, show me some skills.
TOM	Sit on the fucking chair.

DARRYL laughs.

Shut up. Shut up you fucking

DARRYL laughs harder. TOM grabs DARRYL and manhandles him into the chair.

sit on the chair. Sit on the fucking chair.

TOM holds DARRYL by the collar and shouts into his face.

Freak. Fuck up. Fucking fuck up.

TOM breaks away from DARRYL.

Fucking stupid fucking

He throws his own chair over, rubs his eyes and head.

Silence. DARRYL freezes, staring at TOM.

,

TOM looks at DARRYL.

,

listen,

that was wrong.

,

You were winding me up and

DARRYL	I didn't think we used those kinda words Sir, man.
TOM	We don't. That was wrong of me. That was no way to behave. I'm sorry Darryl.

,

DARRYL	That was well funny.

,

TOM	You understand why I shouted, don't you Darryl?
DARRYL	Definitely.
TOM	Good.
DARRYL	'Cause you're mental.
TOM	No.
DARRYL	I thought I was a bit wacky but you is well bats.
TOM	It was wrong of me to
DARRYL	eccentric init? Nutty professor.
TOM	Yeah, alright.
DARRYL	'Sit the fuck down!'
TOM	Yeah, okay. Let's laugh about it and forget I said anything. Please Darryl, accept my apology. That was just, we just
	conflict of personalities.
	Alright?

TOM holds his hand out to DARRYL.

TOM   It's no way to behave and I'm

                   I wouldn't want you to think that I'm that kind
                   of

                   ,

                   I'm sorry. Alright?
                   Darryl?

                   ,

DARRYL   Do you like me?

                   ,

TOM   What?

TOM puts his hand back down.

DARRYL   Do you think I'm alright?

TOM   I

DARRYL   I think I'm alright.

                   ,

TOM   You're alright.

DARRYL   That's what I reckoned.

TOM   A little irritating at times.

DARRYL   Is it?

TOM   At times.

DARRYL   Wind up.

                   ,

TOM   So that's all forgotten then. What just
                   happened is in the past.
                   It's History. Alright?

                   ,

DARRYL   Whatever.

                ,

TOM   Right. Good.
                Listen, forget about the project, let's do a few
                minutes work and you can do whatever you
                want on the computers.

                Alright?

DARRYL   Ain't we going on the computers now?

TOM   We need to do a little bit of work.

                DARRYL mutters to himself.

                Darryl?

DARRYL   You said ten minutes.

TOM   Ten minutes of work.

DARRYL   Gosh man.

TOM   Let's do five minutes.

                ,

                DARRYL stands.

DARRYL   Nah. Fuck that.

TOM   Language.

                DARRYL starts jogging on the spot.

DARRYL   Fuck your fucking language.

TOM   Sit down Darryl.

DARRYL   Fucking lying crazy fuck agency liar.

TOM   Darryl stop it.

DARRYL   Fuck your cunting slut fuck of a
                motherfucking bitch.

TOM	Darryl sit down.
DARRYL	Bet your woman's a whore init?
TOM	Shut up.
DARRYL	Real slosher.
TOM	Darryl stop it right now.
DARRYL	You're the fucking freak, freak boy.
TOM	Calm down.
DARRYL	You've given it your chat, I'm having my ikkle rant now, you get me?
TOM	Don't you want the gold sticker?
DARRYL	Fuck it. Fucking stickers.

,

TOM	Darryl, I'm going to call senior staff.

DARRYL runs towards TOM and jumps onto the table.

DARRYL	Call them. Fucking do it. Bring it on. You're wasting a man's time. You're wasting my fucking time here. What am I doing here? What's the point?
TOM	Get off the table.
DARRYL	Why?
TOM	Because I'm telling you.
DARRYL	And I'm telling you no.
TOM	Get. Down. Now.
DARRYL	My Nan was right. You repping out like you're something special. Frontin' like you better than me. But you're just a fucking savage. Deep down and dirty you're just a gorilla.

TOM	Darryl, get off the
DARRYL	how's this for a project? Let me on the computers *now* and I won't cut you, won't stick a fucking kitchen knife in your fucking eyes.
TOM	Get down.
DARRYL	Carve you up like a fucking animal.
TOM	Please Darryl, calm down.
DARRYL	Cover you in petrol and just watch you burn. Fucking screaming like a bitch.
TOM	Darryl. Sit on your chair.
DARRYL	Are you scared?
TOM	Darryl,
DARRYL	are you though?
TOM	Sit down now.

DARRYL starts to run on the spot on the table.

Darryl, get off the table.
Now.

DARRYL continues to run, increasingly fast. He starts to shout, a sound that rises and rises until he is bellowing at the top of his lungs.

Darryl.
Darryl get off the table.

Darryl, I'm telling you now to get down off the table. Immediately.

Darryl.

,

4

Midday. School.

RITA sits at the table. She wears an angel brooch. She looks around her anxiously, clutching her handbag. On the table is a bunch of flowers wrapped in coloured paper.

,

TOM enters, holding a stack of papers which he places on the table face down.

TOM   Mrs Clark.

TOM holds out his hand for her to shake. RITA quickly shows him the palm of her hand and returns it to her bag.

RITA   Yes, hello.

TOM   Sorry to keep you waiting.
             Thanks for coming in.

RITA   I can't stay long. I'm on my way to church.
             Visit my daughter's grave every week at two.

TOM   I understand.

RITA   I'm not going to get a chance for lunch.

TOM   Really?

RITA   I thought this was probably more important.

TOM   Well, yes.

RITA   I'll grab a sandwich or something later.

TOM   Yes, good idea. I can hang your bag up for
             you if you like.

RITA   It's fine.
             Actually, how long is this going to take?

TOM   Oh, it shouldn't be too
             well,

no, it shouldn't take too long.

TOM sits.

RITA	Good.
TOM	Mrs Clark,
RITA	Rita.
TOM	Obviously this is about Darryl.
RITA	There's a Boots near the cemetery. They do sandwiches and things there I think.
TOM	Yes. Yes they do. I live up near there and I

TOM closes his eyes.

,

Mrs Clark,

He opens his eyes.

as you know, Darryl has been out of lessons officially for more than six months.

RITA	It's the Head of Year. She's got something against him.
TOM	Well, that's not actually
RITA	ego trip. Picking on him.
TOM	Mrs Clark, that's not
RITA	when is he going back into lessons?
TOM	Mrs Clark,
RITA	Rita.
TOM	I have concerns about Darryl.
RITA	You can't expel him.
TOM	That's not what I'm saying.

RITA	God help me I'll sue you. I'll fight you to keep him in this school. He's done nothing wrong.
TOM	I'm not saying that he has, I'm
RITA	he's no different to any of the other boys his age.
TOM	Actually, that's simply not
RITA	it's this school. This school has been nothing but trouble.
TOM	I'm just trying to do the best thing for him.
RITA	Bullying him.
	,
TOM	I assure you that everyone here has Darryl's best interests at heart.
RITA	Really?
TOM	Yes. Absolutely.
RITA	They don't though, do they?
TOM	Yes, yes, they absolutely do. Mrs Clark, you have to understand that Darryl cannot be admitted to normal lessons.
RITA	You won't let him.
TOM	We can't. It's not fair on the other students. He is extremely disruptive. It's hard enough to just get him to
RITA	you saying I don't know my own grandson?
TOM	No.
RITA	I look after him as best I can.

TOM	Of course.
RITA	He'll work harder.
TOM	I don't think it's an issue of that.
RITA	Leave it with me. He'll work harder.
TOM	Mrs Clark, please, you're not listening to me.
RITA	Excuse me?
TOM	If you would just hear me out.
RITA	I don't appreciate that tone Mr
TOM	Tom. Just Tom, please.
RITA	Aren't you a proper teacher?
TOM	Yes. Yes, I am. I'm retraining.
RITA	Oh, that's just great. Poor kid's been fobbed off with everyone and their dog and now they bring in a student.
TOM	Mrs Clark,
RITA	aren't you a bit old to be training? What are you, thirty-odd?
TOM	I don't think it's your grandson's fault.
RITA	Of course it's not his fault. What are you talking about?
TOM	What I'm saying is, I don't think his behavioural problems are entirely his fault. I think he may have certain I think we could be doing more to help him.
RITA	I live for that boy.
TOM	Of course.

RITA	He has a good home.
TOM	The school tries to be as inclusive as possible, but it just we just don't have the resources. As much as we'd like to.
RITA	Here we go.
TOM	Mrs Clark, time is running out. As soon as Darryl turns fifteen his options rapidly diminish. He's then much more likely to fall into the judicial system than
RITA	you're talking another language.
TOM	It means he'll be dealt with by the police and not the school or doctors or
RITA	he's not ill.
TOM	No, but he might he might need special
RITA	he's not crazy.
TOM	That's not what I'm saying.
RITA	It is though, isn't it?
	,
TOM	'Crazy' isn't a helpful word.
RITA	I don't believe this.
TOM	I'd like to suggest that Darryl sees Dr Patterson. She works with many of the schools in the county and
RITA	that's always the answer. Throw pills at it.
TOM	It's not uncommon for
RITA	his mother was drugged up to her eyeballs and ended up hanging from a coat hook.

TOM   Mrs Clark,

RITA   do you believe in God Mr

TOM   Mrs Clark, please,

RITA   after my daughter's death I was in a very dark place.
I blamed myself. I was her mother

I was her mother and I hadn't been able to

RITA opens her bag and takes out a packet of tissues. She takes a tissue and blows her nose.

the world is very cold when you live without hope.
Do you understand that?

,

Now I have my angels.
My belief gives me great strength. It fortifies me.

I can't say I've been convinced by doctors.

,

TOM   Mrs Clark, I

I have hope.
For Darryl.

It's just
it's not just a case of

a number of students, for example, at this school have ADHD, Attention Deficit and Hyperactivity

RITA   he's got one of those.

TOM   One of

72

RITA	he's not allowed in the town centre after he set fire to all those bins.
TOM	Well, that's, no that's an ASBO, an Anti-Social Behaviour
RITA	it's all the same. Just a posh way of saying your kid's messed up.
	,
	I'm not having him take tablets every day.
TOM	I'm not saying that medication would be the entire solution, but we need to be realistic about
RITA	we tried him on Ritalin when he was eleven. Do you know what it did to him? He was a zombie.
	I must say I'm appalled. This school.
TOM	I'd like to suggest that Darryl goes part-time at the school. I can help to arrange for a counsellor to visit him at your home and work with him on
RITA	when will he be going back to lessons?
	,
TOM	Mrs Clark, I'm very concerned about the kind of films Carl has been allowing Darryl to watch.
	,
RITA	What?
TOM	Darryl has seen a number of very graphic films which he has led me to understand have been purchased for him by your partner.

RITA stands.

RITA   I don't believe this.

TOM stands.

TOM   You understand why it would be a concern.

RITA   Carl doesn't know what these films are.
                Darryl says what he wants and Carl gets it
                for him.

RITA looks down.

                ,

                It's hard to say no to him.
                Anything we can do to keep him quiet.

TOM   A lot of these videos simply aren't
                appropriate.

RITA   Every other kid has seen these movies.

TOM   That may be, but Darryl has particularly
                little empathy and a fascination
                no
                obsession
                with violence and torture.

RITA   He's a fourteen-year-old boy.

*TOM turns the stack of papers over and spreads the pages
across the desk. RITA looks at them.*

Silence.

TOM   Darryl had been using the Internet during
                final period yesterday. This morning when I
                turned the printer on, this is what came out.

RITA   That doesn't prove anything.

TOM   I checked the history on his Internet account.

,

RITA	Where were you? Why was he left unsupervised?
TOM	As much as we try to, we can't watch him every second. And I can't be in all day every day, so he's left with a member of senior staff who have their own work to do.

RITA looks at the papers.

RITA	What is all this?
TOM	I'm sorry. I had hoped I wouldn't have to show you these.

,

RITA	Oh gosh.
TOM	This is just some of what he was looking at yesterday. There are some pictures which I thought were too harrowing to include.
RITA	What do you expect? If this stuff is so easy to find on the computer then of course it's going to be looked at.
TOM	We have software to block certain searches, but there are ways round it.
RITA	None of this means anything. He's just curious.
TOM	These pictures aren't pretend. They're not from films or they're real people. Real bruises, and burns and cuts and

RITA	Darryl doesn't know that. He doesn't know the difference.
TOM	That might be true, but
RITA	I've seen enough.
TOM	Mrs Clark, not every fourteen-year-old boy wants to see these images.
RITA	You can't deny my grandchild an education.

TOM singles out a particular piece of paper and hands it to RITA. She looks at it and covers her mouth with her hand.

,

Dear God.

TOM   I'm sorry you have to see this. Particularly because your daughter

how she

,

but it's important that you know.

It's important that you know what is occupying his mind.

,

Listen, Mrs Clark, this would be more than reason enough to expel Darryl. But, so far, I haven't shown this to anyone else.

I don't believe that expulsion would be the best thing for him. Do you?

,

RITA shakes her head.

It would mean more disruption and wasted time and

I think we can really help him. We need
to agree that something needs to be done,
then start working with Dr Patterson. If we
act quickly we can avoid not only expulsion
but put systems in place to stop him doing
something really

RITA   he's haunted.

There's something

there's still something lurking under his bed.
I hear him talking at night.

He
wets the bed.

He still wets the bed. I can't stand it.
He'll be fifteen soon and

I can't

,

I told him I won't deal with it anymore.

I just let him lie in it.
I'm

his room stinks. I don't go in there.

,

A knife's gone from my kitchen.

TOM   Mrs Clark, one-to-one supervision alone isn't
working.

RITA   He's not leaving this school.

TOM   If anyone else in the staff knew about this
there wouldn't be a choice, there would be
nothing I could do.

,

I'm trying to do the right thing.

,

If you want him to stay five days a week at the school, then medication will be unavoidable. And if that didn't work then we'll have wasted valuable time. All that will be left is specialist residential schools or

and neither of us want it to come to that.

RITA is looking at the paper in her hand.

,

RITA   What's the doctor's name?

5

School. Lunch-time. Children are playing loudly outside.

DARRYL is sat at the table, writing. TOM is stood behind him, looking at his work.

Silence.

TOM   You can stop writing now.

Silence.

Do you want a break?

Darryl?

,

TOM looks at DARRYL's bag on the hook.

,

You've been working for a few hours. It's break time.

Do you want to go out? Have a run around?

It is your birthday.

,

Darryl?

Football?

,

Darryl, your mates are out there. Kieran's out there.

DARRYL looks up towards the door, wearily.

Silence.

He looks back down again.

Darryl?

,

How are you feeling since seeing the doctor?

DARRYL shrugs.

,

DARRYL   She axed me about Mum.

,

TOM   Yeah?

DARRYL   And Carl. Lots of questions about Carl.
And Dad.

,

TOM   What did she ask you about Carl?

,

Darryl, is there something you should

DARRYL   nah. Carl's alright.

,

TOM   What have you written?

Can I read it?

*DARRYL shrugs. TOM takes the exercise book from in front of
DARRYL and turns back a few pages.*

,

(*Reads.*) Dog,
by Darryl Clark.

TOM smiles at DARRYL.

My dog is called

what's that word?

,

80

DARRYL   Swastika.

              It's like a cross. Bit spastic. Squished spider.
              See it all over round our way.
              Back a yard people been using it as their tag.

              Nan knows what it is.

              '

TOM   My dog is called Swastika.
              He's bigger than a puppy but not as big as a
              grown-up dog.

              *TOM looks up at DARRYL. DARRYL is staring at the floor.
              TOM looks back at the work.*

              One day we were playing and Swastika was
              jumping up at me and I was pushing him away
              and each time I pushed him he'd bounce back
              harder and show his teeth so I'd push him
              harder and he'd keep

              this is a long sentence Darryl, you can break
              this up.

              TOM makes some marks with his pen.

              He'd keep jumping up at me and then I shoved
              him and his back leg twisted

              his back leg twisted and he
              can't read that word.

DARRYL   Yelped.

TOM   And he yelped and looked at me and

              '

DARRYL   snarled.

TOM   And tried to bite me so I
              smacked him

and it hurt my hand and he barked and I
kicked him and he kept coming at me and I
kept boxing him and I got blood on my hands
that was his and my knuckles all split open
and he kept coming at me and panting with
his tongue out that he'd bit into and his eyes
glaring at me and he kept coming and he was
snapping and barking and I barked back.

And I barked back.

,

TOM looks up at DARRYL.

Is this true Darryl?
Did you ever kick a dog?

,

I'm going to have another chat with your Nan
and suggest that we apply for a place for you
at Greenacres. It's a school, much like this one,
but it's residential, which means that you'd
have your own room and
it's better equipped to deal with
I mean to

it would be better for you there.

DARRYL   Will I still be able to do GCSEs?

,

TOM   Darryl, you've not been in classes for almost

DARRYL   if I don't get GCSEs how will I get a job?

,

TOM   Darryl, I'm sorry, but this school isn't the
best place for you. I'm just thinking about
about what's best for you.

> How would you feel about moving somewhere
> else?

,

DARRYL shrugs.

,

*TOM looks back at the book. He turns the page, scan-reading
for a moment.*

> Swastika dropped back to the floor, dragging
> my arm with him and ripping it open. Red
> everywhere. Dark. I stamped on him and felt
> a crack.

> He was panting and whining and I was crying.

TOM looks up at DARRYL.

> I took his jaw in my hands and twisted it round
> until his neck crunched and he stopped.
> I stood in the living-room without moving and
> watched the little bits of black fur in the air.

,

> Did this happen Darryl?
> It's very vivid. Very descriptive.

> Did you hurt a dog Darryl?

,

DARRYL   Nah.

> I killed a baby rabbit when I was a kid.

> Nan won't let me have a dog.

,

TOM   You've worked really hard today Darryl.

> I think you've earned a sticker, don't you?

Would you like to choose one?

,

Darryl?

,

Interval.

6

Evening. House.

TOM sits at the table wearing a black suit. JODI sits on his knee, wearing pyjamas and a wedding veil. They have their hands on her belly.

A bottle of champagne and two tall glasses sit on the table.

,

JODI

This thing.
This

monster.

,

I'm a house.
I'm a big flesh balloony home for a creature I don't know.

Life-support system.
My heart pumping into another. Little tiny

sharing my food. Giving me backache.
Changing my moods.

Growing.
Listening.

Silence.

How can I get any bigger?
How can I have another eight weeks?

,

TOM takes her hand gently in his and kisses it. She smiles.

,

TOM

You're crushing me.

They smile. He helps her up and stands, staring into space.
She leans against the table and watches him.

,

JODI   Husband.

TOM smiles.

Incredibly odd word.
Husband.

Hus
band.

,

Wife.

I'm a wife.

a
wife.

TOM   You shouldn't have got drunk.

JODI   It's my wedding day.

TOM   You shouldn't have been drinking.

JODI   It's my wedding day and I'm a blimp.

TOM   Jodi, I'm serious.

JODI   Don't start.

TOM   I'm not.

JODI   Don't.

TOM   I just don't want it to

JODI   don't you dare.

TOM   I want it to be

no problems.

JODI	It will be. It will.

JODI looks at TOM.

,

How are you feeling?

,

TOM	Wonderful.
JODI	Really?
TOM	I've just married my soulmate. My best friend. Why wouldn't I be happy?

,

JODI	I'm worried about you.
TOM	I know.
JODI	You're not going to want to go back.
TOM	That's certainly true.
JODI	You should quit.

,

TOM	You're probably right.
JODI	But you won't.

,

TOM	I can't believe that she doesn't want what's best for her own grandson.
JODI	Let's not talk about it. Not today.
TOM	She hates the school but doesn't want him moved.

JODI	Of course she wants what's best.
TOM	Greenacres is fine. It's got staff who are properly trained to deal with kids who are you know, students who are
JODI	crazy? Loony? Mental?
TOM	Stop it.
JODI	Mad? Bonkers?
TOM	It's not funny.
	,
	Sorry. It's just not.
JODI	I know.
TOM	I don't know what I'd do if this one is born
JODI	don't
TOM	born with
JODI	please.
	,
TOM	I can't stop thinking about it.
JODI	No. I know.
	,
TOM	He can't help it.
JODI	Poor thing.
TOM	It's chemical.
JODI	And bad parenting.

TOM	Well,
JODI	isn't it?

,

TOM	I don't know what I'd be like. If we had if our kid was

but we'd still want what's best for him.

JODI	Yes. Of course.
TOM	We'd still make sure he was getting the best support and care.
JODI	Or her.
TOM	Eating the right food.
JODI	Tom.
TOM	I'm a vampire.
JODI	No.
TOM	All those years I spent at that company. Targeting children's cancer wards, vending machines full of
JODI	Tom stop it.

That's all bullshit anyway. That's not why you
quit.

That's not why you

,

seriously sweetheart, who are you talking to?

,

You didn't do anything wrong.
And even if you did, you're making up for it.

,

TOM	Still.
	We've created a whole generation of a whole generation that can't feed themselves.
JODI	He isn't the way he is because of what he's eaten.
TOM	That's not what I'm saying.
JODI	You can't punish yourself.
TOM	Not just the food but everything. It's all colourful and disposable and bad for you. Just listening to him speak is like everything he knows he's got from TV, American TV, and it's all lies. And then we persecute him because he doesn't know how to get on in the real world.
JODI	There must be some hope for him. He's a child, he's not a
TOM	I know.
JODI	Aren't most of these kids really good at maths or something?
TOM	What do you mean, these kids?
JODI	Don't shout at me.
TOM	I'm not shouting Jodi, but seriously you can't just

TOM gestures and JODI flinches.

'

what's that?

'

You just flinched.

JODI	No.

TOM	Shit.
JODI	Stop it.
TOM	Why the fuck are you flinching? What do you think I'm

JODI starts clearing the table.

JODI	stop it.
TOM	Stop what? What the fuck am I
JODI	calm down, please.
TOM	I'm calm I'm

you still don't trust me.

Oh fuck.
You still don't trust me.

I'd never
what happened before,
I'd never again

I'd never hurt you.

JODI	I'm sorry.
TOM	Oh fuck.
JODI	Listen, Tom I'm sorry. I'm tired.
TOM	I'm fine. I'm fine now. I'm doing something I care about and
JODI	I know.
TOM	Oh shit.
JODI	Forget about it. It was just a nervous reaction.
TOM	Jodi.
JODI	I'm jumpy. Like you said. My moods, I'm

hey, I'm fine. I'm sorry.

TOM   You're really worried I might be losing it?

,

Listen, it's pressure, but it's not the same kind of
I'd never

I'm not losing it.
I'm not losing it.

I

,

JODI sits at the table.

JODI   so he isn't good at maths, is that what you're saying?

She tops up her glass.

,

TOM   No.

JODI   And even with a better Mum and Dad he still wouldn't be?

,

TOM   I don't think so.

,

JODI   So whose fault is it?

,

TOM   No one's.

,

JODI   So what hope is there?

,

TOM	If I can get him into this place
JODI	Greenacres.
TOM	Get him into Greenacres and then there's hope.
JODI	But you got him a place.
TOM	Yes.
JODI	They're happy to take him.
TOM	Yes.
JODI	So what's the problem?

,

| TOM | It's up to his Nan. |
| JODI | Oh. Yes, you said. |

JODI rubs her eyes.

| TOM | Otherwise |

,

| JODI | otherwise what? |

,

TOM	I have this horrible feeling.
	I just can't help feeling that one day he's going to
JODI	what?

,

| TOM | He's got zero empathy. You could be having a conversation and start choking to death |

and he'd just think 'well, this conversation's over'.

He'd probably just sit there and finish eating whatever you were choking on.

I can't do anything.

JODI   Then quit.

TOM   I can't.

JODI   Transfer schools.
If you're serious.

Tom, listen,
please.
It's sweet that you care. I love you for it. But I'm asking you, please, to stop it.
For me.

You've got a family now.

TOM   Do you know how many teachers Darryl has had since they kicked him out of proper lessons?

JODI   That's not your problem.

TOM   I've a responsibility.

JODI   You've got a responsibility to me.

TOM   I just want to do something

you know what I mean.
I've got the chance to really

everything I read or watch tells me that I don't care or that I'm
you know, I'm apathetic or

and I'm sick of it.
I'm not. I'm not apathetic.

I just don't know what to do.

There's a difference.

TOM looks at JODI.

,

What happened in the city

I don't understand what happened and
I

but
if it leads to something good. If it means that
this lost kid gets to

a better life

then

JODI looks away from TOM.

,

alright, say it. Say what you need to say. I'm
listening. Let's have the conversation. If you
tell me to quit, if you seriously tell me to just
quit then I'll do it. Give me an ultimatum. Say
it. Tell me. Tell me that you want me to

JODI   it wasn't an accident.

,

I wanted to have a baby.

,

I don't want to be alone in this big house. I
want it filled with children. I want to hear little
voices laughing. I want a family.

,

And I've had to do this all on my own.

And I'm terrified.

I'm hanging by a thread.

And this student is of no relevance to me. He's nothing. From where I'm standing he is of zero fucking importance.

,

TOM   I'm sorry it's got to me so much.

JODI   It's all you've been able to talk about.

TOM   I know. I'm sorry.

JODI   I'm going through something myself.

TOM   Alright.

JODI   He's just a fucked up kid. You can't save them all. There's millions.

         And you're not doing it for him. You're doing it to make yourself feel better and that's selfish and stupid.

TOM   Fine. Alright. I'm sorry.

JODI   You're having a child of your own.

TOM   I know.

JODI   You're never here. You keep escaping.

TOM   I'm not escaping.

JODI   Going for walks or

TOM   I'm not

JODI   even when you're here, you're never completely

TOM   okay. Okay, I'm sorry.

JODI   I need you.

I need you to
I need you to hold my hand.

,

We've just got to hope that this one isn't a
nutter.

TOM   Yes.

JODI   And if it is

TOM   don't.

JODI   If it is,

we'll just have to love it even more.

,

TOM   I know I haven't said, but
having this child is

to have a family
with you

never knowing my real parents,
there's a huge part of my history that I don't
feel I

to have that with you
to look at a child and know that it's mine
my own

that scares me to death.

,

I can't quit Jo.
I have to just see this through. Get him into this
residential place and then I won't be needed at
the school.
I'll be all yours.

,

JODI   Okay.

            Listen,
            soon he'll be gone and it won't be your
            problem.

JODI touches her stomach.

TOM   What?

            ,

JODI   I think I just felt it kick.

7

Night. RITA's house. There are angel figurines around the room.

Rain.

RITA is crying. She is bleeding from her head and very shaken.

RITA	And then he came at me.
TOM	Where is he now?
RITA	His eyes.
	Just tiny black dots in the white. Cruel, angry
TOM	Rita, listen to me.
RITA	I'm shaking. I'm sorry.
TOM	Rita, where is Darryl?
RITA	I'm sorry I called you.
TOM	It's fine. Rita,
RITA	I didn't think, it's
	what,
	it must be four in the morning.
TOM	You did the right thing.
RITA	I couldn't call the police.
TOM	No.
RITA	Not on my own grandson.
TOM	I understand.
RITA	What kind of person would that make me?
TOM	Rita, did Darryl not take his medication?

RITA   I don't know.

TOM   Rita, this is very

RITA   I don't know, I leave it to him. It's been fine, he's been fine so I've left it to him this past few weeks. See how he'd get on.

You've been away.

,

TOM   Alright.
Alright.

Rita, where is Darryl?

RITA   I'm so scared.

TOM   Where is he?

RITA   Upstairs.

,

TOM looks up.

What are you going to do?

,

TOM   How long has he been up there?

RITA   When did I call you?

TOM   About

RITA   he was up there then, banging around. I heard breaking.

TOM   When did everything go quiet?

RITA   About

TOM   do you think he's hurt himself?

RITA   Oh.

TOM	Is it possible?
RITA	I hadn't thought.
TOM	Did he take the knife with him?
RITA	Oh no.
TOM	Rita. Where is the knife now?
RITA	I

,

TOM	alright. Listen, are you sure you're not hurt?
RITA	Bleeding but no. Just shaken.
TOM	Okay. Call an ambulance. Just in case he's

I'll

TOM stares at the ceiling.

,

listen, Rita,
I'm sorry,

I can't

my wife is pregnant. She's got five weeks.

,

I can't go up there.

I'm sorry. I

she'd never forgive me.

RITA	He'll listen to you.
TOM	I'm just his teacher.

I can't risk my child growing up without a father.

There is a loud crash above them.

,

RITA   Is it your first?

,

TOM   Yes.

RITA   Boy or girl?

TOM   We don't know. We didn't want to know until

Rita, Darryl needs to be at a residential school.

RITA   Talk to him. Please.

TOM   I really don't think

RITA   you have to.
I can't

I can't do this on my own.
I can't do it anymore.

TOM   I know.

RITA   What's got into him?

TOM   Rita, at Greenacres there are trained, professional people who can

RITA   no.

TOM   Darryl needs to be

RITA   you don't understand.

TOM   No, I don't. I don't understand.
What will it take to make you

RITA   I just want him to have a normal life, go to a normal school.

TOM	Of course, but
RITA	he's my daughter's son.
TOM	I know. I know that Mrs Clark but
RITA	he found her.

,

She didn't pick him up from school. He walked home and found her in the living-room.

The coat hanger had cut into her throat. Her whole face was dark blue, eyes wide open.

He was so little.

,

I can't fail him.
I can't fail my daughter.

,

More sounds from above.

,

TOM	Keeping him at the school is not fair on him Rita.
	I'm just trying to do what's best.
	,
RITA	Yes.
TOM	Greenacres will take him.
	You don't have to do this on your own anymore.
	,
RITA	If you talk to him.
	If you talk to him, then

,

then okay.

,

A loud crash. They look up.

8

Morning. School. Bright sunshine streaming through the windows.

Children playing outside.

TOM is sat at the table.

,

DARRYL enters. He drops his bag on the floor.

DARRYL	Boom!
TOM	Darryl.
DARRYL	A'ight agency.
TOM	Tom.
DARRYL	Yeah, yeah. Tom.
TOM	You can call me Tom you know Darryl. You've not done up until now you may as well on your last day.
	You said goodbye to your friends?
DARRYL	Yeah. Yeah we had a gathering.
TOM	Did you?
DARRYL	Going away party. A rave.
TOM	Good.
DARRYL	Believe. Some tunes. Some bitches. It was heavy. Me bleach *hard.*
TOM	Right.
DARRYL	Cristal. Celebrities.
	You should've come. Was pure fiyah. Solid. Hyphy. You get me?

TOM	Sorry I missed it.
DARRYL	It was off the hook. Could've brought your gyal.
TOM	My
DARRYL	your woman. Girlfriend, whatever.
TOM	Actually, she's my wife now Darryl. We got married last month.
	,
DARRYL	Your wife. Whatever. You could've brung her.

DARRYL sits down.

TOM	Maybe next time.
DARRYL	F'shizzle ma nizzle. Can I axe you a question?
TOM	Darryl, sit on your chair properly.
DARRYL	Can I though?
TOM	What do you want to know?
DARRYL	I bet you got a well nice house init?
TOM	Why do you ask?
DARRYL	Nan saw you up at the cemetery init? Saw you coming out of one of those big houses. Dem old ones. Lakeside Mansions.
TOM	It's alright.
DARRYL	Is it a mansion though? Proper massive manor?
TOM	No. No, it's actually
DARRYL	fountains and limousines and shit.

TOM laughs.

TOM	No.
DARRYL	Bet you can see the lake though init?

,

TOM	From the top bedroom you can see the far west corner of the lake.
DARRYL	Reckon I'll have a view in this new place?
TOM	You looking forward to going?

,

DARRYL	Yeah. Yeah, it'll be a'ight.
TOM	It'll be much better for you at Greenacres than here.
DARRYL	Yeah. It'll be good init?
	Had a look around.

,

	Dem's all spazzas init?
TOM	All the students have certain specific
DARRYL	spastications.
TOM	No, they are all
DARRYL	retarded.
TOM	No.
DARRYL	They are though init?
TOM	No.
DARRYL	Except they are though.

TOM smiles, despite himself.

,

Gonna be in with the ruffnicks init?

,

TOM	I'm sure it won't be too bad.
DARRYL	Yeah. Whatever.
TOM	How's the new meds?
DARRYL	Yeah. I'm taking them if that's what you're asking.
TOM	Good. Good. And you're not as drowsy? Not as out-of-it?
DARRYL	I's on this planet bruv.
TOM	Glad to hear it.
DARRYL	Focused, you get me? It's like your shoes.

TOM looks at his shiny black shoes.

TOM	What about my shoes?
DARRYL	Brand new brand new. Wicked steez. Spic and span, y'get me?
TOM	Right.
DARRYL	In your case though, they just make everything else look cheap init?
TOM	Do they?
DARRYL	Classy shoes, granddad trousers.
TOM	So you're feeling alright?
DARRYL	Superstar.
TOM	Great. Keep taking them.

DARRYL   You got it brah.

TOM   Good.

           ,

DARRYL   What about you?

           ,

TOM   What about me?

DARRYL   If I'm gone then your project's over init?

TOM   Yeah. Yeah, that's right.

DARRYL   Your last day an' all.

TOM   That's it.

Silence. They look at one another. TOM smiles, DARRYL stares at him.

DARRYL   So, that it?
           Can I go now?

           ,

TOM   Well, it's early, but,
           yeah. Go on.

           ,

DARRYL   Bless up.

DARRYL stands.

           ,

           I'm sorry about that time I called you a
           monkey.

           ,

TOM   Gorilla.

DARRYL   Yeah. Yeah.

,

TOM   Goodbye Darryl.
             Look after yourself. Alright?

,

DARRYL   Yeah.
             Yeah. Peace.

,

TOM watches DARRYL leave.

,

9

Night. House.

JODI enters, carrying a bottle of wine and a large glass. She is heavily pregnant.

She stands at the table, takes the cork out of the bottle and fills her glass. She looks at her watch then stares towards the door.

She nurses the glass with both hands and takes a sip. She stares at it.

,

She takes a big swig.

,

She drains the glass.

The doorbell rings. She puts the glass on the table.

JODI   It's open babes.

She exits to the kitchen.

,

DARRYL enters.

He looks around. His eyes are wide.

> *(Off.)* You're back early.
> How was today?

> I was just about to eat without you.
> I would've waited but,
> when you gotta eat, you gotta eat.

> But at least I'm awake. Sorry about the last
> few nights. Sorry about the sofa. I just can't get
> back to sleep once I wake up.

> You know.

I packed my suitcase today ready for

JODI enters, carrying a plate of food and some cutlery. She sees DARRYL and freezes.

Silence.

hello.

DARRYL   Alright?

JODI   Are you with Tom?

,

DARRYL   Is Tom here?

JODI   He's not here?

DARRYL   Is that a question?

,

JODI   Sorry. He
                he must still be

                perhaps you could come back another time.
                Or better yet, do you have the number?

DARRYL   Telephone.

JODI   Just give us a bell later in the week and

DARRYL   nah, nah.
                Wanted to see the man in person, you get me?

She places the plate and cutlery on the table. She is very frightened.

JODI   Are you his student?

DARRYL   When's he back?

JODI   He should be back any minute.

DARRYL   Cool. I'll wait.

,

JODI	I didn't get your name.
DARRYL	Didn't get it.
JODI	No.
DARRYL	Nah.
JODI	I'm Jodi.
DARRYL	Yeah, yeah.
	Darryl. You got a well nice crib init?
JODI	Thing is Darryl, it's very late and as you can see I'm
DARRYL	yeah. You're massive. Up the duff init?
	Gonna be a Mum.
	,
JODI	Yeah. So I think you should just come back another time.
	,
	Alright?
DARRYL	Can you see the lake from your bedroom?
	,
JODI	No.
DARRYL	I think you can.
	,

113

JODI	Will you please leave?
DARRYL	Once I seen the lake init?

,

JODI	Get out please.
DARRYL	You being moody? You picking a fight?
JODI	No.
DARRYL	Because I don't think that's wise, do you?
JODI	I'm not picking a fight.
DARRYL	State you're in.
JODI	I'm sorry, I didn't mean

,

would you like something to drink?

DARRYL	Trying to get me drunk?
JODI	No.
DARRYL	You are though init?
JODI	I'm definitely not.
DARRYL	Except you are though. Dutty gyal.
JODI	Are you hungry? Why don't you wait for Tom? Sit down. Have something to eat.
DARRYL	Ain't hungry.
JODI	Watch TV then?

,

DARRYL	You got any DVDs?
JODI	We've got some videos.

DARRYL	Can I see the lake?
JODI	It'll be too dark now, you won't be able to see anything.
DARRYL	Won't see anything?
JODI	It's pitch black.
DARRYL	It is well dark init?
JODI	Tom's thinking of getting a little boat. You should call up in a few weeks and maybe Tom'll take you out on it.

,

DARRYL	What videos you got?

JODI is moving slowly towards the table.

JODI	What kind of thing do you want to watch?
DARRYL	Do you like me?

,

JODI	I don't know you.
DARRYL	Is it?
JODI	I'm sure you're very nice.
DARRYL	You're sure.
JODI	As I say, I don't know you.
DARRYL	As you say. You trying to pick up that knife?

,

JODI	No.
DARRYL	What you want that for?
JODI	Nothing. I wasn't.

DARRYL   You wanna slice me up?

JODI   No.

DARRYL   Gonna cut me is it?

JODI   I wasn't.

DARRYL   Slice my throat?

> *DARRYL mimes his throat being cut, making a loud ripping noise. JODI is too frightened to speak.*

,

Have you got 'Pearl Harbour'?
It's well good.

Skip the chapters for about an hour anyway.
First part's shit.

,

Pick it up.

JODI   Hmm?

DARRYL   The knife. Pick it up.

,

JODI   No.

DARRYL   Go on.

JODI   Now listen to me, if you don't leave now I'm
              going to call the police.

DARRYL   Is it?

JODI   Yes.

DARRYL   And say what?

JODI   Just
              I'll just ask them to remove you from my
              property.

DARRYL	Is it?
JODI	So please leave.
DARRYL	Pick it up.
JODI	No.
DARRYL	Pick it up.
JODI	No.
DARRYL	It's well poxy.
	Ikkle fing. Bet it's blunt as fuck.
	Come over here.

JODI shakes her head.

Silence.

Look at this.

He unzips his bag and pulls out a large carving knife with a serrated blade.

It's my Nan's. It's excellent.

Have a look at it.

JODI shakes her head.

Don't you like me?

JODI	Please
DARRYL	please. Please.

You look a bit like my Mum.
Like how she used to look.

Your hair and that.

,

JODI	What do you want?

,

DARRYL   Can you put your arm around my shoulder?

                  ,

JODI   Alright.

                  ,

DARRYL drops his bag on the floor and walks towards JODI, still holding the knife.

She puts her arms around him. He puts his free arm around her.

                  ,

                  Alright Darryl.

DARRYL starts to cry.

                  Sssh.
                  It's okay Darryl.

                  Sssh.

                  Sssh.

                  Sssh.

                  Darryl,

                  why don't you put the knife down on the table?

                  Why don't you give me the knife?

DARRYL looks at her.

DARRYL   You want it?

JODI   Yes.

DARRYL   You want me to give you the knife?

                  ,

JODI   Yes.

                  ,

DARRYL   Okay.

                ,

                He hands it to her, she takes it and puts it on the table.

JODI   Thank you Darryl.

                ,

                Still embracing him, she looks at her watch, then to the door.

                ,

DARRYL   I've got to go back to my Nan's.

JODI   Yes. Good.

DARRYL   It's well past curtain time.

JODI   She'll be worried.

DARRYL   I'll just look at the lake and go.

                JODI closes her eyes.

                ,

JODI   Alright.

DARRYL   Come on.

JODI   It's through the kitchen, up the stairs and
                straight ahead.

DARRYL   After you.

JODI   I'm alright here.

DARRYL   Ladies first.

JODI   I can't really

DARRYL   yes you can.

                DARRYL picks up the knife.

JODI   Listen, please

DARRYL   no.

JODI   Please.

               I'm due in eleven days. I'll just wait here and

DARRYL   do you think I'm stupid?

JODI   No.

               I don't think you are.

DARRYL   You're well scared init?

JODI   Please.

DARRYL is smiling.

DARRYL   Are you going to piss yourself?

JODI is crying.

               You were going to knife me init?

JODI shakes her head. She is too scared to speak.

               Nah. Nah.
               You're just scared init?

               ,

JODI nods. She has tears in her eyes.

               ,

               Yeah. Me too.

               ,

JODI   Get out of my house.

               Get out.
               Now.

DARRYL stares at JODI.

               Get out of my fucking house.

,

I don't like you Darryl. I hate you. I don't want
to bring my baby into a world with you in it.

,

Why are you standing there?
What do you want?

I can't help you.
I'm sorry that you've been fucked around by
your school. I'm sorry that the whole education
system is fucked, but you know what? Most
people cope with it. I'm sorry you've seen
lots of nasty films and been lied to and fed
bad food and gangster rap. I'm sorry that you
blame yourself for your father leaving and your
mother killing herself, and I'd like to say that
it's not your fault but

it is. I'm sure neither of them could stand you.

I'm sorry that you've got nothing to look
forward to.

But I'm not going to stand here and be
intimidated by a stupid, ugly, messed-up little
boy.

Because of you I've barely had a moment
to speak to my husband during my whole
pregnancy. I'm alone and terrified and I don't
need this. I'm at the end of my patience.

So get out.
Now.

I'm going upstairs to call the police. I suggest
you leave.

,

JODI exits.

Silence.

DARRYL picks up his bag and stands still, looking at the door.

Silence.

He looks in the direction JODI left.

,

He walks to the table and stands looking at the plate of food.

10

Graveyard. Lunch-time. Bird-song.

TOM sits on a bench, his head in his hands.

Silence.

RITA enters holding a plastic carrier-bag and a bunch of flowers. She doesn't see TOM. She walks to a small gravestone beside which is a small porcelain angel and some flowers, identical to those RITA is carrying but a week old. She crosses herself and stands for a moment staring at the stone.

TOM watches her.

RITA kneels and replaces the flowers, putting the old ones in the plastic bag. She spends a moment arranging the fresh ones.

,

She stands, with difficulty, brushes herself down and picks up the plastic bag. She turns towards the bench and sees TOM looking at her.

,

TOM   Mrs Clark.

,

I'm sorry, I didn't mean to

I didn't want to disturb you.

,

I live just up the road.
I come out here sometimes. Get out of the house.

,

Would you sit down?

,

RITA sits on the bench, as far from TOM as she can.

,

I think spring's coming. Mild today.
It'll be summer before we know it.

,

How are you? Are you well?

RITA   That's my daughter's grave.

TOM   I know. I'm sorry, I

RITA   did you follow me here?

,

TOM   I live just over the way.

RITA   Getting some fresh air.

TOM   Yes.
Just

,

my wife is
she's asleep. She's been up all night with the
baby.
They're getting some rest.

,

RITA   Boy or girl?

,

TOM   Boy.

,

RITA opens her plastic bag and takes out a packet of sandwiches, opens them and starts to eat.

,

	It's so quiet here. There's nowhere in the city this peaceful.
	Good place to just sit and think.
RITA	Escape the family. Get some peace and quiet.
	,
TOM	I'm not escaping.
RITA	Oh.
TOM	I'm not escaping.
	I often come down here with Howie, my son. Give my wife a break.

Silence.

	Rita,
	How's Darryl?
	,
	How's he getting on at the home?
RITA	It's not a home.
TOM	The secure child's home.
RITA	It's a remand centre. Borstal with a posh name.
	It's a nightmare.
	He's much worse since he's been there.
	,
	They barely let me see him.
	,
	He wants to go back to school.
TOM	Right.

RITA   Do his exams.

TOM   Yeah.

RITA   They won't let him.

              ,

              They can't decide if he's crazy or just

              if they should keep him locked up or

              ,

              he's a *child*.

              ,

              Greenacres don't want him now.

              ,

              I worry about him.

              ,

TOM   Mrs Clark,
              Rita,

              I heard there'd been a fire.

              At the home.
              I heard that part of the home had burnt down
              and

              ,

              I just wanted to know if he was alright.

RITA   You wanted to know if he'd done it.

              ,

TOM   Where is he now?

              Is he back with you?

              ,

RITA	Do you want the other half of this sandwich? I shan't eat it.
TOM	Rita?
RITA	Mexican Chicken.
TOM	I'm fine thanks.
RITA	Well it's there if you want it.
TOM	Rita, where is Darryl?
RITA	You still teaching?
	,
TOM	No. No, me and Jodi, my wife, we're going back to the city. I'm going back to my old job.
RITA	I thought you were here to apologise.
	,
TOM	Apologise for what?
RITA	Darryl was let down by that school. He was betrayed. Particularly by you. You let him down. Turned him into a
	,
	but I've forgiven you.
	,
TOM	Mrs Clark
RITA	Rita.
	,
TOM	My wife

127

my wife could have been

it's lucky she didn't

,

whatever they decide, I think it's too late for
Darryl. I can't see any hope for him. He's a
mess. He's

unfixable.

If he didn't start this fire, he'll start the next
one.
He'll never go back to school. Never sit exams.
Never have a job.
He'll spend his life in and out of institutions.
Psychiatric hospitals. Prisons.
And there's nothing we can do but shake our
heads. Nothing.

,

I sometimes think
and I hate myself for it
but I sometimes think we should just take them
all, all the Darryls of this world and lock them
in a room. Give them all the knives and guns
and matches they want and let them sort it out
amongst themselves. Drown them in petrol.

I think what your daughter did was a terrible
shame. What she put you through and what
she condemned Darryl to.
But someone like her shouldn't have been
allowed to have children. She should have
been sterilised.
It's not fair on Darryl and it's not fair on
anyone else.

My child has to live in this world.

Darryl is a fucking virus. Do you understand
me?
I lie awake at night listening out for him.
Knowing he's out there.

My wife barely leaves the house.

Soon you'll be under the ground somewhere in
here and then what will happen to him?

,

RITA   Perhaps he should just be more like you.

,

Children shouting nearby. RITA looks over towards the school.

,

Break time.

,

I wanted to be buried in here, but I don't think
I will now. It's full up.

I'll be in the new place over the other side of
town.
By the motorway.

,

She looks back at TOM.

,

I love my grandson.

,

Go on. Have the other half.

,

> *TOM takes the sandwich. They sit and eat. RITA takes a packet of crisps from the bag and opens them. She offers the packet to TOM and he takes one.*

,

TOM   Thanks.

,

> *JODI enters, carrying HOWIE, a sleeping baby. She stands watching TOM and RITA. TOM sees her.*

,

JODI   I came to find you.

TOM   You were sleeping.

,

                This is Mrs Clark.

RITA   Rita.

,

JODI   Hello.

,

> *TOM stands.*

TOM   You were sleeping.

JODI   Woke up.

,

TOM   How is he?

JODI   Alright.

                He's been screaming.

,

                I don't really know what I'm doing.

RITA smiles politely at JODI. JODI smiles cautiously back.

,

TOM   It was good to see you again Rita.

RITA holds her hand out to TOM. He looks at it.

,

He takes her hand and shakes it.

,

Thanks for the sandwich.

RITA   Take care.

It was nice to meet you.

,

JODI   Yes.
You too.

RITA   Good luck.

,

JODI   Right.

TOM kisses JODI on the top of her head.

TOM   You're out of the house.

JODI   I came to find you.

TOM   I didn't go far.

JODI   Can you please take him?

JODI passes the child to TOM and leaves.

,

TOM turns back and he and RITA look at each other.

,

TOM leaves.

RITA watches him go, then looks at her daughter's grave.

It begins to snow.

RITA wraps her jacket around her, and looks up.

The sound of children playing increases as the lights fade.

LUNGS

For Effie

Acknowledgements

Thanks to Daniel Evans, David Muse, Aaron Posner, Richard Wilson, Adrien-Alice Hansel, Annie MacRae and all at MTC, Simon Stephens, Roxana Silbert, Pippa Hill, George Perrin, James Grieve, Tara Wilkinson and all at Paines Plough and Sheffield Theatres, Linda McLean, Mike Bartlett, Lyndsey Turner, Amy Rosenthal, Dan Rebellato, Clare Lizzimore, Nick Gill, Charlotte Westenra and Lucinda Burnett.

Thanks to David and Jean Heilman Grier and Jon and NoraLee Sedmak Thanks also to Jessica Amato, Rachel Taylor and Jessica Cooper.

Special thanks to Christina Pumariega.

This play is written to be performed on a bare stage. There is no scenery, no furniture, no props and no mime. There are no costume changes. Light and sound should not be used to indicate a change in time or place.

A forward slash mark (/) marks the point of interruption in overlapping dialogue.

A comma on a separate line (,) indicates a pause, a rest or a silence, the length of which should be determined by the context.

The absence of a full stop at the end of a line indicates a point of interruption, a trailing off or an interruption of thought.

There is no interval.

****

The play should be set in the city it's being performed in. Any references in the text that suggest another place should be amended.

The letters 'W' and 'M' are not character names. Any programme materials should simply list the actors and not who they are playing.

Lungs received its first performance at the Studio Theatre, Washington D.C. USA on Wednesday 28th September 2011, directed by Aaron Posner in a rolling World Premiere with Paines Plough/Sheffield Theatres. The cast of the Studio Theatre production was:

Brooke Bloom

Ryan King

A Paines Plough and Sheffield Theatres production was first performed on 19th October 2011 at the Crucible Theatre, Sheffield, directed by Richard Wilson with the following cast:

Kate O'Flynn

Alistair Cope

A second production was directed for Paines Plough by George Perrin with the following cast:

Sian Reese-Williams

Abdul Salis

The German-language premiere, 'Atmen', was directed by Katie Mitchell and entered the Schaubühne rep on the 4th December 2013 with the following cast:

Lucy Wirth/Jenny König

Christoph Gawenda

Lights up.

W	A baby?
M	Breathe.
W	A baby?
M	I was just thinking.
W	About the future.
M	We'd have to change how we live.
W	The planet, use less
M	no, that's, well yes but that's not
W	okay.
M	I'm freaking you out.
W	Not / freaking me out.
M	Completely. You thought you'd be the one.
W	No.
M	The one to say it, yes. To say yes, yes okay, I'm ready, yes, let's do it, yes.
W	That's
M	to put the pressure on, yes, / to try to convince me to
W	pressure? Put the pressure on, I'm not a a a a
M	we're having a conversation. That's all that's happening. All that's happening is we're having a conversation.
W	You're having a conversation.
M	We're having a conversation.
W	A conversation you're starting.

M	A conversation I'm, yes, that I'm trying to start.
W	A conversation that you're deciding to start now.
M	Yes.
W	In Ikea.
M	I hadn't planned to.
W	No. Okay. Yes. Okay.
M	Do you want some water / or
W	that kid with the panda is staring.
M	You're hyperventilating.
W	Don't exaggerate.
M	If it's too much
W	it's not / too much.
M	If it's too much we can put it back in the box, just put a lid on it and lock it away and then later when you're feeling less freaked out / we can
W	I'm not freaked out.
M	Alright fine okay.
W	I'm not freaked out I'm just surprised. I'm surprised I'm fucking shocked actually. I'm
M	freaked out.
W	I'm not.
M	You are.
W	I'm completely freaked out yes because why don't you ever, how can you, why didn't

you, why would you not talk to me about
this / I wish you'd let me IN I wish you'd
let me IN to your head. Into your fucking
impenetrable fucking

M   I'm talking to you now. I'm telling you now.
We're talking, we're talking now, we're
having a conversation. When should I have

W   we're not. We're not. This isn't a
conversation.

M   Okay.

W   It just isn't.

M   Okay.

W   I don't know what it is but I know for fucking
certain it's not a

M   right okay okay.

W   Can we at least get out of the queue?
Everybody's

M   of course, I'm sorry, I didn't mean to just

      ,

W   yes. I need a minute. Can we put it back in
the box?

M   There's no rush.

W   Just to

M   there's no hurry.

W   Catch my breath.

M   It's a conversation.

W   Bit of a walk or something. Ten minutes.
Meet you back at the car.

M	Okay.
W	What's wrong?
M	You said ten minutes.
W	I needed to think.
M	It's pitch dark. You stink of fags.
W	It's snowing. Is it snowing?
M	You've not got a coat.
W	This weather is insane.
M	Coldest winter ever they've just said. Hottest summer, coldest winter.
W	And you left the engine running.
M	I was listening to the radio.
W	I'm okay.
M	I know I just
	worried.
W	No need.
M	Good.

,

W	Did we get any of the stuff we came here for?
M	I went back but they'd
W	shit.
M	Yeah.

,

W	A baby?

,

M	I was just
	thinking.
	,
W	Can we just
	we will talk about it but
M	I know.
W	not right now. I'm too
M	yeah, me too.
W	Can I drive?
M	Course.
W	You can play your tape. Let me hear your new songs.
M	They're not finished.
W	Okay, well,
	let's just sit and not say anything then okay? Just be silent, just not have to deal with this right away because
M	good.
W	I don't have the
M	it's okay. Whenever you want to talk about it we / can
W	no okay of course good but not now I don't have anything to say about it right now because it's such a shock, it's such an enormous, you can't just say something like that to someone you can't just say that to me and expect me to just be fine and rational and clear-headed / and not

M   when would be the right time to / mention

W   I don't know I don't have the answers I just
know that
that
wasn't
it.

           ,

           I'm sorry.

M   I shouldn't have said anything.

W   No, no, you're right. You're right.
It is something we should

M   should we?

W   We should be, yes, be talking about, because,
fuck, we're not getting

M   I know.

W   Any younger.

M   No.

           ,

           So are we talking about it or

W   no.

           ,

           Yes.

           ,

           Go on.

M   With what?

W	With, you were saying, with, you know, what?
	What were you saying?
M	I've said it all.
W	Then say it again because I couldn't hear you before because people were staring and I was pushing a trolley and holding a lamp and I couldn't breathe.
M	You got the gist.
W	I think so.
M	Or you wouldn't have got as freaked out as you did.
W	Touché.

,

Touché.

,

So.
Where do we go from here?

M	Well, we should try to leave the car park.
W	Sarcasm? Right now? You think that's going to
M	I'd like to hear your opinion.
W	Yes.
M	Of course.
W	Of course yes.
M	It's a two-way
W	I know.

M	It's a two-way thing and so
W	but
M	go on.
W	Alright, it's *this* it's
	I have no idea. I don't opinion? I don't have it's like you've punched me in the face then asked me a maths question / while I'm still on the
M	like I punched you in the face?
W	You know what I mean.
M	No.
W	Okay. Yes. Let's do it. Let's do it. Yes. Let's do it. Yes.
M	I'm not
W	I'm saying yes.
M	I'm not asking a question.
W	Aren't you?
M	No.
W	You're starting a conversation.
M	I'm not sure if
W	well it's started and now it's happening and I'm saying yes.
M	Right.
W	Look, alright, listen, you have to understand alright, I'm thinking out loud here so please just let me talk just let me think it through

out loud please alright don't just jump in
if I say something wrong or stupid just let
me think okay because I've always wanted
alright and I'm talking in the abstract I've
always wanted I've always had a sense or an
idea of myself always defined myself okay
as a person who would, that my purpose in
life that my function on this planet would
be to and not that I ever thought about it
like that it's only now because you're asking
or not asking but mentioning, starting the
conversation only because of that that I'm
now even thinking about it but it's always
sort of been a given for me an assumption
ever since I was a little girl playing with dolls
I mean long long long before I met you, it's
never been what I guess it should be which
is a a a a a a an extension of an expression
of you know, fucking *love* or whatever, a
coming together of two people it's always
been this alright and this will sound stupid
and naïve but it's always been an image, I
guess, of myself with a bump and glowing
in that motherly or pushing a pram or a
cot with a mobile above it or singing to it
reading Beatrix Potter or Dr Seuss, I don't
care, never cared about it being a boy or girl
just small and soft and adorable and with
that milky head smell and the tiny socks and
giggles and yes *vomit* even it's all part of it,
looking after it, caring for it that's I think
that's the impulse and there's always been
a father in the picture but sort of a blurry
background generic man, I'm sorry, it's
just this picture of my life I've always had
since I was able to think and I've never ever
questioned it. Never. And I've pushed it all
down and focussed on my career, on my

studies, on myself and now it's becoming,
potentially becoming a bit real I'm going to
have to think about it for a second please
just a a a a a a or much longer in fact
because well because I'm not an idiot, I'm
a thoughtful, very thoughtful person and I
want to do everything for the right reason
or at least a good reason and I believe in
questioning and never just blindly accepting
or and it's going to take a lot of effort to
unravel or to to to to to to excavate not
excavate but excavate all of those previously
held beliefs and assumptions because it's
important probably the most important thing
you could do to bring another person a yes a
person an actually living breathing thinking
because they won't stay small forever and
I think don't they I think a lot of people
think about them being small, just tiny and
sweet and unconditional with their eyes and
giggles and tiny little fingers gripping your
thumb and I do I did I think I thought like
that because it's too hard like we're not quite
designed to be able to fully comprehend the
the the the

M   enormity

W   or whatever which is a maybe it's a survival
mechanism perhaps an inbuilt thing because,
fuck,
if you thought about it if you really properly
thought about it before actually doing it
then you'd never ever actually fucking do it
because it's too fucking too fucking

M   enormous

W   it is it is it is it's fucking enormous,
fucking enormous fucking the purpose of

life itself, the purpose, the meaning, the
meaninglessness, the love and the horror
and the hope and the fear and everything
the volume of all of it turned right up, the
rest of your life the rest of someone else's
life committing someone to something
forever, ancestry, the seven and a half
thousand generations of human history and
I don't even know much about my own
*grand*parents, let alone my *great* grandparents
or or or or and it's *their* genes, their genetic
stuff, really, them, these dead people moving
around making choices for this little, this
tiny, but that's not the whole thing,

M   breathe.

W   This is what I'm saying this is what I'm
           saying because they don't stay small, they
           grow up and become people, they become
           grown-ups like everyone else, they become
           their own grown-up people and they think
           their own thoughts and they buy their own
           clothes and they leave home and they hate
           you.
           Alright, because I'm thinking out loud.
           I'm thinking and talking.

M   I didn't say anything.

W   We're having a conversation.

M   Yes.

W   That's all that's happening.

M   Look, let's get home and drink some gin and
           pretend I never said anything.

W   And the planet.

M   I don't want ice. Take my ice.

W	The planet. Because you worry about the same things I do, you care about the same
M	do I?
W	And they say don't they that if you really care about the planet, if you really care about the future of mankind then don't have children.
M	Do they?
W	I mean, they actually say if you really care about the planet then kill yourself but I'm I mean,

I'm not going to do that.
So,
because there's, what, there's seven billion people or so, there's too many people and there's not enough of everything so really the right thing to do, the ethical thing to do is to not contribute to that, particularly people like us. |
M	People like
W	car driving, plastic bag using, aerosol spraying, avocado importing, Western,
M	but we're good people.
W	Exactly. We are we are we are good people yes we are. Good.

Are we? |
| M | You can't think about that stuff. |
| W | No I know. It's not our responsibility. And anyway, so much about it is unknown. And what if this kid, this hypothetical what if she, or he, this imaginary little Edwin or Hannah, |

M	Edwin?
W	What if she or he was the person to work it all out and save everything, everyone, the world, polar bears, Bangladesh, everything, we don't know so
M	no, but
W	or we could plant a forest. We could work out the carbon footprint of the expanding nappies in the landfill and the Baby Gap hoodies flown in from the Congo or wherever and we could plant trees, entire forests, make something pure and and and oxygenating, so
M	how do you factor that in?
W	Exactly.
M	The world is going to need good people in it.

With everything that's happening.
We can't just leave it to the people who don't think, the people who just have child after child without ever properly examining their their their their *capacity for love.*
I mean, that's what's wrong with everything isn't it? |
| W | Yes. I know. Exactly.
Hang on what?
Are you saying some people are too stupid to have children? |
| M | No. No of course not. But
yes.
Some people, lots of people, aren't thinking it through, not fully, and maybe the smartest, most caring, most informed people aren't having children. |

W	Right.
M	So it's their genes that aren't surviving. So things are getting less caring and less informed and more savage.
W	So, to save the planet it'll be, what, eugenics or
M	no, no.
W	Sterilise? Exterminate?
M	Not what I'm saying.
W	Camps? Enforced
M	no. Of course not I'm not I don't have the answers. Yes, some people are saying that maybe that will happen but we'll be long dead by the time that's I mean, you know more about this stuff than I do. You're the one doing the PhD. But, yes, if we're being honest, really, teen mothers in tracksuits with fags in their mouths, smacking their kids in supermarkets, being a gran by thirty, multiplying like rats,
W	rats?
M	Meanwhile the people who read *books*, the people who *think* and try to help and I know I'm being a bit fascist here, I'm just playing devil's advocate here of course I am but there are some thoughtful people who are waiting for the perfect circumstances and there's no such thing as perfect so the world is overcrowded and people think well I don't want to bring my child into this world full of

crack dealers and pimps and homeless, and
I know this sounds reactionary but let's not
be politically, you know, correct about this
for a second, there are *some people* who just
shouldn't have children. They just shouldn't.

And would it be such a great loss if those
people, you know,
couldn't
have
children? Or
I mean,
isn't this what you were saying? I'm only
carrying on from what you were saying.

W   I think I'm going to be sick. No I'm not. I am
actually I think yes.

M   I was only

W   I know that's what I feel, what I think
sometimes, but when you say it out loud it
sounds like the worst, cruellest, sickest, most
hateful

M   what do you want me to do?

W   Just a cuddle and shut up for a bit I think
would be good actually.

M   Is that okay?

,

W   We should adopt then maybe, probably,
shouldn't we?

,

Why aren't you saying anything?

M   Yeah, you're right, you're absolutely
the best thing to do, absolutely, with the

	world as it is would be to
W	so many unwanted, unloved
M	and it's completely irrational, I know it is, but I
	I don't want to do that.
	I know that makes me sort of a
	terrible person. I just don't think I'd be
W	what if it's something I really want to do?
M	Then we can talk about it.
W	But not do it.
	,
M	Yeah.
	,
W	Right.
	,
M	I worry I might be one of those fathers who doesn't notice his kids unless they're winning stuff or getting in trouble.
W	I don't want to be one of those mothers who only lives through their children. I want to still read books and do things. I will not use having a child as an excuse for becoming an idiot.
M	You're not your mother.

W   You're not your dad.

M   I want to be able to play with my kids
           without it having to be competitive or
           educational.

W   I want to still have sex. We mustn't let it ruin
           our

M   people get so boring and it doesn't have to
           be like that.

W   I don't want to have to host the best birthday
           parties or make the best Chewbacca costume
           for Halloween.

M   Or push our kids to do stuff they don't want
           to do.

W   Harp lessons or

M   but it has to value learning and be able to
           think for itself.

W   But not so thoughtful that it gets depressed
           and lonely.

M   Autumn babies get picked first for sport.

W   No princesses or soldiers. No guns and tiaras.
           Disney will not dictate what our

M   and the schools are a mess, we'd have to
           get on the board of governors or parents
           associations.

W   We're talking about it. Look at us.

           ,

M   Are we too young to be thinking about this?
           To be worrying about all this? We used to do
           stuff. Go to the zoo. Go clubbing.

W   We still do.

M	When?
W	How about tonight?
M	Not tonight.
W	Friday.
M	It'll be too hectic on Friday.
W	Wednesday.

,

M	Okay.
W	I'VE MISSED THIS!
M	WHAT?
W	I SAID I'VE MISSED THIS. BEING OUT.
M	BEING OUT, YEAH.
W	WE'VE GOT SO BORING. STAYING IN. TELEVISION.
M	TELEVISION.
	WHAT?
W	IT'S VERY LOUD IN HERE.
M	I CAN'T HEAR YOU.
W	IT'S GREAT.

,

	ARE YOU READY TO GO HOME?
M	Fresh air.
W	My feet still hurt. Used to love those boots.
M	Look at those llamas.
W	Everyone here has a pram.

M	Shall I grow a beard?
W	Yes okay yes it's yes let's make another person. I gave myself a week to think it through and yes I think we should do it. I think we should try.
M	You're sure?
W	Yes. Aren't you?
	,
	You're not or you wouldn't be
M	I'm sure. Yes.
W	Okay.
M	And you're sure.
	,
W	Yes.
M	Okay.
W	Let's go to bed.
M	Okay.
W	Can we stop a second?
M	Again?
W	I think I just need
M	it's been weeks.
W	I'm sorry I'm just
M	not again.
W	If we're / going to do this

M	there's no *if* there's no so don't please don't / start with that.
W	I'm not starting I'm just I'm talking, I'm saying that if *because* I mean, not if, *because, because* we're doing this
M	we are we are
W	you're going to have to
M	I am.
W	Let me finish, you're going to have to relax because this should be beautiful and
M	I'm fine.
W	You're fine okay good good because it's just, and maybe I'm reading this all wrong maybe I'm seeing something that's not really happening, but it feels like you're sort of feeling quite a lot of that the way you're being towards me is sort of giving off a lot of hate.
M	I don't hate you.
W	No I know I know you don't I know that I know that I know you don't.
M	I don't hate you.
W	Please don't take that the wrong way.
M	Might go for a walk.
W	I'm sorry I'm sorry I've ruined it I'm tense and it's not just your fault
M	what isn't? Fault? What is?

W   No, stop, okay look all I'm

okay. So.

,

We're trying. We're trying and it's
that's wonderful, it is and it's
scary it's wonderful and scary and not just
for me because it's my body it's going to be
happening to, not to but inside or whatever
but for both of us it is isn't it, and we're not
talking about it and there's this atmosphere
isn't there or is it just me who's

,

maybe it's just me then.

M   I was there. I was ready.

W   Yes. Yes.

Yes I know.
I know and I'm sorry.
I know.

,

But it's
alright.
Deep breath.
I want our
it's about making a person. What we're
doing.
It's about this amazing
miracle, not miracle but you know what I
mean, miracle yes miracle it's about this
miracle happening and it
I want it to
need it to feel

I don't know
sacred or
not sacred but
yes.

,

And you've got that porno look in your eyes.

M   I can't help the way I look.

W   That look that murderers and men in porn
films have.

M   It's just
I'm concentrating.

W   Scares me.

M   Really?

W   No.
No of course it doesn't.
But yes, a bit.

M   Fucking hell.

W   Don't feel bad about it I don't want you to

M   do you feel this a lot? When we

W   no. No. No. No.

M   You've said it before.

W   Sometimes but

M   you've mentioned it. It's one of your things.

W   Only sometimes it
things? One of my things?

M   I want you. Sometimes I get this
when I want you

get this animal fucking
horrible you know
lust
I suppose,
want to
fucking
you know.
Hard.
Want to
yes, hurt you maybe. A little. Make you
scream.

W   I know baby and sometimes that's really

M   you want it.

W   Sometimes I do I do sometimes I do but

M   sometimes I want to get inside you so much,
      want to open you up, split you apart / like
      you're a

W   okay okay okay and that's
      in the right *context* that's fine, that's more
      than fine that's

      but this is different, this is
      I'm thinking about
      aren't you thinking about
      what it means? What we're doing? The thing
      beyond
      the moment?

M   Honestly?

W   Yes honestly.

M   Honestly I'm just thinking about the
      moment.

W   Okay.

M	In that moment I'm not thinking I'm just my cock and my mouth and my / hands and looking at your
W	yes alright alright alright okay, good okay.
M	So squeamish about this stuff.
W	I'm not I'm just
	just want a
	I don't know. Connection. Is that what I mean?
	Some
	like it's the two of us together and not something you're
	doing
	to me.
	Did you know in those scanning machines the same bit of a man's brain lights up when he looks at a woman as when he looks at a spanner?
M	What does that mean?
W	Sorry. Sorry.
	Sometimes that look you do is sexy. It is.
	Sometimes it makes me think
	oof.
	And your shoulders and your noises and the weight of you and the danger, the
M	danger?
W	the way you need me, that there's nothing else on the entire planet for you at that moment, bombs could be going off, an earthquake or whatever and it wouldn't matter to you in that moment and I love I can make you feel that way and I do, often, usually, lots of the time I'm there as well, I'm absolutely

the world's not there it's just us and
we're the whole universe.
And then sometimes
and I'm just being honest here okay but
sometimes it looks like you're about to hack
off my limbs.
You know? Like you're going to smash in my
teeth, throw me into bin bags and bury me in
the woods.
Not always but that's how it feels sometimes.

M   Fucking hell.

W   Only sometimes. And only for a second.

M   Fuck.

W   I shouldn't have said anything.

M   No.

W   I should have just

M   no it's

W   shit.

,

I'm sorry I'm just scared and I'm not

,

I don't know what I'm talking about. I never
feel that way.

Let's

,

woo. Fucking hell.

I need a big laugh or a big cry.

,

Know any good jokes?

,

We won't sleep now will we? Not for a bit.

,

We can try again. I'm glad we talked about it.
We can try again.

M   Yeah.
We will.
Not right away though.

W   No. Okay.

,

I / love you.

M   I'm going to read for a bit. Watch TV maybe.

W   Do you want me to come with you?

M   No.

Get some sleep.

W   Okay.
Sweetheart,

just,

sorry but

don't

you know.

I know you're
that you didn't

M	what?
W	Doesn't matter.
M	I wasn't going to masturbate if that's / what you're asking.
W	All I'm saying is we need all the help we can get so please don't
M	fuck sake.
W	I'm just saying.
M	Okay.
	,
W	Okay.
M	Good morning.
W	You're cheerful.
M	I think spring's here.
W	You made breakfast.
M	We should move. Go to Brighton. Isn't that what people do? Get some outdoor space. Fresh air. Room for goalposts. Trampoline. Paddling pool. Trees. We should plant some trees. Put a bit more oxygen into the world. Like you said. Do our bit.
W	We should get married.
M	Let's think about it.
W	You don't want to?
M	One thing at a time maybe.
W	I'll make coffee.

M	You should get a job.
W	Once I've got my PhD my / prospects will be
M	we can't both be
W	I know this isn't very feminist of me but actually sweetheart I think you should, if we're serious about this, you should get something a bit more full-time and I know you get free records and time off to do gigs but we've both got to make sacrifices and I'm not going to be able to work once I get bigger and then for a lot of that first year and we're going to need to
M	plenty of musicians have children.
W	Plenty of successful musicians have children. Sorry. I didn't mean that. It's just the economy is in freefall and nobody's buying vinyl anymore. You really don't want to get married?
M	What do you mean happening to? Last night when we were talking you said it's your body, that it's your body it's happening to.
W	Well it is.
M	Talk about it like it's a
W	it is my body that when it happens, yes, it'll happen to me.
M	Alright I know yes of course but do you want some of this?
W	I'm not hungry.
M	You make it sound like a I don't know

damage,
violence,
an act of terrorism or

W   well,

M   you see it as

W   yes.

M   Threatening.

W   Not just that but
actually I will have some
but, yes I'm fucking terrified. If I'm honest.

M   That's
it's a shame.

W   It's realistic. I'm trying to be
I'm readying myself.
Yes I'm excited about growing bigger and
getting scans and yes giving birth as well
of course but it's going to be painful and
uncomfortable and my feelings, my thoughts
are going to be all over the place.
And I've got anxiety about that. Of course I
do.

You get that right?

,

I'll stretch, expand, become a a a a a house,
my breasts will swell, ache, hurt like hell then
get drained and lose their shape forever, my
you know, my

I mean,
that's bound to change with what it has to go
through.
Have you ever seen a real birth? It's not like

TV. It's blood and shit and mess and I'll be
torn and bruised like I've gone under a truck.

This must be how a caterpillar feels as it
cocoons itself.

M   I'm sorry I can't
that I can't do it.

W   You don't have a womb.

M   That's what I'm saying.

W   You wish you could be the one who gets

M   yes.

W   Pregnant?

M   Don't laugh at me.

W   You wish you could gestate the foetus to full
term then birth it through your

M   a bit yes I do. I feel already that we're not
equal somehow, that I can never quite know
what it feels like and you'll know that I can't
and why are you looking at me like that?

W   You're sharing your anxieties.

M   I'm sorry.

W   No. I love it. This is delicious, is there more?

M   Have mine.

W   No.

M   I'm done.

W   What's wrong?

M   Nothing.

,

You should quit smoking.

,

If you're serious / about

W   yes you're right.

M   You're going to be a home, an ecosystem and you're / polluting

W   I've said yes shut up yes I've said yes alright so / please just

M   it doesn't make sense to me that you could want to be a mother and still be smoking.

W   You don't understand because you've never been addicted to anything.

M   Those two impulses seem to me to be completely

W   you're right.
So shut up.

,

Good luck.

M   I'm doing it for you.

W   For us.

M   That's what I mean.

W   You look handsome in your suit.

M   I feel sick.

W   How did it go?

M   Find out Monday.

W   Keep checking your email.

M	Here goes.
W	Well?
M	You're looking at the newest cog in the corporate machine.
W	I'm so proud of you.
M	Will you drive me?
W	How many do you think?
M	Left here. How many
W	trees. Few weeks ago you said about planting trees. Do you know? I do. How many trees would we have to plant to counteract the
M	left again.
W	I did some maths. How many plane trips? London to New York?
M	I
W	two thousand five hundred and fifty.
M	two / thousand
W	I could fly to New York and back every day for seven years and still not leave a carbon footprint as big as if I have a child.
M	You're having second thoughts.
W	Ten thousand tonnes of CO_2. That's the weight of the Eiffel Tower. I'd be giving birth to the Eiffel Tower.
M	You / wouldn't be giving
W	and if we had a second it doesn't just double because the chances of them reproducing and how many they might have and how many their children's children might

have and how many their children's
children's children might have that goes
up exponentially. Fuck recycling or electric
cars, fuck energy efficient fucking light bulbs,
unless educated, thoughtful people like
us stop making babies the world is totally
fucking fucked.

M   We should talk about this.

W   We are talking about it, it's fucking nuts it's
fucking terrifying it's the taboo, the last real
taboo. / There is no incentive to save lives
right now, there is no incentive to to to to to
cure AIDS or whatever, to keep people alive,
what we need is the planet to fucking *purge*
us, fucking drown us, burn us, cull everyone
by about two thirds.

M   What's happening now? What's actually
happening in your mind? What have you
been reading? Because really it's important
to check your sources thoroughly. There's a
lot of scaremongering and I know you know
that, I know you know all of that. You tell me
off for the stuff I read because it's too too too
I don't know.

W   Fucking, hurricanes. Floods. Fucking
volcanoes. Earthquakes. Tsunamis. Bring it
on.

M   Up here on the right.

W   And we're just letting it happen. We're so
caught up with our little fucking lives and
we're killing everyone.

M   We're not killing everyone.
We're not killing everyone.

,

W	I got my period.
M	Oh sweetheart.
W	That doesn't mean I'm not right.
M	I know.
W	I'm going to smoke a cigarette and I don't need you judging me, alright? I'm going to smoke 'til I vomit.
M	Do you want me to take the day off?
W	Yes. No. Your first day? Don't be stupid.
M	I can.
W	We're here now. Go on. Just come straight home after.
M	Okay.
W	And bring cake.
M	Here.
W	What's that?
M	Cake.
W	I missed you.
M	Why? I mean, thanks, you too, but
W	lately it's feeling more and more odd when we're apart.
M	Sorry I've barely been here. My appraisal's coming up.
W	I wish I could come to work with you.
M	You could meet me for lunch. We could make it a regular thing. Tuesday thing.
W	Okay.

M	What's that?
W	Sandwiches. Picnic.
M	Shit.
W	It's Tuesday.
M	I forgot.
W	Made us a picnic. This weather. Let's sit on the grass. Find some shade.
M	Look, I can't.
W	Didn't make it. Bought it. Got you a donut and a Ribena too.
M	I forgot, I'm sorry.
W	And an apple to counteract the donut. What do you mean forgot? It's Tuesday.
M	There's a meeting.
W	At lunch?
M	Carbon efficiency, ethical blah blah blah.
W	Skip it.
M	I asked for it.
W	Go in late. You / asked for it?
M	Offsetting, that sort of thing yes I asked for it. I think we should plant trees. The company. Lots of them. Forests of them. Try to offset our you know, our footprint, our
W	yes.
M	I've been reading that book of yours. Was up half the night. I've overtaken you with it I think. I've got to that bit about how since the Industrial Revolution we, people, everyone,

	we've put half a trillion tonnes of pure carbon into the air. Twenty seven billion tonnes a year.
W	I had to stop reading it.
M	Apparently an elephant weighs a tonne. So there's half a trillion elephants worth of carbon up there. And it'll only take us forty years to burn the same again. Our kid would be middle aged, maybe have kids of their own. Grandkids even. It's actually pretty interesting when you get into it, when
W	sex we should have sex. Find somewhere. Now. Walk and eat. Have donuts and if we find somewhere a a a a I don't know, a secluded bush or wooded area, or a you know, a public toilet,
M	not a public
W	we could be quick. You could make your meeting.
	,
M	What kind of donut?
W	Iced.
	,
M	Alright.
W	Well.
	Well well well.

M	We haven't done that in a while.
W	Needed to.
M	You're loud.
W	Was I loud?
M	Where did that come from?
W	What does that mean?
M	I'll have some explaining to do.
W	There'll be other meetings.
M	Yeah.
W	Proud of you. It's good, it's a good thing that you're trying to do.
M	I missed the meeting.
W	Are we good people?
M	Yes.
W	I mean, yes I know but are we actually though?
M	Yes we are.
W	How?
M	How?
W	In what way are we?
M	We just are.
W	Yes. Okay.
M	We're going to be great parents.
W	I think it's okay to ask the question.
M	So do I.

W	Good.
M	It's part of what makes us good people.
W	But I don't we don't believe, do we, in good and bad. Right and wrong.
M	Don't we?
W	Don't believe in evil.
M	Not evil no, we don't condemn people, we try to empathise, to put ourselves in their / position.
W	Shoes I know we do yes but doesn't everybody think that they're good? Doesn't everyone believe they're
M	some people wouldn't ask, wouldn't question it.
W	Hitler or Rupert Murdoch or
M	everyone thinks they're doing the right thing. Pretty much.
W	So what makes us sure?
M	You're worrying too much.
W	Yes.
M	You're thinking too much.
W	Okay.
M	Okay?
W	We must be very certain, arrogant even, to want to create another person out of our genes and to teach / it and to bring it up as

M	we are we are we are certain. We're not bad people.
W	Okay. Good.
M	I'm going back to work now.
W	Okay. I love you.
M	It's going to be very lucky to have such thoughtful parents who care about things and who will love it very much.
W	It?
M	Him or her.
W	We recycle.
M	We do.
W	We don't keep the tap running when we brush our teeth.
M	That's right.
W	We watch the news. We vote. We march. We recycle.
M	Yes.
W	We support the smaller coffee shops against the larger chains.
M	Even when it tastes like soil.
W	Does it? Sorry.
M	I'll see you tonight. I'll run you a bath and we can sit and talk. How's that?
W	More hot.
M	Okay. Move your feet I don't want to scald you.

W	We watch documentaries. We read books about proper things. We read the classics. We watch subtitled films.
M	We ride bikes. We buy fair trade.
W	We give to charity.
	,
	What?
M	I didn't say anything.
W	We do. We give to charity. I do fun runs. I've done one anyway and I'll do another one.
M	I didn't say anything.
W	You have a red credit card for Bono's AIDS in Africa thing.
M	I didn't say / anything.
W	You gave five hundred pounds to the crisis appeal when that horrible thing happened. Okay too much hot now.
M	Sorry.
W	We shouldn't feel guilty about having things when really in the grand scheme of things we are not spoilt, we don't live beyond not too far beyond our means it's not swimming pools and sports cars and
M	I'm not saying anything.
W	We live pretty simply actually, we spend money on food and books and music and films and holidays sometimes and our mortgage and we don't just throw it away and yes it would be lovely to give more I do feel like we should, I wish we could give

178

more but it's just not, we don't have any
more

M   hey, just
alright, you're

W   am I being mental?

M   You're somewhere on the spectrum.

W   Oh fuck it's maybe it's hormones maybe it's
my hormones I do feel crazy I do feel like
some, I don't know, some chemicals some
foreign chemicals are

M   alright still, you're still

W   sorry I'll stop I'll stop I'll just sit for a second
I'll just try to calm down, just soak for a
second do you think that's what it is? Do you
think the garage is still open do you think
they'll, they sell condoms and things don't
they but a pregnancy test do you think they'll

M   do you want me to go and see?

W   Don't ask please don't ask that why are you
having to ask me isn't it obvious, isn't it
sometimes you look at me like I'm a cryptic
fucking crossword. Do I have to say it? Yes,
yes, yes go, check, go and check now why
are you not putting your shoes on why are
you just staring at me like I'm a

M   is this still the hormones do you think or are
you just being nasty now?

W   I'm sorry oh fuck I'm losing my mind this
is amazing does this happen? Is this what
happens or am I just having a breakdown? I
fucking better be pregnant because otherwise
this is terrifying.

M	Isn't it vomiting? Isn't that the first thing? Or missing a period?
W	It's been keeping track of what date is it?
M	It's
W	thirteenth, fourteenth
M	when did you
W	cinema when did we go and see that film?
M	You mean the
W	that shit film that you liked and I fell asleep in?
M	That was
W	was that three, four weeks ago already?
M	You didn't like that film?
W	Five. I think it was fuck I think yes it was fuck fuck fuck it was I should have already had go. Go. Go. Why are you still here? I'll come with you. I need a towel. Give me a kiss.
M	How long does it say?
W	A minute. Two minutes.
M	Alright.
W	Let's leave it for three just to make sure.
M	Check it each minute but then keep checking.
W	Good good yes good. I'll come and get you.
M	Right okay. What?

W	I can't go when you're right there.
M	You've peed in front / of me before, you've
W	I know but I've got performance anxiety as it is and
M	some water I could get you some
W	please yes but then will that count if it's come / straight through you
M	or will it have to sort of percolate I see what you're saying.
W	It doesn't say in the instructions.
M	Do I really have to leave?
W	This isn't one of the special bits. Pissing on a plastic stick isn't one of the sacramental
M	yes. I want to, I want to see all of it I think it's all
W	fine okay okay okay run the tap or
M	how's that?
W	Ssshhh.
M	Gush or a trickle?
W	Please.
M	Sorry.
	,
	Shouldn't keep it running like this.
W	Can we not think of the planet for one second?
M	Sorry.

W	Okay that's I think yes,
	,
	right.
	Now we wait.
	,
	How long's that been?
M	Thirty seconds.
W	Really? Wow.
M	A minute.
W	How about
M	two minutes.
W	Right.
M	Three.
W	Okay, here we go.
	,
M	Where's my phone?
W	You hate your parents.
M	That's not true.
W	Okay, I hate your parents but I mean they're not like mine, mine are
M	you could have called them already.
W	I'm going to dial. Do you want to speak to them?

M	No.
W	After, I mean, they'll want to speak to you.
M	Why?
W	I don't know, they might, they might want to say, you know
M	I could call mine at the same time.
W	You could of course you could, just let me, I just, let's just get this first call done and then, you know, then people know, then it's out and
M	you want them to be the first to know.
W	Is that okay?
M	Before mine.
W	I just
	yes.
M	Okay.
W	I'm tingly. What is it I'm feeling? Like, naughty a little bit, like
M	you shouldn't feel naughty.
W	Like embarrassed almost, like I'm
M	it's a secret that's why.
W	It is it is it's our secret. It's our secret. Fucking hell I just had this fucking massive, ooooaar, shiver up my spine.
M	You've gone white.
W	Fucking goose bumps I'm shaking look I just had this and this is going to seem so weird but I just

had this thought which was that it's not just
you and me any more, in this room, it's you
and me and then there's this other thing here
now which is half you and half me and half
completely something new.
It's happening. It's happening. It's
happening.

M	Yes.
W	You look normal or is it just that I'm not seeing clearly?
M	No, I feel I'm happy. I'm ecstatic.
W	Good. Good.
M	It's not sunk in yet I don't think.
W	No. I know. I know. What do you mean it's not sunk in?
M	Nothing, it's I've been preparing myself for it, bracing myself and now
W	shock.
M	Exactly.
W	But you are you're feeling something of course you are, you're not just
M	I'm yes I'm it's the eye of the hurricane maybe or
W	no, I know I know.
M	I'm watching *you*.
W	Right.

M	Getting everything from *you*, you're
W	buzzing.
M	Should we call your parents?
W	Okay.
M	No, I mean, should we?
W	Because
M	they do say don't not straight away because it's still very early and a lot can
W	why are you saying this?
M	Just, they say it for a reason because, you know, they say one in four pregnancies ends in
W	can we for just one second feel invincible and reckless before we start saying words like miscarriage?
M	I just think
W	do we have to be thinking right now? Can't we just live inside this perfect little bubble of happiness for a moment? You're stood so far away ,
M	Yeah, this is this is all a bit I'm just a bit
W	ignore me, that was you don't have to feel or react any particular way or you're right you're right, you are. I'm just really

	I'm not smoking as well so
	cranky. First day of school feeling. The world just got bigger and I can see us from space and we're just a
	speck. I'm going to call my mum.
M	Do you really hate my parents?
W	Yes.
	,
M	Because why?
W	The thought of our offspring sharing their genetic code. That I could look into my son's eyes and see your father makes me no. I'm being emotional. Ignore me. They're fine. I'm fond of them in a way. Of course I am.
M	We never stay. Not long.
W	That's because don't you feel this that in their own way they're lovely, they're once you get attuned to their you know, but if I stay there for any length of time I worry that I might just put some scissors though their necks.
M	Right.
W	Don't you feel that way?
M	What, about your parents?
W	No, about

	why would you feel that way about *my* parents?
M	I don't.
W	Why would you say that? My parents have never been / anything but
M	they have I know. I'm not
W	you should be careful.
M	Sorry.
W	And our kid is going to have their genes too so be careful.
M	Can we just never mind.
W	What?
M	Never mind.
W	What?
M	Can we I need to just put this on pause, just put this argument / on pause and say I love you.
W	Not an argument it's a / conversation.
M	if we're going to be tearing bits off each other it's good that we take a second just to
W	can you not do this?
M	we're parents now.
	,
W	Yes. Okay.
M	So do you want to hug or maybe
W	no let's save that for

M	no, okay.
W	I don't feel like doing that right now.
M	Fine.
	,
	Let's call your mum and dad.
	,
W	Maybe later.
M	Yeah.
W	Okay.
M	So what did she say?
W	Oh, you know. She's happy. Of course she is.
M	Except
W	nothing. She's pleased, she's happy.
M	They didn't want to speak to me?
W	No.
M	Congratulate me?
W	She was crying.
M	Good crying?
W	Crying for, I don't know. I don't think she means what she said.
M	What did she say?
W	She knows I love you.
M	What did she say?
W	She's just anxious for me that's all.

M	Wishes you were having someone else's baby.
W	I didn't say that.
M	Well you're not, you're having mine so she can go fuck herself.
W	Please don't / talk about
M	bitch bitch bitch bitch.
W	No.
M	Thinks I'm boring that's what you said.
W	No.
M	Because I told her I was reading a book on radiation.
W	No.
M	Because I tried to talk to her about food scarcity and economic incentives for capping emissions.
W	Now you *are* being boring.
M	They were *your books.*
W	She didn't say anything.
M	Give me the phone.
W	Okay.
M	I'm going to call her.
W	Fine.
M	I will.
W	Go ahead.

,

M	I'm going to prove her wrong.
W	I know you will.
	,
	I know you will.
	Come here.
	,
	What's the matter?
M	I can't sleep.
W	Try.
M	I've been trying for hours.
W	Switch your brain off.
M	It's just disaster scenarios playing out in my head.
W	Oh baby.
M	Keep drifting off but it's explosions and helicopters and chunks of land collapsing into the sea.
W	Anxiety dreams.
M	No shit.
W	You've seen too many crap films.
M	We should at least / consider
W	I know but just
M	when then, when? We need to be equipped for if they

W	I'm not going to know until they say. I can't plan for how I'm going to feel in that moment if they're saying our child is
M	okay but
W	that there's something wrong with
M	We should have thought about it before. Talked about it.
W	Okay alright here it is.
	I want it whatever. If it's I don't know I'm not comfortable with flushing it away and starting again until we get one that's perfect.
M	I'm not saying that but let's be / realistic about
W	I'm saying I know what I want. I don't care if it's born without bones or limbs, legs or a face just a a a a a an amorphous blob of skin and a mouth which just screams and screams I don't care if it's like the thing in Eraserhead it's mine, ours and it's part of us and we'll love it, we will, we'll love it no matter
	no matter.
	,
M	No. I know.
W	Won't we?
	,
M	Yes.
	,

Let's try to sleep.

,

Are you asleep?

,

I can't sleep.

I'm trying.

,

I've always thought

I'm okay, I'm an okay person. A normal
enough person. Basically, you know, good.

,

I wish I'd read more when I was younger.
Or just, maybe slept with more people. Or
travelled. It's going to be harder to travel
now you know, with

,

nothing's ending. It's the start of something.
I'm young. We're young. It's exciting.
Can't tell if my eyes are open. Am I keeping
you awake?

Just can't stop thinking. Everything. Life. The
universe.

Death.

Try to picture what I'll look like. Dead.
Stopped. Just another object in the room.
Who'll see me like that.
What my expression will be.

When the face just relaxes it looks sort of
sarcastic I think.
My dead face.

If it's going to happen, the solution to it all,
the survival of mankind, it will happen in
our lifetime. It has to. And we'll be alive to
witness it.

When we're talking I can't take my eyes off
you. You're so honest with me and it hurts
sometimes but I remind myself you only say
these things because you trust me. That I'm
an anchor or something, I'm a nucleus to
your proton, is that right? I think sometimes
you think we're having a conversation and
that I'm listening and responding but really
I'm only silent because I have no idea what
to say. You're like an animal, a hungry, wild
animal and you're circling me and snarling
and you're beautiful and exciting and you're
trusting me because I'm standing still but
really I'm just frozen to the spot, really I just
don't know what else to do and I worry that
sometimes you think that that's strength and
it's not, it's not, it's just

I dreamt that the baby had been born but it
was just a cloud. A little thunder cloud. Or a
squirming little creature with fangs and claws
and flashing eyes.

I'll take a book off the shelf, any book
and you'll have turned down the pages
and underlined things. Put stars in the
margins. And I stare at the sentence you've
highlighted. I'll reread the paragraph. I'll
think what has she seen that I can't see?
What is it that I don't understand?

W   Go to sleep.

193

M	What time is it?
W	You've been snoring.
M	What are you doing?
W	Vomiting. Feel poisoned. Burst a blood vessel in my eye, look.
M	Oh. Yeah.
W	Look, my stomach. I'm definitely
M	no, you are I can see it.
W	I'm
M	massive.
W	Oh. I wasn't thinking
M	no I mean,
W	massive? Really?
M	Just, no, showing, you're
W	I just meant
M	I mean you can see it, you can, you're definitely
W	you can see it, you can definitely
M	there's a bump.
W	A bump. I've got a bump.

,

According to the Internet, my uterus is the size of a grapefruit.

Why do they use food to explain everything? And why do they call the baby 'baby'. Not 'your baby'?

'Baby is the size of a lentil.'
'Baby is the size of a kidney bean.'
'A peanut.'
'An olive.'

M	Are you hungry?
W	Famished.
M	I'll make you breakfast.
W	I want bacon and washing powder.
M	You can have bacon.
W	Close your eyes.
M	What have you done?
W	We have a nursery.
M	Green?
W	We don't want pink or blue and yellow is so
M	you're covered.
W	I've painted little trees.
M	I brought you chilli chocolate.
W	You're my hero.
M	Is it crazy I've been looking into local schools?
W	Do you want to know? Boy or girl? Or should / we
M	should it be a surprise on the day?
W	Not that the day won't be special enough as it is.
M	I'm too curious to wait.
W	Me too.

,

I was thinking.
It's silly.

What if I don't
what if I can't

love it?

What if I look in its eyes and I let it grip my
little finger and I hold it in my arms and I
don't feel a thing? That happens doesn't it?

M   Not to us.

W   I'm so terrified. I have no idea how I'm
going to be.

M   You're going to be a wonderful mum.

W   You don't know that.

M   Yes I do.

,

W   Thank you for being my person. For putting
up with me when I'm

,

we should get married. I know that's old
fashioned or whatever. I know you're against
the idea.

I love you. I don't say that enough.

M   You look beautiful.

W   Not fat?

M   Fat and beautiful.

,

W   Going to get bigger.

M   I expect so.

W   Much.

M   Yes.

W   I'll be a planet.

           So
           you know.
           Brace yourself.

           ,

M   Okay.

W   Ouch.

M   What is it?

W   Oh.
           Oh no.

M   Blood.

W   Not this. Not to us.

M   Hospital. Now.

W   I can't bear this.

M   I'll wait outside.

W   No.
           I need you.

M   Okay.

           ,

W   At least I can start smoking again.

M   Oh sweetheart.
           Shit.

W	You were right. We shouldn't have got excited.
M	Don't be silly.
W	We shouldn't have told anyone. We knew this could happen. Do you have change for the coffee machine?
M	Give me the keys.
W	I'm not an invalid.
M	What do you want me to do?

,

W   It's for the best probably isn't it? Would have completely taken over our lives. So much time and money, so much that could go wrong. End up sleepless with worry or with our heads in the sand.The world. Who'd want to have a child now? We should be happy. This is a relief it is it is it is we should take a deep breath and give a huge sigh of thank fuck for that because we're not going to add to any of it, we're not going to add yet one more lost person into this crowded little world so good for us. Let's crack open some champagne. Let's fly somewhere. Spend our money on *us* before the global economy completely implodes. When the riots start let's join in. Let's smash something. Start some fires. If we see an electric car with a baby on board sticker let's ram it off the road the fucking hypocrites. The damage they're doing.

,

It's a relief for you I suppose.

,

M   Why would you say that?

W   Just
                   you never quite seemed as

M   that's not true.

W   It wasn't as necessary or

M   it was my idea.

,

W   Yeah. I'm just trying to

                   I'm just trying

,

M   get some sleep.

,

I'm here.

I heard you get up, can I sit with you?

You fell asleep. I brought you in here.

Goodnight.

Good morning.

Goodnight.

I made some tea.

I'll see you after work.

Have you been sat there all day?

It's getting dark.

It's getting light.

Come to bed.

You fell asleep.

I woke up and you were gone.

You've not said a word to me for days.

,

Baby.

,

We need to get on with things.

W	Please don't.
M	It feels like you're punishing me.
W	I'm not trying to.
M	You're angry with me.
W	No. No I'm not I'm

yes. Alright I must be I suppose. I'm angry at this.

This everything. I hate it.

M	We can try again.
W	No.

I can't bear it.

Sorry.

There it is.

,

Should we stay together do you think? Or should we

I don't know.
Not.

,

M   I

W   I'm not saying this because I want to break
           up.
           I don't know what I want.

           I just think it would be
           I think it's a good opportunity for us to
           you know,
           talk.
           Have a conversation.
           Ask ourselves some serious
           you know,
           difficult

M   opportunity?

W   You know what I'm saying please fucking
           help me out here.

M   No. I know what I want.

W   We should, no, we should take some time
           and really think about this because right now
           I don't want to look at you. I need you to just
           fucking put your arms around me but you're
           not and don't, please, not now, not because
           I'm telling you to, I don't want that, not

M   sorry.

W   Fucking apologising you don't know do you
           what you're apologising for, so
           I need some
           just
           space.

M   Space?

W   Space. Fucking space. Yes. The fucking final
      frontier why are you / repeating things I'm
      saying?

M   Sorry I'm
      just
      getting my head around it that's all. Just
      trying to catch up a bit, trying to fucking

W   get your head around it.

M   Yes. And it's taking me a second so I'm sorry.
      I love you. I'm
      I don't know what you need or what you
      this is difficult for me too.

W   Oh fuck off / I'm not saying it's not, I'm not
      saying it's easy for you I know it's
      don't put that on me don't
      look we're both in the same
      we've both

M   just I need some help I need some help a
      little fucking
      I need you to give me some clues here as to
      what you need because honestly I feel like
      you're standing behind a glass wall just this
      sheet of glass and I can't reach you.

W   Don't cry for fuck sake because
      look,
      for fuck sake.

      ,

      It's okay.
      Fuck. It is.
      There are people in the world with real
      problems. This is just
      people go through this everywhere. All the
      time. Through time.

	We'll we could try again. If that's what we want to do.
M	It is.
W	I don't know.
	,
	Feel like I've had my skin peeled off.
M	I kissed someone else. At work. The new girl. The temp. I didn't talk to her about you and I don't know why, didn't say I had a
	,
	she was nice to me. She was nice to me. We talked about music.
	And she kissed me and I didn't stop her.
	However hurt you feel and raw and angry that's how I'm feeling too and that I love you more than anything. I'd cut off my arms for you. I'd pull my eyes out. And I'm sorry. And I know that if I go back in on Monday and she's there I might do it again.
	I could see our future together, this picture of what our lives were going to be like and it feels like I've been burgled and I have to live in this stupid angry version of the world where the person I adore, my best friend in the world can't even look at me and where I can't look at myself.
	I miss you.
	I want to sit opposite you in a restaurant, share a bottle of wine. I want to go to the

cinema and hold your hand. Run around in the park.

We can try again.

Adopt maybe.

,

Why are you smiling?

W   For the first time in ages I feel a little clarity. I'm sad. I've been really sad and I don't know if that's ever going to go away completely. I'm sorry I've not been able to tell you what I've needed.
I don't know what I needed.
Yes I do.

I needed you to be patient with me. To wait as long as it took. I needed you to be braver than me and put your own feelings second and to understand, even when you didn't understand. To use your initiative for once and not need instructions. To try to imagine what it's like to miscarry. To realise that there are certain feelings I'm trying to cope with and protecting you from and I'm working *hard*.

Most of all I needed you to not kiss someone else.

,

So, I'm being sensible for both of us. That's it.

Lucky we don't have kids.

,

So there you are.

M   You look good.

W   No I don't, shut up. Thank you.

M   No, it's

W   thanks for meeting me.

M   Oh, it's
no, of course. I was surprised when you
asked

W   right.

M   Starbucks.

W   Oh. Yeah. Well. You know.

M   Didn't seem like you.

W   Beard.

M   I know.

W   It's good.

M   Oh. Yeah.

W   I didn't know who else to tell.

M   No, I'm glad you did.

W   Mum was very fond of you.

M   I thought she hated me.

W   Yeah.

                   ,

M   How was the funeral?

W   It's tomorrow.

M   Oh.

W	Come with me. Will you come with me? I mean, if / you want to.
M	Really? Because
W	weird? Too weird, forget it. Sorry.
M	Of course, I'll, yeah if you want me to.
W	I do yeah that would be good. You don't need to check with
M	check with what? What?
W	Nothing.

,

M	My dad died. Few months back.
W	You never said.
M	No, I know I didn't know if
W	oh, no, that's

,

We're getting to that age now.

Scary. Be just us left soon.

,

Fuck. Look at you.

M	You too.
W	Just want to just take just a second.

Mental picture.

Click.

M	It's alright.
W	No, I know. I know.
M	Oh, please don't you don't need to oh.
W	I'm sorry, I promised myself I wouldn't
M	it's okay. It's okay.
W	Mess. Already. Brilliant. Well done me.
M	You're okay, just you're okay.
	,
W	How are you anyway? How's life? How's work? Good? Everything good?
M	Yeah / it's
W	how's the temp?
M	Oh. Yeah. No, we're not
W	no?
M	No we're, we, / I mean we
W	that's really I'm really I'm sorry about that.
M	No no no, I mean after we, you and I once we I just wasn't I didn't have the energy for another not right away, not

W	so you didn't I mean with the temp that didn't you didn't
M	oh, well, yeah but I mean, that was just fucking hell. That was this whole other
W	right.
M	Thing.
W	Right. Yeah.
M	How about you?
W	Do we really want to talk about this? I mean, I don't want to talk about this. I know that we're not that you and I are no longer but I still don't want to hear about your your your sex life or
M	no okay.
W	So you're not together now?
M	No. Fuck. No. No. No. No.
W	Right. Okay.
M	Now I'm with
W	oh okay.
M	Yeah.

W	You don't have to
M	I don't mind.
W	I don't want to hear it.

,

So okay.

This is horrible.

I don't know what I was expecting.

I think I might leave before we start talking about the weather.

M	It's fucked.
W	It is. It's impossible. Sweat's pouring off me like
M	everything's shut down. City can't cope with it.
W	Keep passing out.
M	What?
W	Dehydration or I carry a bottle around with me but I just go through it like
M	yeah.
W	So I take two but then I'm just lugging around all this water and it's
M	I know I'm the same it's
W	we weren't right together were we? We were good people, weren't we, but it just wasn't meant to be.
M	You don't believe in any of that predetermination, destiny stuff.

W   I do now.

M   Oh,
           sorry. Really?

W   Yes.
           No.

           I think what with the world how it is,
           I think if I didn't think someone was going to
           fix it all, that some superhuman genius was
           going to work out how to fix it all then

           I think I'd just entirely lose my mind.

           I don't know.

           I'm different.

           We both are.

           I quit smoking.

M   Yeah?

W   It's shit. I feel so much better.

M   I started.

W   You're kidding.

M   I look cool.

W   No.

           No.

M   How about your course?

W   Oh. Yeah. Finished. Done.

M   You're a doctor.

W   Technically.

           ,

M   I've been playing again. Couple of gigs in a
           friend's band. Nothing big.

W   Yeah?

M   It's a sort of electronic thing, a new direction.

W   Right.

M   I think I've got stupider.
           Since we

           ,

           I don't know what books to read, I don't
           really read anything.

           I have no idea what's happening in the
           world.

W   It's fucked.

M   I can't remember how to think.

           And it feels, you know, really

           wonderful.

           Not having to worry about stuff I have no
           control over. I used to get so angry at people
           who didn't read or think or care about
           anything but I completely get it now.
           Sometimes I'll be driving. No, it's stupid.

           ,

           Sometimes I'll have this thing, I'll just sort of
           like I wake up.
           While I'm driving. Not that, exactly, because
           I'm not tired, all I do is sleep. It's not that.
           It's just

who's been driving? I don't remember
anything from the last twenty minutes. You
know. Like I've been on autopilot. Zombie or

and I have *days* like that.

Days.

,

Now I'm here with you and

,

W   yeah.

,

M   Yeah.

W   Well.
Well well well.

Fuck.

M   Yeah.

W   Well.

M   Yeah.

W   Well well well.

M   That was

W   it was. It really was.

M   I don't feel bad about this.

W   You,
what? You don't

M   not at all.

,

W	Oh.
M	What?
W	Nothing.
M	What?
W	No, nothing I'm I was being I was thinking something.
M	What?
W	Just letting myself get carried away for a bit. I forgot for a second. About her.
M	Oh. No, I didn't mean
W	it's fine.
M	I no I'm I wasn't thinking, I was just
W	no of course.
M	Just talking just
W	it's just it felt right. Didn't it? I mean to me anyway.
M	Yeah, no, of course it was yes. It did. , It did. But

W	can we save the buts? I think we both know.
	Can we just
	for a minute
	just lie here and pretend that we're years ago
	and nothing's happened. That we'll get the
	papers and maybe go to the pub for a roast.
	Play the quiz machine. Have a quarrel about
	some book I've been reading that I explain
	badly and sound like I'm advocating
	I don't know,
	compulsory euthanasia of the old or
	you know, I kept a drawer of your socks and
	things.
	It's stuffy in here. Sorry. Can't breathe. I'd
	open the window but it's just as bad out
	there.
	I've not slept with anyone else since you.
	You don't need to know that. It doesn't
	matter. It doesn't matter that you slept with
	two people.
	,
	What, more?
M	We were apart for
W	no I know. I know.
	It doesn't matter. How many? It doesn't
	matter.
M	You want to know?
W	Yes. No. I've not so much as kissed anyone
	else.
	I'm crying again. Shit.
	I tried to. I went for a drink with this guy.
	But he was horrible.

,

M   Don't tell me her name. Your girlfriend.

,

M   Fiancée.

,

W   Oh.

M   Yeah.

,

W   Let's never see each other again. Okay?

,

You look startled.

M   You said we shouldn't see each other.

W   Yet here I am. Why might that be?

M   It's raining.

W   Do I look different?

M   You've not got a coat. Different?

W   I thought I might, yes
           look
           different.

           Glowing maybe.

,

M   You mean

W   yep.

,

215

So, okay, that's as far as I planned. I got as
far as telling you then I hoped you'd maybe
jump in and save the day, be all manly and
know what happens next because this is
I mean,
come on Superman. Swoop down. Save the
day.
Anything.

,

Nothing.

I've broken you. You've shut down. It's too
much.
Can I come in at least? I'm drenched.

,

It'll be born by the time you've said
something. It'll plop out of me and be
slippering, squirming around in the afterbirth
can I at least come in or

M   listen,

W   it speaks.

M   Okay, listen, I'm sorry but can I

           can we talk later? I'll come round, I'll

W   she's here isn't she?
           Of course she is. I'm an idiot. This is
           horrible.
           I'm going.

M   Wait, just

W   I can't do this.

M   Please.

W	Don't.
M	I knew I'd find you here.
W	How?
M	I looked everywhere else.
W	You know me so well.
M	Shouldn't be out here at night.
W	We had sex in those toilets do you remember?
M	I'm sorry I couldn't speak before.
W	I made you miss your meeting.
M	Obviously I'm going to do I want to do the right thing.
W	The right thing. Good.
M	I'm going to support you.
W	Support. Great.
M	Will you just please, I'm sorry, but just be quiet because it's you're making it impossible to think and I really need to think.
W	No. I won't. You shouldn't need to think. You shouldn't. You should just fucking know what to do. Say what you want. Say what you're feeling. Don't tell me what I need to hear.
M	I don't know what you need to hear.
W	Then it shouldn't be a problem.
M	What I'm feeling, what I'm thinking is there is no perfect outcome of this. I have to tell my fiancée.

W	Yes you do.
M	And I please, shut up for a second. I'm sorry, just give me a chance here.
	,
	Thank you.
	,
	Right.
	So okay,
	let's get married.
W	No.
M	Why?
W	Okay, one, because you're already engaged to someone else. Two, because that's the least romantic proposal in the entire sad sorry two hundred thousand year history of the human race and three, because I don't want to. Fucking hold your horses I don't even know whether I'm going to keep it yet so let's not get ahead of ourselves.
M	You're not / going to
W	I've not decided yet and don't tell me your opinion because it's fucking irrelevant. What's your opinion?
M	All I'm saying is
W	you think I should abort it.

I wish you were dead.
I wish I was dead. I need an earthquake. A
tsunami.

M   I'll do what it takes. I'll do whatever you
           want, whatever you need.

W   I need you to call your fiancée.

M   I'm not going to tell her on the phone.

W   Because you don't want to hurt her feelings.

M   Because she deserves better than that.

W   Better than her husband-to-be impregnating
           his ex-girlfriend?

M   Than being told by phone.

W   How touching. You must love her very
           much.

M   Yes. Actually I do. Is that surprising, she's
           my fucking fiancée. We're getting married in
           three months.

W   I must buy a hat.

M   Were. We were. Obviously we can't now.

W   And you loved her even when you were
           fucking me on my sofa?

M   Yes.

W   You loved her when you were coming inside
           me?

M   Yes.

W   Which is why you were with her whilst your
           sperm was fertilising my egg. As I sobbed
           on my own. Sobbed so hard I burst all the
           capillaries under my eyes. Vomited. Took

	an earring and pushed the metal point into my arm, drew blood, a lot, here look, it got infected.
M	What happened with me and you wasn't to do with her.
W	You and me, you really have stopped reading.
M	I still loved her, yes, at that moment. I didn't want to hurt her.
W	You just weren't thinking.
M	I didn't think she'd find out.
W	Wow. Okay. Well that's completely fine then. Obviously you loved her very much, it's just at that particular moment, ejaculating was a little bit more important to you than her sanity and wellbeing and now this is happening, a chain of events which is going to culminate in the miracle of childbirth and it's going to grow up and behave like you and leave armies of sobbing women puncturing themselves alone in their rooms. Give me your phone I want to talk to her.
M	No.
W	I want to apologise to her. When we had sex I thought how sad you seemed, how lonely and desperate and how much you missed me, how much I missed you and how horrific this two-dimensional idiot fiancée of yours must be but I bet she's lovely. I bet she's just extremely

nice.
Give me your phone.

| M. | No. |

W This day this day this fucking wedding day
she's planned since she put a napkin on a
Barbie and now here I am, my fucking belly,
swelling by the minute, the evidence that her
entire world is bullshit. She'll probably off
herself, be one of those people under a train,
one of those station announcements, I would,
I fucking would, I'd open up every vein and
write on the wall big and red 'this is not a cry
for help'. Give me your phone.

M No.

W How did I become this person? I used to be
a good person and now I'm evil. I'm actually
evil. Give me the phone, I'm serious, I want
to talk to her.

M That won't help.

W Give me the phone.

M No.

 ,

W No you're probably right. I don't think I'd
handle it well.

M I'm going to talk to her. Now. Face to face.
Okay? I'm doing it.

 ,

 Can I come to yours once I've seen her?

W Why?

M Because I want to.
And I'll have nowhere else to go.

 ,

W	Okay.
M	Okay.
W	You're bleeding.
M	She was upset.
W	And there was
M	kicking. Screaming. Hitting.
W	Did she hurt you?
M	Scratching. She caught me on, under my ear, her ring
W	good.
M	Yeah, I suppose.
W	No she deserved to. She deserved to really fucking
M	yeah.
W	Cripple you.
M	No, you're right.
W	For what you did.
M	Yeah, but
W	should have cut your fucking dick off.
M	Okay.
W	I must be insane. You clearly can't be trusted.
M	I
W	you're clearly unable to overrule your prick.
M	I'm not entirely to blame for

W	yes actually yes fucking yes you fucking are, yes.
M	It was both of us who
W	I'm not engaged to her.
M	Nor am I now.
W	Touché.
	,
	Touché.
	,
M	So what now? We just what? Go back to normal?
W	Normal? What normal? What?
M	No, just
W	we're not a couple.
M	Oh.
W	We're not we're not going to be like
M	no, right.
W	Not like before. We need to start fresh. If at all.
M	I just sorry, I thought
W	I don't know you. You're a fucking stranger now. A fucking deceitful, immature evil little stranger.
M	I just assumed.

W   Well don't. This is all just going at a hundred
                miles an hour and I need a second to
                breathe.

M   No. If we think about it too much we won't
                do it.

W   Do what?

M   This. Now. Us.

                Yes it's not the perfect circumstances, but
                let's go into this with open arms. I love you.
                Okay? I always have. When I'm away from
                you I forget how to enjoy anything and when
                I'm with you I feel at home.

                We've never worked out how to be together
                without making each other feel a bit shit and
                I want to find a way to not do that. You've
                got to stop ripping bits off me and I've got
                to grow up and behave like an actual human
                being.

                You've needed me to know what you need
                without having to ask.
                You've needed me to be aware of how I'm
                feeling and to let you in to my head.
                Right now I know exactly what you need to
                hear and it's absolutely what I'm feeling.

                We're not going to overthink this.

                We're doing this.

                We're going to get the books and go to
                classes and work out how to be parents. And
                we're going to grow old together and look
                back on all this and laugh because it will
                seem like a different lifetime.

And we'll have a conversation and we'll just
try to do the right thing. Because we're good
people. Right?

And we'll plant forests. I mean it. We'll cycle
everywhere. We'll grow our own food if we
have to. We'll never take another plane.
We'll just stay right here. And we'll plant
forests. You and me.
You, me and the little speck. The ten
thousand tonnes of CO_2 waiting to be
unleashed onto the planet.

,

W   Thank you.
           I needed to hear that.

,

           I'll think about it.

,

M   Breathe in.

W   Okay.

M   Breathe.

W   They're getting more frequent.

M   Every few minutes.

W   Get the keys.

M   We're here.

W   Don't leave me.

M   I'm right here.

W   I'm scared.

M	You're so brave.
W	Hurts.
M	I forgot the camera.
W	Here it comes.
M	He's so beautiful.
W	Let me hold him.
M	Of course.
W	We're a family.
M	I'm so tired.
W	It's your turn.
M	Shall I bring him in with us?
W	He's got to wean.
M	I know.
W	The books all say so.
M	Good marks all round.
W	I'm so proud of him.
M	I forgot my camera.
W	There he goes.
M	Don't cry.
W	He's never slept away from home.
M	We're going to be fine.
W	You shouldn't let him see that.
M	I'll talk to him.
W	He needs to hear it from his father.
M	Are we going up this weekend?

W	I just want to see him before he's off because, what with the world as it is,
M	I know.
W	Have you got your camera?
M	Let's get married.
W	I do.
M	We need to be prepared.
W	It won't be as bad as they're saying.
M	He hasn't called.
W	They've suspended all flights.
M	It's so hot.
W	The planet's fucked.
M	He looks so different.
W	He wants to help out.
M	We're fine.
W	That's what I told him.
M	It's a standard operation.
W	I know.
M	Just goes with old age.
W	He's going to drive you.
M	I'm going to be okay.
W	I'm scared.
M	You're fine.
W	He's found me a home. They have classes and things there. Art and things. It's nearer to him so a long way from here. He gets

cross with me sometimes. You know how he
is. I think a lot of people are angry at me.
At us. Those of us still around. I forget more
and more. I don't know what they're so upset
about.

I miss talking to you. Here I am talking to
myself.
Your forests have gone. I don't watch the
news any more, it all just gets worse and
worse.
Everything's covered in ash. He tells me to
stop dusting. Snaps at me.
I'm tired. Fed up.
But I'm okay. Listen to me moaning on. It's
a nice cool day today, like we used to have.
Fresh air. No sirens. No noise. Nothing.
It's good.

,

Anyway, I just thought I'd stop by. Change the
flowers.

I don't know if I'll get much of a chance to
pop back here so

anyway.

,

I love you.

,

Lights out.

2071

Note from the authors

Climate science is a complicated, emotive topic. Attempts to dramatise it often over-simplify the issues and compromise the integrity of the data, or sensationalise the possible future outcomes. The element of fiction can also allow an audience to dismiss what they're hearing.

For many years, director Katie Mitchell explored various approaches to communicating climate science in a theatre context. Her conclusion was to place the scientist onstage, to explain the data with clarity and objectivity from a position of authority.

The following text was co-written by Chris Rapley and Duncan Macmillan, following more than a hundred hours of conversation. It was written to be performed by Chris Rapley at the Royal Court Theatre in London and the Hamburg Schauspielhaus in late 2014, in a production directed by Katie Mitchell.

As a performance text, it can be performed by one or more people, of any age, gender, class or ethnicity. Productions should include the following text at the beginning and end:

* * *

What you're about to hear was originally delivered by Professor Chris Rapley at the Royal Court Theatre, London, and the Hamburg Schauspielhaus in 2014, with some updates made in mid 2015.

Since this text was written, the 21ˢᵗ annual meeting of the world's climate negotiators took place in Paris. On December 12, 2015, representatives of 195 countries approved the Paris Agreement, which seeks to fulfill the United Nations Framework Convention on Climate Change's mandate to 'avoid dangerous anthropogenic interference with the climate system.' The agreement is ambitious. It will require the elimination of practices that destabilise the climate system, while ensuring ongoing and expanded prosperity for people around the world. For the agreement to work, we shall all have to play our part.

DM and CR

I'm here to talk about the future.

As a climate scientist, it's part of my job to explore what it might bring.

My career has been unusually varied.

It has included developing rocket and satellite instruments, initially to study the Universe and the Sun, but then to observe the Earth, particularly its polar regions.

It has also included running the International Geosphere-Biosphere Programme that coordinates the activities of over 10,000 scientists in 75 nations.

I have run the British Antarctic Survey, and in that role have been to the Antarctic and the Southern Ocean many times.

I was President of the international scientific body that coordinates research in the Antarctic, and was one of the architects of the International Polar Year 2007-2008 – an exercise by thousands of scientists from over 60 countries to build up a 'snapshot' of the polar regions.

My work has enabled me to travel to parts of the planet visited only by a few and to meet experts from all over the world – to see and assess things for myself.

As Director of the Science Museum I moved away from running research projects and instead sought out ways for scientists and the public to discuss complex and controversial subjects.

Perhaps the most complex and controversial subject of all is that of our climate – if it is changing, in what way and on what timescale.

It is an extremely emotive issue, and we are all susceptible to bias and irrationality when confronting it.

The issues are often oversimplified. But it is a subject of enormous complexity.

The climate system itself is very complex, the most complex system we know of.

There are gaps in our knowledge, and many scientific uncertainties, some of which are fundamentally unknowable.

This makes it extremely difficult to predict precisely what the future holds and to determine exactly what, if anything, we should do.

In addition there are economic considerations, political implications and ethical questions that are not easily answered.

But decisions are being made on our behalf at various levels of government and we all need to be part of that process.

One of my current responsibilities, as Chair of the London Climate Change Partnership, is to draw together organisations within the public, private and civil sectors to make London the best prepared and most resilient capital city in the world with respect to climate change.

On some issues, such as flood protection, our planning horizon extends forward 100 years.

The future is also being planned for at the national and international level.

In December this year, 195 nations will meet in Paris to agree on a course of action to respond to climate change.

Their discussions will be informed by a detailed summary of the latest climate science.

The decisions they make will affect us all.

I'm here to communicate the results of the science, their implications, and the options we have before us.

…

A lot has changed in my lifetime.

When I was ten years old my mother gave me an Atlas in which large areas of the Antarctic were marked 'Region Unknown to Man'.

But in that same year an unprecedented sequence of scientific and technological advances began to open up that continent and render my Atlas obsolete.

It was 1957, and the Commonwealth Trans Antarctic Expedition embarked on the first ever crossing from coast to coast via the South Pole.

At the same time, despite the ongoing cold war, 67 countries, including the USSR and eastern bloc nations, collaborated in the International Geophysical Year – an intensive scientific campaign to study the Earth.

Major advances were made in oceanography, meteorology, magnetism and a host of other research fields.

One of the greatest advances was in the Antarctic where airborne surveys using ice penetrating radars revealed, for the first time, the staggering depth of the ice sheet – up to 4km deep – and began to map out the mountainous terrain that lay below.

Then, on October the 4th 1957, the Russians launched Sputnik 1, the first ever satellite.

I helped my father set up a short-wave radio set so that we could listen to Sputnik's faint bleeps amongst the hiss and crackle of static as it passed overhead.

Only 4 years after Sputnik, Yuri Gagarin became the first human in space, and just 12 years later – on July 20th 1969 – Neil Armstrong and Buzz Aldrin stood on the Moon.

By that time I had trained as a Physicist at Oxford and was at home with my parents awaiting my degree result.

We watched the blurry footage of the moon landing together on a Murphy black and white TV set.

A few years later, in 1971, I began my research career designing and building my own rocket and satellite instruments to study the cosmos.

I went on to work with NASA in America designing and operating a satellite mission to study solar flares – explosive energy releases that occur in the Sun's atmosphere.

After 6 years, as we started work on a follow-up project, I saw some data from another pioneering NASA satellite mission called Seasat.

It was a contour map of the very edge of the Antarctic ice.

Instead of looking away from the Earth, Seasat looked back at it.

It carried radar instruments that imaged and mapped the oceans and polar regions.

It had the ability to map the ice sheet shape and, over time, to monitor its changes.

I knew I had to be part of this.

For the next 15 years I built up a research group specialising in the design and use of radar altimeters to map the polar regions from satellites.

At the same time I was a member of a small group of scientists from across Europe working with the European Space Agency to develop their series of Earth observation satellites.

This work culminated in the Cryosat satellite, which is operating as I speak, taking hundreds of millions of measurements of the polar ice with pinpoint accuracy and unprecedented resolution.

Maps of Antarctica produced from Cryosat cover 96% of the continent.

Very little of the region remains 'Unknown to Man'.

...

It hasn't just been polar research that has benefitted from satellite technology.

The advanced instruments available today allow us to probe and map the key components of the Earth: the Atmosphere, the Oceans, the Ice, and the Land - in unprecedented ways.

For example – space radars are unaffected by cloud cover or darkness, and unlike human researchers on the surface, can continue to observe in the depths of the polar winter.

Imaging systems can see detail at the level of metres, and instruments with exquisite sensitivity can detect tiny changes in the Earth's gravity that allow us to measure changes in mass of the ice sheets and oceans.

We combine the space data with the myriad of measurements made from aircraft, ships, buoys and a host of specialised instruments on the ground.

By using computer models to bring together the data with our understanding of the underlying physical laws, we can begin to make sense of what we observe.

This provides us with a grand perspective of the Earth's system as a whole, of its component parts and the interconnections between them.

The component parts are:

– The Atmosphere – the layers of gas surrounding the planet.

– The Hydrosphere – the oceans, lakes and rivers.

– The Cryosphere – the ice on land and sea, the snow and the permafrost.

– The Lithosphere – the outer layer of the rock that makes up most of the planet's mass.

– The Biosphere – all living material, including us.

The system behaves in complex and often counterintuitive ways, but the fundamental principles of it are quite simple:

Its component parts interact with each other, exchanging energy in ways that operate in an overall *Dynamic Balance.*

…

Dynamic Balance applies to many features of the system, such as the balance of carbon between the atmosphere, ocean, land and vegetation or the amount of ice on land and water in the ocean.

But it especially applies to the *energy* balance of the planet – meaning that, over time, the amount of energy leaving the planet is equal to the amount entering it.

The primary source of energy is the Sun.

About a third of the solar energy is reflected away by clouds, haze, and the surface.

About a quarter is absorbed by the atmosphere.

Over 90% of the remainder is absorbed by the oceans, since they cover the majority of the Earth's surface and are dark.

The rest of the energy goes into the land and ice.

More energy is accumulated in the equatorial regions than at the poles, and it is the action of redistributing this energy that drives the circulation of the oceans and atmosphere.

Heat energy radiated by the Earth's surface is partially absorbed in the atmosphere by trace gases – water vapour, methane and Carbon Dioxide.

The interactions between the atmosphere, the oceans, and the ice on land and sea drive the natural variability of the climate.

The system is very responsive, and even a small change in one component can trigger a chain of consequences in the other parts.

When such changes alter the Energy Balance, the effects are felt throughout the entire system.

Such changes include variations in the energy received from the Sun – either from fluctuations in the solar brightness or from small variations in the Earth's orbit and tilt that change its distance and orientation relative to the Sun.

They include increases or decreases in the Earth's reflectivity due to variations in the cloud cover, or volcanic eruptions that inject haze into the upper atmosphere, or changes in the surface cover of snow or vegetation.

And they include changes in the concentrations of water vapour, methane and Carbon Dioxide that alter the planet's loss of energy to space.

Whenever one of these changes takes place, the climate system adjusts until a new energy balance is reached.

Some changes are amplified. An especially important effect occurs in the polar regions where, as highly reflective ice and snow melt, dark, heat-absorbing land or ocean is revealed beneath.

This increases the rate of melting and amplifies the warming.

...

Since the majority of the energy is absorbed by the ocean, any imbalance would be most observable in the Hydrosphere.

To detect an energy imbalance in the oceans, we can analyse data from the worldwide system of ocean buoys – known as the Argo floats.

Over 3,500 of these have been deployed by 30 nations throughout the world ocean since the start of the millennium.

The instruments measure temperature, pressure and salinity down to a depth of 2000m.

We can combine their measurements with contemporary and historic data from ships and other systems of buoys to allow us to estimate the ocean heat content and its variations.

Additionally, we can measure sea-level, which rises as temperature increases, acting as a global thermometer.

A history of global sea-level can be constructed from studies of beach structures worldwide, and from archaeological data, for example the location and height of Roman era harbours, all of which hold a record of past sea levels.

There is also information from a worldwide network of Tide Gauges installed at harbours on coastlines around the world over a century ago, to provide data on local tides for seafarers and civil engineers.

The number of such installations has increased over the years to nearly 300 sites worldwide, creating the official 'Global Ocean Sea-Level Network'.

More recently – over the last two decades – Satellite Radar Altimeters have revolutionised sea-level measurements.

They provide almost complete ocean coverage, and they have the ability to detect changes in the global average to within millimetres.

The combination of all these data shows that over the last several thousand years, global sea level was virtually static.

However, in the late 19th Century, sea level began to rise. Over the 20th Century the rate of rise averaged 1.8mm per year.

Over the last two decades, the rate of rise has increased to 3.3mm per year.

This may not sound much, but it indicates that the Dynamic Energy Balance of the climate system has been disrupted.

...

To understand the implications of this imbalance, we have to put it in the context of geological time.

Stored in the rock and ocean sediments of the planet is a record of the past – often patchy and indistinct – but a record nonetheless.

When we investigate this record, we find that the world's climate has varied on many timescales and for many reasons.

Little is known of the early history of the planet after its formation 4.5 billion years ago.

We do know that the Biosphere emerged as soon as the physical conditions permitted - about 3.5 billion years ago.

Like the other components, the Biosphere interacts with the rest of the system, in particular the atmosphere, in complex ways.

In the 'Great Oxidation', which started about 2.3 billion years ago, living organisms began producing oxygen in substantial quantities by photosynthesis.

This ultimately transformed the atmosphere to the oxygen rich state that we experience today.

Over the last 500 million years – the climate has varied between a warm state – much warmer than today – and a so-called 'icehouse state', in which ice sheets formed at one or both poles.

Between 360 and 300 million years ago, in the Carboniferous Period, conditions of temperature and moisture supported the formation of vast swamp forests.

Over time their vegetation decayed, and was gradually overlain by sediments, compressed and baked, creating deposits of coal, oil and gas.

250 million years ago – in the age of the reptiles – the temperature of the planet was much higher than today, and so was the Carbon Dioxide concentration of the atmosphere.

The Age of the Mammals began about 65 million years ago following an asteroid impact in which more than three quarters of all plant and animal species on Earth went extinct.

Life gradually recovered.

As it did so, the planet slowly cooled, and by about 34 million years ago ice sheets had developed at the South Pole.

The system then went through another warm phase, after which, about 20 million years ago, we entered the 'icehouse' world we experience today.

Over the last 2.5 million years the ice sheets at both poles have waxed and waned, initially on a 40,000 year cycle and, more recently – over the last million years - a 110,000 year cycle, triggered by small variations in the shape of the Earth's orbit and in its orientation to the Sun.

As the ice sheets wax and wane they have a huge impact on global sea level.

During the transition from the peak of the last ice age 18,000 years ago to the beginning of the current warm interglacial period, the oceans rose 120 metres at a sustained rate of about 1m per century – 10mm per year.

...

12,000 years ago, as the transition from the last ice age came to an end, the Holocene Epoch began.

Global average temperature stabilised, declining since then, very gradually, by about a degree centigrade, with natural variations of no more than a degree.

The Holocene has been an extraordinary stable period. We find nothing else like it in the climate record.

It is argued that this relative equilibrium has enabled our species to flourish, first establishing agriculture, then civilisation and then the modern world.

But the equilibrium is delicate.

There have been small climatic variations, which have had human consequences.

For example, over the northern hemisphere, between the 10th Century and 13th Century, regional warmings of up to a degree centigrade took place.

This was the Medieval Warm Period, when the Vikings established substantial settlements on Greenland.

It was followed by a cooling from the 16th Century to 19th Century, known as the Little Ice age, when the Thames was repeatedly frozen and the Viking settlements in Greenland were abandoned.

The climatic variations during the Holocene Period had significant human impacts. But they were small compared with the changes that took place over the 110 thousand year Ice Age cycles.

During the latter part of the Holocene, sea-level changes did not exceed 0.2mm per year.

In the context of this, the 1.8mm per year observed last century, and the 3.3mm per year we observe today are geologically significant.

The current rate is approaching that which occurs during the transition from an Ice Age to a warm interglacial, a major climatic shift.

And it is occurring during the warm interglacial, and at a time unrelated to the natural ice age cycle.

…

To understand what is causing this change in the Hydrosphere we can first look to the Cryosphere, in particular the Ice Shelves.

Ice shelves are platforms of ice 100s of metres, or sometimes even a km thick, that extrude off the main ice sheet on the land.

Both the ice sheet and the ice shelf move towards the ocean under the action of gravity.

The ice sheet moves over land, and the ice shelf moves over the sea.

Ice shelves commonly run aground in the shallow continental waters, and when they do so their movement is slowed, causing a build-up of pressure in the ice sheet behind them.

If ocean temperatures rise, the water warms the underside of the ice shelf, which then collapses into smaller sections – Icebergs.

As the ice shelf collapses, the pressure of the ice sheet behind is relieved causing the ice sheet to flow more rapidly into the ocean, raising sea-level as it does so.

…

In 1995 the most northerly ice shelf of the Antarctic Peninsula collapsed.

For the first time in thousands of years it was possible to sail a ship around James Ross Island, which until then had been linked to the Trinity Coast of the Peninsula by the ice shelf.

The northern Peninsula ice shelves have waxed and waned even during the Holocene, so this event was not necessarily climatically significant.

However, since then, there has been a progressive southerly wave of collapses; the Larsen A ice shelf in 1995, the Wilkins in 1998, the Larsen B in 2002.

The Larsen B collapse was particularly significant, since the evidence from sediment cores is that it had been in place since the last Glacial Maximum 20,000 years ago.

In 2008 and again in 2009 parts of the Wilkins ice shelf – the largest on the Peninsula's West Coast – collapsed. In two years it reduced to one third of its original size.

I flew over the Wilkins ice shelf in 2009 and looked down on the vast area of shattered ice – it looked like pieces of a broken window.

The pilot, who had been flying in the region for more than 20 years said he'd never seen anything like it.

In 1978 John Mercer, a US glaciologist with much Antarctic field experience described how, in a warming world, we might see a successive collapse of ice shelves extending down the Antarctic Peninsula.

He suggested that this would be a warning sign of a more worrying sequence of events to come.

The Antarctic Peninsula connects to an area of the Antarctic called West Antarctica, and the chief feature of West Antarctica is that its massive ice sheet sits on bedrock that is up to 2km below sea level.

For this reason it is called a *marine* ice sheet.

Mercer's concern was that if the successive collapse reached as far as West Antarctica, the pressure of the warmer water at depth would lift the ice sheet, causing water to penetrate deeper and deeper below the ice, reducing friction between the ice and rock, and so leading to an unstoppable collapse.

This would result in a rise in sea level over time of many metres, since the total volume of ice in West Antarctica is equivalent to a 6 metre rise.

As Mercer feared, the ice shelf collapses along the Peninsula have occurred and parts of the West Antarctic Ice Sheet are now starting to collapse.

Disturbingly, in East Antarctica, the Totten glacier, which is also marine based, is showing accelerated ice loss too, which no one predicted.

And in the northern hemisphere, the satellite and surface data show that the loss of ice from the Greenland ice sheet increased by

600% – from about 34 Gigatonnes per year in the late 1990s to 215 Gigatonnes per year just a decade later.

One Gigatonne is *a thousand million* tonnes.

Greenland's fastest flowing ice outlet, the Jakobshavn glacier, is now flowing in the summer at speeds of 17km per year - nearly 50m per day – the fastest rate for any polar glacier or ice stream that has been recorded.

This glacier drains about 7% of the ice sheet, and about 35 billion tonnes of icebergs calve off and pass out to sea every year.

It was one of these that is thought to have sunk the Titanic in 1912.

In addition to this ice loss in the Antarctic and Greenland, satellite image data reveal that 90% of the world's glaciers and small ice caps are shrinking.

In Alaska alone, the rate of glacier ice loss over the last decade has been measured as 75 Gigatonnes per year – about half the net ice loss from all of Antarctica.

There is evidence from historical records that some glaciers, especially in Europe, began retreating as long ago as the mid 19th Century, probably in response to the end of the Little Ice Age.

But the satellite data show that the retreat globally has gathered pace over the last 30 years.

…

By analysing variations in the Earth's gravity field due to changes in the mass of the ice sheets and the ocean, it has been calculated that, at present, the melting of ice sheets and glaciers contribute to about half of the observed sea level rise.

Apart from a small contribution from human use of aquifers, the rest of the sea level rise is due to thermal expansion.

The water is getting warmer.

We know that this warming is not due to the Sun's brightness increasing, because satellite instruments have been accurately measuring the Solar energy flux since the late 1970s.

We also find that while the lower atmosphere and surface are warming, the upper atmosphere is cooling.

If the Sun were the cause, the upper atmosphere would be warming too.

...

To understand what is causing the ice to melt and the oceans to warm, we need to look at what is happening to the Atmosphere, in particular the trace gases – water vapour, methane and Carbon Dioxide.

These gases are present in relatively small quantities in our atmosphere, in comparison to Nitrogen and Oxygen, but they have a significant impact on the temperature of the planet.

Water vapour, methane and Carbon Dioxide obstruct the loss of heat from the surface as it passes upwards.

This effect, referred to as the "Greenhouse Effect", causes the Earth's surface to have an average temperature of 15 degrees.

Without it, the surface would be 15 degrees below freezing.

Life as we know it would be impossible.

We can observe the change in atmospheric concentration over time, by looking at data from ice cores drilled from ice sheets and glaciers in the Antarctic and Greenland.

The ability to study these ice cores is regarded by many as the most important advance in Earth science of the 20th century.

Each year the snowfall creates a layer that compacts to ice and traps bubbles of the contemporary air.

The deepest ice cores extracted from the Antarctic are more than 3km long, and contain a record stretching back 800,000 years.

As the Director of the British Antarctic Survey on one of my Antarctic trips in 2002, I visited the European drill site at a place called Dome C.

I watched as a 5m section of ice core, nearly half a million years old, was extracted from a depth of just under 3km.

It took an hour to lower the drill, a few minutes to drill the core section, and an hour to winch it up to the surface.

There are offcuts, small chunks of the core, which aren't useful to science.

I picked a piece up.

As a scientist I try to remain objective and dispassionate.

But here I was, in a part of the world that had fascinated me since I looked at that area marked 'Region Unknown to Man' as a child, holding a piece of ice that had not seen the light of day since before the dawn of mankind.

I listened to the air bubbles pop and crackle as the ice melted from the heat of my hand.

I breathed the air coming out of it, air that was trapped at the time of freezing.

By measuring this air it is possible to study the composition of methane and Carbon Dioxide over time.

We melt the ice and measure the ratios of different atomic isotopes in the water. This provides us with a history of global temperature.

We can then study the relationship between the trace gases and temperature.

The ice core data show an almost perfect match between the time curves of global temperature and atmospheric concentrations of Carbon Dioxide and methane.

As temperature increases, Carbon Dioxide and methane are released from the ocean and land Biosphere, causing further temperature rise through their enhancement of the Greenhouse Effect.

The opposite takes place during the cooling phase.

During each recent cold phase, when on average global temperatures have decreased by 5 degrees centigrade, the Carbon Dioxide concentration of the atmosphere dipped to about 180 parts per million.

In the warm phases it peaked at around 300 parts per million.

Last year, the Carbon Dioxide concentration of the atmosphere passed *400* parts per million.

Take a deep breath.

We're the first human beings to breathe air with that level of CO2.

It is unprecedented in the recent record.

…

The rise over the last century is already 100 parts per million – the same as the natural change between an ice age and an interglacial warm period, but at a rate more than 100 times faster.

And it is in the 'warm' direction of increased concentration not experienced by the planet with certainty over the last 800,000 years based on the ice core data, and probably over *2 million years* from the geological record.

The Atmosphere is warming because the global Carbon Cycle has been disrupted.

…

The global Carbon Cycle consists of large seasonal exchanges between the carbon reservoirs of the Atmosphere, the land Biosphere, the Lithosphere and the Ocean.

The exchanges occur as a result of a variety of chemical, physical, geological, and biological processes.

For example, as plants grow on land and in the sea in the Spring, they draw down CO_2, which is later released as the green matter dies and decays.

Within the ocean, biological processes cause a fine rain of carbon to descend to the sediments, where it becomes trapped and stored.

Volcanic eruptions ultimately return Lithospheric Carbon Dioxide to the Atmosphere.

Physical exchanges take place between the Atmosphere and the ocean as CO_2 is absorbed into cold dense waters that sink to depths, and is released from areas where warmer water upwells.

These exchanges are much greater in magnitude than our own carbon emissions – but prior to industrialization, they were in Dynamic Balance.

...

In 1712, the invention of the Newcomen Steam Engine started a chain reaction of innovation, technology and science that spread across the globe, driven by a desire for profit and the pursuit of a better life.

This revolution built the modern world.

It has been fuelled by cheap and accessible fossil energy, which had been accumulated over 100s of millions of years during the Carboniferous Period, and stored underground as coal, oil and gas.

Since the 1950s, population, GDP, fertiliser use, water use, the number of cars, airline travel and many other human activities have all increased in what has been called 'The Great Acceleration'.

This has lead us to the point where we are currently burning 10 thousand million tonnes of carbon per year – a figure that has been increasing at a rate of 2% per year.

To date, we have burned an estimated 530 thousand million tonnes of carbon.

A quarter of the resulting Carbon Dioxide has been absorbed by vegetation on land, which has bloomed as a result, and just over a quarter by the ocean, which has become more acidic.

The remainder will stay in the atmosphere for hundreds to thousands of years because it takes that long for natural processes – mainly rock weathering – to draw CO2 out of the atmosphere.

Consequently, since the beginning of the Industrial Revolution, atmospheric concentration of CO_2 has risen by 40%.

Human impact on the planetary system has been so profound that many feel we have irreversibly brought the climatic stability of the Holocene to an end and entered a new epoch:

The 'Anthropocene'.

...

The energy imbalance revealed by the ocean, confirmed by rising temperatures and loss of ice, is being driven by us. It is the unwitting result of our use of fossil fuels.

To me, the evidence seems compelling.

But the implications are so profound that a deeper evaluation is merited.

To make such an evaluation requires a gargantuan effort.

This is the task given to the Intergovernmental Panel on Climate Change – the IPCC.

The IPCC was set up in 1988 by the United Nations Environment Programme and the World Meteorological Organisation.

Its job is to provide a comprehensive summary of the scientific data to inform the policy decisions of the United Nations Framework Convention on Climate Change.

This is an international treaty negotiated by 195 nations at the Earth Summit in Rio in 1992.

Its objective is to "stabilize greenhouse gas concentrations in the atmosphere at a level that will prevent dangerous human interference with the climate system."

The IPCC has three working groups. Working Group I reviews and assesses the physical science information relevant to human induced climate change.

Working Group II addresses the related impacts on people and the environment.

And Working Group III focuses on the policy options for adaptation to and mitigation of human induced climate change.

Since its establishment the IPCC has produced five Assessment Reports, approximately 1 every 5 years.

Each consists of a lengthy technical report, and a brief Summary for Policy Makers, which is scrutinized and agreed by representatives of the governments participating in the IPCC process.

The most recent Working Group I report – the 5th – was released in September 2013.

It is arguably the most audited scientific document – and possibly *the most audited document* – in history.

The work was led by 209 scientists, who are regarded as the world experts in their respective fields.

They were supported by more than 600 'contributing authors' from 32 countries, and 50 review editors from 39 countries.

Of the tens of thousands of publications sifted more than 9200 were cited.

The authors responded to 54,677 comments from 1089 reviewers worldwide. And the final text was approved by representatives from 195 governments.

The full Working Group I Technical report has 1535 pages and weighs four and a quarter kilos.

…

So what do they conclude?

Concerning the Atmosphere: Each of the last three decades has been successively warmer at the Earth's surface than any preceding decade since 1850.

In the Northern hemisphere the 30-year period from 1983 to 2012 was likely the warmest in the last 1400 years.

They add that the globally averaged combined land and ocean surface temperature measurements show a warming of 0.8 degrees Centigrade over the period 1850 to 2012.

They note that despite the warming at and near the surface, the upper atmosphere has cooled, ruling out the Sun as the cause.

They note that an increase in the frequency of heatwaves and heavy precipitation events has occurred in many regions since the 1950s.

...

Concerning the Cryosphere, they report that the rates of loss of ice from the world's glaciers and from the Greenland and Antarctic ice sheets have all increased dramatically – especially over the last 30 years.

While glacier losses have increased globally by about 20%, the ice sheet losses have increased over that 10 year period as much as 600%.

They report that the summer minimum sea ice extent in the Arctic decreased over the last 30 years at a rate between 9 and 14% per decade.

There is evidence that this level of ice retreat is unprecedented in the last 1450 years.

In contrast, winter sea ice extent in the Antarctic has increased slightly, at a rate of about 1.5% per decade.

This appears to be driven by changes in the southern ocean winds, that have intensified in response to the planetary energy imbalance.

Other evidence of warming is provided by the loss of Northern hemisphere snow cover at a rate of nearly 12% per year in summer, and increases in permafrost temperatures too.

The warming since the 1980s has been 3 degrees Centigrade in parts of North Alaska, and up to 2 degrees Centigrade in parts of Russia, where a considerable reduction in permafrost thickness and geographic extent has been observed.

…

Concerning the Hydrosphere, they report that ocean warming dominates the increase in energy stored in the climate system, accounting for more than 90% of the energy accumulated between 1971 and 2010.

Over the period 1993 to 2010 global mean sea-level rise is consistent with a 39% contribution from thermal expansion, 48% from melting ice and 13% from a decrease of land water storage.

They confirm that the ocean has absorbed about 30% of the cumulative anthropogenic Carbon Dioxide emissions, causing it to become progressively more acidic.

…

In November last year the IPCC released their overall Synthesis Report.

The report states that: "Warming of the climate system is unequivocal, and, since the 1950s, many of the observed changes are unprecedented over decades to millennia. The atmosphere and ocean have warmed, the amounts of snow and ice have diminished, [and] sea level has risen."

It observes that "In recent decades, changes in the climate have caused impacts on natural and human systems on all continents and across the oceans. Impacts are due to observed climate change, irrespective of its cause, indicating the sensitivity of natural and human systems to the changing climate."

On the causes of climate change, the IPCC state that solar influences cannot account for the observations.

They add that "It is extremely likely that more than half of the observed increase in global average surface temperature from 1951 [to] 2010 was caused by the anthropogenic increase in greenhouse gas concentrations and other anthropogenic forcings together."

They continue that "the best estimate of human-induced contributions to warming is similar to the actual warming observed."

In other words, there is evidence that *all* the warming that has occurred since 1950 is due to human actions – due to *us*.

…

They conclude that: "Continued emissions of greenhouse gases will cause further warming and changes in all components of the climate system. Limiting climate change will require substantial and sustained reductions of greenhouse gas emissions, which together with adaptation can limit climate change risks."

John Kerry, the US Secretary of State, summarised the findings as follows:

"Boil down the IPCC report and here's what you find: Climate change is real, it's happening now, human beings are the cause of the transformation, and early action by human beings can save the world from its worst impacts."

…

The cut-off date for published material considered by the IPCC Working Group I was July 2013. But science never stops, and there have been some important results since.

Evidence from the Argo floats and ship-borne surveys shows that despite a 15 year pause in the rate of surface and atmospheric temperature rise, energy has continued to accumulate in the oceans unabated, with the prospect that some of this energy will be released to the atmosphere in the future.

New data from the Cryosat satellite show the recent rate of ice loss from Greenland and Antarctica has doubled in just 3 years.

Some experts have concluded that the loss of ice from the West Antarctic ice sheet is now irreversible, and that this will raise sea-level by 1 to 2 metres in as little as a few hundred years.

…

Based on a combination of scientific analysis, assessments of the impacts and related value judgments, the nations negotiating under the terms of the United Nations Framework Convention on Climate Change have set a limit beyond which climate change will be "dangerous."

That limit is 2 degrees Centigrade above the pre-Industrial average.

We are currently at 0.8 degrees Centigrade.

Two thirds of that increase has occurred since 1980.

In order to stay below the 2 degree Centigrade 'guardrail', human carbon emissions have to drop to 50% of the present level by 2050 and thereafter drop to zero.

Nothing.

This would mean leaving 75% of known fossil fuel reserves in the ground. They would become economically worthless.

…

The temperature at which the system will stabilise is determined by the *total quantity* of carbon we emit to the atmosphere, not the rate at which it's emitted.

So reducing carbon emissions to zero won't lower temperature, it will just prevent the temperature rising beyond the 2 degree Centigrade level.

Temperature will then remain at that 2 degree Centigrade level for a very long time because CO_2 remains in the atmosphere for 100s to 1000s of years.

This sets a limit on the total carbon that we can burn.

The IPCC calculate this to be 800 Gigatonnes of carbon.

They estimate that we have already burned 530 Gigatonnes of carbon.

This leaves 270 Gigatonnes for us to use.

At our current rate, which is 10 Gigatonnes of carbon a year, we only have 27 years left, after which time carbon emissions would need to cease.

Suppose we begin reducing our emissions this year and don't exceed the overall 800 Gigatonne limit –

Then the atmospheric CO_2 concentration will stabilise at 450 parts per million.

Temperature will take longer to stabilise because it responds to CO_2 concentration – but it will eventually stabilise at our Guardrail of 2 degree Centigrade.

The oceans will continue to warm and the ice will continue to melt, so the sea-level will continue to rise.

It will take hundreds of years but will eventually stabilise at a level, based on evidence from past warmings, some 2 to 3 metres higher than today.

…

If we leave it longer to start reducing our emissions, we'll have to reduce them more rapidly to avoid exceeding the overall 800 Gigatonne limit.

Calculations show that if we leave it until 2020 – only 5 years away – the subsequent reductions would be of order 6% per year

– year on year – to stay within the 2 degree Centigrade limit.

6% may not sound much but annual reductions of carbon emissions greater than *1%* have in the past been associated only with economic recession or upheaval.

The UK conversion from coal to gas and the French conversion to nuclear in the 1970's and 80's only achieved reductions of 1% per year.

A temporary 5% reduction was achieved in the Soviet Union when it collapsed.

The 6% annual rate of reduction required is of *global* emissions.

We in the developed world have to reduce our emissions even more rapidly to accommodate growth in the developing world.

So it is noteworthy that in 2014, because of a 20% shift from coal to gas and a fall in overall energy use, the UK achieved a 9% reductions in emissions.

This shows that progress can be made within a national context.

Also, the International Energy Agency recently reported that while the global economy grew by around 3% in 2014, energy-related Carbon Dioxide emissions stayed flat – the first time in at least 40 years that such an outcome has occurred outside an economic crisis.

In spite of these encouraging results, achieving emissions reductions at the enormous scale and pace necessary to stay within the 2 degree guardrail will require a major collaborative effort on a global scale.

It will require the greatest collective action in history.

...

In December 2015, 195 nations will meet in Paris to forge a deal to put the world onto a path to a 2 degree centigrade maximum rise.

The new agreement aims to obtain credible and fair emission reductions and legally binding commitments from all countries – reflecting GDP, mitigation potential and contributions to past and future climate changes – with the most advanced economies making the most ambitious commitments.

There is justified cynicism surrounding this year's meeting in Paris.

These nations have been meeting for decades and overall global emissions haven't yet decreased.

However, there are hopeful signs from world leaders and governments and a growing pressure on them from an increasingly informed populace.

Last year, a million people around the world marched in various capital cities to demonstrate their concern.

In the lead up to Paris 2015, President Obama and Chinese President Xi Jinping have announced joint measures to fight climate change.

The US aims to reduce its carbon emissions 26-28% below 2005 levels by 2025 – nearly doubling its previous commitments.

Despite not having signed up to Kyoto or Copenhagen, the USA is already on track to cut its emissions by 17% between 2005 and 2020.

China, partly driven by serious air pollution problems, has committed to cutting the proportion of energy it generates from coal and has set up pilot carbon markets and low carbon zones.

It has set a date of 2030 for when it plans to 'peak' its emissions, and has pledged to ensure the share of non-fossil fuels in its energy mix will be around 20% by 2030.

To do this will require the installation over the coming 15y of 1000Gw of carbon-free power, equivalent to the current entire generating capacity of the USA.

Prime Minister Narendra Modi of India has committed to expand solar energy to provide electricity to 300 million of his country's citizens, who have no access to power at present.

The European Union has agreed a package to achieve a 40% reduction in its domestic emissions by 2030.

The aim is to boost the use of renewable energy to 27% and to increase energy efficiency by at least 27%.

And Germany has committed to curbing its emissions by 40% by the end of 2020, with the longer-term goal of supplying 80% of its power from renewable sources by 2050.

The UK Climate Change Act, passed in 2008 with cross-party support, is the world's first long-term, legally binding, national framework for reducing emissions – setting 5-year carbon budgets to cut UK emissions by 80% by 2050.

Around the world, almost 500 climate-related laws have been passed in 66 of the world's largest emitting countries.

...

Although the long history of negotiations by the United Nations Framework Convention on Climate Change is regarded by many as a chapter of failures, others argue that it has created the conditions in which national legislators and decision makers have been able to take actions that have had a positive effect.

In 2005 the Mayors of the worlds 40 largest 'Megacities' – including London – met and formed the C40 Cities Climate Leadership Group.

These cities have a combined population of 297 million people, and they generate 18% of global GDP as well as 10% of global carbon emissions.

Collectively they have taken 4,734 actions
to tackle climate change. Over 3 quarters of
these actions have been implemented.

Many individuals have taken measures to
reduce their own climate-related impacts –
by making changes in their personal,
professional and public lives – installing
solar panels, increasing the energy efficiency
of their homes, vehicles and appliances,
by using public transport and avoiding
unnecessary travel, by changing diet and by
choosing to forego activities that generate
emissions.

They have encouraged changes to be made
in their workplaces and written to their MPs.

They have sought to educate themselves
about the issue and to talk about it with their
friends, families and communities.

But despite all these measures, projections
of future emissions reveal a substantial gap
between what is required and what is likely
to be achieved.

...

Suppose we fail to take the action needed
to stay below the 2 degree Centigrade
guardrail?

The IPCC Working Group I predicts
that by the end of the Century we could
have committed to more than a 4 degree
Centigrade rise.

A 4 degree Centigrade world would be one
of unprecedented heat waves, severe drought
and major floods in many regions, with

serious impacts on ecosystems and food and water supplies.

Given that uncertainty remains about the full nature and scale of impacts, there is no certainty that adaptation to a 4 degree Centigrade world is possible.

A 4 degree Centigrade world is likely to be one in which communities, cities and countries would experience severe disruptions, damage, and dislocation, with many of these risks spread unequally.

The International Energy Agency's 2012 assessment indicated that without further mitigation action there is a 40% chance of warming exceeding 4 degree Centigrade by 2100 and a 10% chance of exceeding 5 degree Centigrade.

No nation would be immune to the impacts of that level of climate change.

Our infrastructure was built for the climate system we inherited, and is not designed to cope with the climate system we are provoking.

Our food and water supplies, housing, industry – our entire wellbeing and prosperity depends on access to energy – and our primary source, at present, is fossil fuel.

…

So we are confronted with a need to totally transform the world's Energy System.

At the same time we need to ensure energy security, equity, sustainability and growth.

The amount of carbon that we emit is determined by four things:

The number of people on the planet.

The size of the global economy.

The amount of energy it takes to power that economy.

And the amount of carbon it takes to create that energy.

There's little we can do about population which continues to increase, albeit at a decelerating rate, and is projected by the UN to peak at about 9 billion later this century.

There's little we can do to reduce the global economy. All governments are committed to increasing it and, in any case, our prosperity and wellbeing depends on it.

So there are only 2 areas in which we can take action to reduce emissions.

The economy can become more energy efficient and less wasteful.

This can be achieved through energy standards legislation, and by changes in behaviour at a personal and societal level.

Many policies are already in place, and progress is being made.

But we haven't got close to the reduction we need.

Which leaves us with reducing the amount of carbon we emit as we generate energy.

This involves renewable power sources – Wind, Solar, Biofuels, Nuclear - and, if feasible, 'clean' – or 'Carbon Abated' – fossil fuels.

Around the world, renewable power grew at its strongest ever pace in 2014, accounting for nearly half of all new installed generating capacity.

In China, the authorities have set green energy as a strategic priority. Their aim is that it will account for more than half of China's energy production by 2050.

This explains why investors are increasingly confident and keen to put their money on alternative energy.

The growth rate of wind farms and solar plants in China, India and an array of smaller developing nations is starting to outpace that in the world's richest nations.

But, in the UK, despite our best efforts to move to green, renewable and nuclear, coal and gas still provide about 70% of the energy to our grid and more in transport.

To achieve the necessary magnitude and rate of reduction in carbon emissions will require all the clean energy options available to us, as well as the invention and mass roll-out of new technologies, which, at this present moment, do not exist.

...

It's a daunting challenge, but my experience at the Science Museum, with its legacy of technical innovation on public display and held in its reserve collection and archives, convinces me that on a finite planet human ingenuity is unbounded.

My hope lies with the Engineers.

But the right conditions need to be in place for innovation and exploitation to occur.

I would like to see governments, investors and the engineering profession itself, create the conditions for a massive effort of innovation and rollout of energy technologies that will make existing fossil fuel redundant – energy which is cheaper and cleaner than unabated fossil fuels.

Once available, the markets will drive its exploitation.

But progress is hard when other economic drivers inhibit the transformation.

Fossil fuels are estimated by the International Energy Agency to receive subsidies of 500 billion dollars per year, 6 times the incentives to develop renewables.

...

I think back to the remarkable collaborative efforts of the International Geophysical Year, culminating in the first satellite and the obsolescence of my childhood Atlas – the 'Region Unknown to Man' that I would go on to visit personally dozens of times.

I look at my eldest grandchild who is now the age I was during that world-changing year.

I tell her I think she should become an Engineer.

She will reach the age I am now in 2071.

I try to imagine 2071, and then I find myself thinking what 4071 will look like.

Or 100,71.

We are all dependent on energy. Almost everything we do depends on it.

By being here tonight – by travelling to this theatre, by using these lights, the heating, the amplification of my voice – we have contributed to the amount of CO_2 in the atmosphere.

There will be carbon atoms that were generated by this event that will still be in the air in 2071, in the air that my granddaughter will breathe.

That's our legacy.

Science can't say what is right and what is wrong.

Science can inform, but it cannot arbitrate, it cannot decide.

Science can say that if we burn another half-trillion tonnes of carbon the atmospheric content of CO_2 will go up by another 100 parts per million, and that will almost certainly lead to a warming of the planet greater than two degrees, with major disruption of the climate system, and huge risks for the natural world and human wellbeing.

But it can't answer moral questions. Value questions.

Do we care about the World's poor? Do we care about future generations? Do we see the environment as part of the economy, or the economy as part of the environment?

The whole point about climate change is that, despite having been revealed by science, it is not really an issue about science, it is an issue about what sort of world we want to live in.

What kind of future do we want to create?

EVERY BRILLIANT THING

For Dad

Acknowledgements

George Perrin and Jonny Donahoe.

Anne McMeehan and Jim Roberts.

James Grieve, Elizabeth Freestone, Alicia White, Hanna Streeter, Francesca Moody, Benedict Lombe, Natalie Adams, Tara Wilkinson, Claire Simpson, Aysha Powell.

Jean Doumanian, Scott Morfee, Tom Wirtshafter, Patrick Daly, Preston Copley, Saul Nathan-Kazis, Kathryn Willingham, Kate Morrow, Victoria Gagliano, Amy Dalba, Richard Hodge, Charlene Speyerer, Matt Allamon, Josh Kohler.

Rosie Thomson, Ace Lawson, the Miniaturists, the Apathists, Lucy Prebble, Gugu Mbatha-Raw, Paul Burgess, Simon Daw, Kanatip LoukGolf Soonthornrak, Tom Dingle, Jamie Cullum, Sophie Dahl, Poppy Corbett, Ali Mason, Emma Campbell-Jones, Imogen Kinchin, Camilla Kinchin, Sian Reese-Williams, Stef O'Driscoll, Sean Linnen, Dominic Kennedy, Becki Willmore, Nikole Beckwith, Tom Richards, Robert Icke, Katie Mitchell, Josie Long, Daniel Kitson, Mark Thomas, Jessica Amato.

Mike Bartlett, Clare Lizzimore.

Paddy Gervers, Anna Knight.

Will Young. Rachel Taylor.

Michelle Beck. Effie Woods.

The play also owes a debt to those who have contributed to the list over the years.

Every Brilliant Thing is a collaboration between myself, George Perrin and Jonny Donahoe. It is an adaptation of my short story 'Sleeve Notes', originally written for the Miniaturists and performed by Rosie Thomson at Southwark Playhouse, Theatre503 and the Union Theatre and by myself at Trafalgar Studios, the Old Red Lion and Village Underground, by Gugu Mbatha-Raw at 93 Feet East and by various people at the Latitude Festival. George and I worked for over a decade to turn it into a full-length play. During this time it has been through several incarnations, including an installation created by Paul Burgess and Simon Daw for Scale Project. This particular incarnation was developed with Paines Plough and Pentabus with support from Anne McMeehan and Jim Roberts. The play wouldn't exist were it not for George's persistence, his enthusiasm for the story and his openness to work in an entirely new way.

It also owes a particular debt to Jonny Donahoe who, drawing on his experience as a stand-up comedian, found ways to tell the story and use the audience that George and I couldn't have conceived of. By its nature, the play is different every night and, as such, Jonny essentially co-authored the play while performing it.

This text was published after two years of devising, several trial performances around the UK, runs in Edinburgh and London and a four-month run at the Barrow Street Theatre in NYC. It has been filtered through Jonny's interactions with hundreds of audiences. I've provided footnotes throughout to explain certain aspects of the play in performance and to give examples of some of the things that have happened unexpectedly.

DM

NOTE

The NARRATOR can be played by a woman or a man of any age or ethnicity. In the first production, the NARRATOR was performed by a man, so appears as such in the text. The play should always be set in the country it's being performed in and references should be amended to reflect this.

The word NARRATOR is included for ease of reading. It is never heard by the audience and shouldn't be included in programmes or production materials.

There is no interval.

*****

The first performance of *Every Brilliant Thing* took place on 28th June 2013 at Ludlow Fringe Festival with the following cast:

Jonny Donahoe

Direction	George Perrin
Producer	Hanna Streeter
Line Producer	Francesca Moody
Stage Managers	Alicia White
	Charlotte McBrearty
	Hamish Ellis

The houselights are on full and will remain so throughout. There is no set. The AUDIENCE are seated in the most democratic way possible, ideally in the round. It is vital that everyone can see and hear each other. Music is playing, some upbeat jazz – Cab Calloway, Cannonball Adderley, Hank Mobley or Duke Ellington perhaps. The NARRATOR is in the auditorium as the AUDIENCE enters, talking to people and giving them scraps of paper. As he does so, he explains that when he says a number he wants the person with the corresponding entry to shout it out.[1]

Eventually, when everyone is seated, the music fades and the NARRATOR begins.

NARRATOR   The list began after her first attempt. A list
                of everything brilliant about the world.
                Everything worth living for.

                1.   Ice cream.
                2.   Water fights.
                3.   Staying up past your bedtime and
                        being allowed to watch TV.
                4.   The colour yellow.
                5.   Things with stripes.
                6.   Rollercoasters.
                7.   People falling over.

                All things that, at seven, I thought were
                really good but not necessarily things Mum
                would agree with.

                I started the list on the 9th of November,
                1987.[2] I'd been picked up late from school
                and taken to hospital, which is where my
                Mum was.

                ,

---

1   The AUDIENCE will be involved throughout and need to feel relaxed and safe.
    Greeting them also helps the NARRATOR cast the play. Jonny would be in the
    theatre for at least half an hour before the start of the show to speak to as many
    people as possible and work out who he was going to use in performance. The
    pieces of paper should look like authentic parts of the list – ones written during
    childhood could be written in crayon for instance, others should be written on
    napkins, beermats and the backs of envelopes (for example).
2   This date should be amended to correspond to the NARRATOR's age.

285

Up until that day, my only experience of
death was that of my dog, Sherlock Bones.[3]

Sherlock Bones was older than me, and he
was a central part of my existence. He was
really sick and so the Vet came around to put
him down.

The NARRATOR speaks to someone from the AUDIENCE.

Would you mind, I'm going to get you
to be the Vet, it's just that you have an
immediate... *Veterinary* quality.

The NARRATOR gets the VET to stand.[4]

It's alright, I won't ask you to do very much.
Just stand here.

And would you mind if I borrowed your
coat?

The NARRATOR takes a coat from someone else.

Thank you.

Okay, so you're the Vet, and I'm me as a
seven-year-old boy, and this here...

*The NARRATOR holds the coat carefully in his arms, as if it's
a docile animal.*

...this is Sherlock Bones. I know you because
you're one of the parents from school. And
you say something reassuring, like:

*'You're doing the kind thing. It's not a moment too
soon.'*

---

3   Originally the dog's name was Ronnie Barker but we had to change that for the
    US. Other possible names included Charles Barkley and Edward Woofwoof.
4   The Vet can be a man or a woman.

VET	You're doing the kind thing. It's not a moment too soon.[5]
NARRATOR	And I don't know what that means because I'm seven. I've no real concept of finality. Or mercy.

But you are clearly a very kind man, so I trust you.

Now do you have a pencil or a pen on you?

The VET has one or the NARRATOR asks him to get one from someone in the AUDIENCE.[6]

So that pencil is the needle.

And inside that needle is an anaesthetic called pentobarbital. The dose is large enough to make the dog unconscious and then depress his brain, respiratory and circulatory systems, and to put him to sleep forever.

(To the owner of the coat.) It's completely blunt so we won't draw on your nice coat okay?

When you're ready I want you to come over here and inject Sherlock Bones in the thigh.

The VET approaches the NARRATOR and attempts the task.

No, the thigh.

If the VET is smiling or laughing:

Now I'm going to stop you for a moment there. There is one hard and fast rule while euthanising a child's pet and that is you

---

5   Throughout the play, AUDIENCE members will be invited to play characters. They are allowed to say whatever they wish and the NARRATOR has to work with what he's given. Though improvisations shouldn't go on too long, the spontaneity of these interactions is a central element of the show.

6   There are several props used during the play but they should all be sourced from the AUDIENCE.

really mustn't laugh as you do it. Totally changes the tone of the situation.

So um, no...let's do this again. Go back to the start and try to respect the solemnity of the situation.

Maybe take a moment.

Okay. Let's try this again.

The VET completes the task.

Okay, now stroke his little head.

Could someone with a watch tell me when thirty seconds has passed?

I held Sherlock Bones, who I'd known my entire life. I held him as he died.

The NARRATOR looks at the coat, stroking it gently.

And I thought about the walk we'd had that morning. And about the smell of him in my room. His toys in the garden. The recently opened packet of dry food. His bed under the stairs. All the things that could now be thrown away.

The NARRATOR looks at the coat for a little longer.

And he became lighter. Or heavier, I'm not sure. But different.

An AUDIENCE MEMBER tells the NARRATOR that thirty seconds have passed.

And that was my experience of death.

A loved one, becoming an object...

The NARRATOR hands the coat to the VET.

...and being taken away forever.

Thank you.

The VET returns to their seat.

It's the 9th of November, 1987. It's dark and it's late. All the other kids had gone home long ago.

Eventually, my Dad pulls up.

The NARRATOR speaks to someone in the AUDIENCE.

I'm going to ask you to be my Dad if that's okay. You don't have to do much, just sit here on this step.

The NARRATOR indicates where DAD should sit.[7]

Now, normally it's my Mum who picks me up and normally she's on time. Normally I travel in the back because I am seven and I make things sticky.

But this time it's Dad. And it's late. And he opens the door to the front passenger seat.

The NARRATOR indicates to DAD to open an imaginary passenger door.[8]

Dad looked at me. I looked at him.

When something bad happens, your body feels it before your brain can know what's happening. It's a survival mechanism. The stress hormones cortisol and adrenalin flood your system. It feels like a trapdoor opening beneath you. Fight or flight or stand as still as you can.

I stood very still, looking at my Dad.

---

7   If the DAD can be seen by everyone, and if the NARRATOR can sit next to him, there's no need for him to move.

8   In the US Jonny would correct DAD: 'Actually, it's a British car, so –' and they would mime opening the other door.

> Eventually, I got into the car. Dad had the radio on. He'd been smoking with the window down.

The NARRATOR sits down next to the man.

> Now, actually what's going to happen is that I'm going to be my Dad and you're going to be me as a seven year old. You don't have to do much, you just say 'why'. Okay?

The NARRATOR speaks as the DAD. He doesn't alter his voice.

DAD   Put on your seatbelt.

AUDIENCE   Why?

DAD   Because cars can be dangerous.

AUDIENCE   Why?

DAD   Because other drivers don't always pay attention.

AUDIENCE   Why?

DAD   Well, because there's lots to think about when you're a grown up. There are bills to pay and work to do and relationships to sustain and there's never enough time to do it all.

AUDIENCE   Why?

DAD   Because there are only twenty-four hours in a day.

AUDIENCE   Why?

DAD   Well, because that's how long it takes for the Earth to rotate.

AUDIENCE   Why?

DAD   Because...I don't know.

AUDIENCE   Why?

DAD	Because I don't know everything.
AUDIENCE	Why?
DAD	Because that's impossible.
AUDIENCE	Why?
DAD	Because there's only so much anyone can know.
AUDIENCE	Why?
DAD	Because if you were able to know everything then life would be unlivable.
AUDIENCE	Why?
DAD	Because then there would be no mystery, no curiosity, no creativity, no conversation, no discovery. Nothing would be new and we'd have no need to use our imaginations and our imaginations are what make life bearable.
AUDIENCE	Why?
DAD	Because in order to live in the present we have to be able to imagine a future that will be better than the past.
AUDIENCE	Why?
DAD	Because that's what hope is and without hope we couldn't go on.
AUDIENCE	Why?
DAD	Because...can you just put your seatbelt on?
AUDIENCE	Why?
DAD	Because we're going to the hospital.
AUDIENCE	Why?

DAD	Because that's where your mother is.
AUDIENCE	Why?
DAD	Because she hurt herself.
AUDIENCE	Why?
DAD	Because she's sad.
AUDIENCE	Why?
DAD	I don't know.
AUDIENCE	Why?
DAD	I just don't.
AUDIENCE	Why?
DAD	Put on your seatbelt.
AUDIENCE	Why?
DAD	Because your mother is in hospital.
AUDIENCE	Why?
DAD	Because she can't see anything worth living for.
AUDIENCE	Why?

'

NARRATOR	At least, that's how I like to remember it. But we actually just sat in silence. The only thing he said to me was:

The NARRATOR feeds the 'DAD' the following line:

DAD	Your Mother's done something stupid.
NARRATOR	I didn't know what that meant.

'

The NARRATOR thanks the DAD and, if relocated, indicates for him to return to his seat.

> At the hospital, Mum saw me and said 'not him'. So I sat in the corridor next to an old couple…

The NARRATOR sits next to an OLD COUPLE in the audience.

> …who bought me a carton of juice and some chocolate from the machine.

He acquires a drink and some chocolate from the OLD COUPLE.[9]

> I don't know exactly when I had the idea for the list but it was here, with the old people, that I started to write it down.

The NARRATOR eats the chocolate and calls out numbers.

> 1. Ice cream.
> 2. Water fights.
> 3. Staying up past your bedtime and being allowed to watch TV.
> 4. The colour yellow.
> 5. Things with stripes.
> 6. Rollercoasters.
> 7. People falling over.

The NARRATOR does the following entries himself.

> 8. Juice.
> 9. Chocolate.
> 10. Kind old people who aren't weird and don't smell unusual.

I don't like it.

---

9   In performance 'chocolate and juice from a machine' changed depending on what could be acquired from the AUDIENCE – 'a cup of tea and a sandwich' for instance, or 'some water and an apple.' These then have to be included as items 8 and 9. Jonny would often take someone's wine and react as a child would, saying 'spicy' and handing it back. In New York, we shortened it to just 'chocolate' and Jonny would hand one of the couple a bar of chocolate and then hold out his hand to get it back.

The NARRATOR hands the drink and chocolate back to the OLD COUPLE.

> Dad was in with Mum for ages. When
> he finally came out I followed him down
> the corridor, I followed him out of the
> hospital, I followed him to the car park, I
> followed him in to the car, I followed him
> up the driveway, I followed him in through
> the front door, I followed him down the
> hallway, I followed him up the stairs until
> we reached his study, where he went inside
> and closed the door before I could follow
> him any further.
>
> I waited to see what music he put on.
>
> I knew the rules. If it was this woman
> singing I could go into the room.

'Gloomy Sunday' by Billie Holiday plays, beginning with her vocal.

> If it was the sort of music you could sing
> and dance to, it was okay to go in but I ran
> the risk of being hugged and spun around in
> his chair.

Some upbeat vocal jazz plays – Cab Calloway perhaps.

> If no one was singing it meant Dad was
> working so I should be quiet.

Some melodic instrumental jazz plays, John Coltrane or Bill Evans perhaps.

> And it if sounded like all the instruments
> were just falling down the stairs, it meant I
> should leave him alone.

'Free Jazz' by Ornette Coleman plays – loud and chaotic. After a moment it fades to silence.

,

So standing outside his door, I waited to see what he put on.

,

'Free Jazz' by Ornette Coleman plays. After a moment it fades.

I went downstairs and made myself some dinner. A ham and mayo sandwich. Just without the ham. I sat down in front of the TV and continued with the list.

It occurred to me the list should be presented in no particular order. There was no way of saying that, for example, Danger Mouse was objectively better than Spaghetti Bolognese.

23. Danger Mouse.
24. Spaghetti Bolognese.
25. Wearing a cape.
26. Peeing in the sea and nobody knows.

I stayed up late writing and fell asleep in the living room. Dad must have carried me upstairs.

Mum didn't come home for a week or so.

While she was away I had to speak to the school counsellor, which was actually just Mrs Patterson from upper school. She was a wonderful woman, the sort of woman you looked at and immediately trusted.

The NARRATOR looks at a woman in the AUDIENCE.

I'm going to ask you to be Mrs Patterson if that's okay. Now, what she'd do is, and it seems a little weird now but remember this

was the Eighties and she got results, what
she'd do is she'd take off her shoe...

*The NARRATOR waits for MRS PATTERSON to take off her
shoe.* [10]

Then she'd take off her sock.

The NARRATOR waits for her to take off her sock. [11]

Then she'd put it on her hand and talk to
you through her little sock-dog which she
called – what did you call the sock-dog?

The AUDIENCE member says a name, for instance 'Mostyn'.

Yes! That's it, I remember now. What
Mostyn would do is he'd ask questions like
'how are you feeling today?'

SOCK   How are you feeling today?

NARRATOR   I'm very well thank you Mostyn, how are
                you?

SOCK   I'm fine, thank you.

NARRATOR   You're brilliant. What kind of dog are you?

SOCK   I'm a... *(She specifies a breed or colour.)*

NARRATOR   Wow, that's amazing. When I was little we
                had a dog called Sherlock Bones, and he
                was a cross between a Border Collie and a
                Doberman, because a Border Collie and a
                Doberman lived next door to each other in
                our street and there was a very low hedge.

---

10 So far, nobody has refused to do this. In performance it sometimes took quite
a while however. Jonny would acknowledge this, saying things like 'she liked to
create a real sense of dramatic tension. She was a double-knotter, that's one of
the things we always liked about her, very thorough.'

11 At one performance, MRS PATTERSON explained that she had a bad toe. Jonny
added 'I remember her telling me how worried she was about her toe. It was
a skydiving accident wasn't it?' MRS PATTERSON replied 'Yes that's right.'
Jonny then included her in the list '165, Mrs Patterson and her extreme sports
hobbies.'

You're brilliant, by the way. I really like you. I'm going to put you onto my list. 164. Mostyn the sock dog. Have I told you about my list?

SOCK   No, tell me about it.[12]

NARRATOR   I'm making a list of a thousand Brilliant Things. I'm not certain but I think I might be a genius.

If MRS PATTERSON wishes to ask more questions that's fine, if not the NARRATOR moves on to:

It's been very nice talking to you, but can I go now?

SOCK   Yes.[13]

NARRATOR   Mum did eventually come home from the hospital, and by that time the list was eight pages long and had three hundred and fourteen things on it. I left it on her pillow with the title:

'Every Brilliant Thing.'

She never mentioned it to me, but I knew she'd read it because she'd corrected my spelling.

,

I kept speaking with Mrs Patterson and Mostyn once a week, then once a fortnight, then once a month and then one day I left the school and I never saw them again.

---

12   Occasionally, the sock dog would say that, yes, he had mentioned the list to which Jonny would reply something like 'well, I'd still like to recap'.
13   If the SOCK/MRS PATTERSON insist that the NARRATOR stay and talk, the NARRATOR can beg childishly until they are released.

I don't want to make it sound like my
Mother was a monster or that my childhood
was miserable because it wasn't.

We had a piano in our kitchen. It wasn't a
big kitchen but it was the warmest room in
the house and we'd gather around it and
sing soul songs. There's a Ray Charles song,
'Drown In My Own Tears' that she sang a
lot. There's a moment halfway through that
sends shivers down my spine.

*This moment of the song plays – the drums building
and Ray Charles singing 'why can't YOU...' The song
continues, quieter.*

The way he sings the word 'you' gets me
every time. It's like it's coming out of
someone else. We all used to howl it like
wolves.

313.   Having a piano in the kitchen.
314.   The way Ray Charles sings the word
       'You'.

*The music swells and continues to play for a few moments
longer. The NARRATOR listens. It fades.*

I forgot about the list until her second
attempt, just over ten years later.

Dad showed up halfway through Chemistry.
The same trapdoor feeling. Fight or flight.
The same wordless drive to the hospital.

As a teenager I dealt with it less well. I wore
my heart on my sleeve.

The night she came home, she sat at the
kitchen table and said that if it wasn't for the
ham and pineapple pizza lining her stomach

from the night before she'd be dead. And I
said:

*'You took three weeks' worth of anti-depressants,
a packet of Aspirin and half a tub of
antihistamines. You're probably healthier than I
am. If you're going to kill yourself go jump off a
bridge.'*

Rather than storm off I sat there and started
to shovel food into my mouth. I'd spent
ages on this meal and I was furious that she
was sitting there, wishing she was dead and
letting it go cold.

There was a moment of absolute, deafening
silence. And then she started to laugh. It
was such a genuine laugh that after a while I
found myself joining in. Eventually, Dad got
up and left the table, going into his study to
listen to records.

I couldn't sleep that night. I started to
clear out my room, packing up the things
I wanted to keep and throwing away the
things I didn't.

I started shaking. Have you ever had that?
Where you notice that your hands are
shaking and your breathing is deeper and
you're surrounded by bin bags full of your
things and you realise that, you know, *I'm
really upset.* I must be really upset.

'

And then, inside a box under my bed,
underneath some sticker albums, sea shells
and action figures, I found the list. I sat on
the floor and I read it through.

1.   Ice cream.

The younger me had dealt with this so much better. He wasn't self-righteous. The younger me was hopeful. Naïve, of course. But, hopeful.

So once I got to the end of the list I picked up a pen and continued where that little boy had left off.

315.   The smell of old books.
316.   Andre Agassi.
317.   The even numbered Star Trek films.
318.   Burning things.
319.   Laughing so hard you shoot milk out of your nose.
320.   Making up after an argument.

The next morning I sat at the end of Mum's bed and I read the list to her, and she got up and left the room. I followed her and read louder.

516.   Winning something.
517.   Knowing someone well enough to get them to check your teeth for broccoli.

Over the next few days and weeks I would leave messages on the answer phone. I would turn off the radio or stand in front of the TV. I spent a lot of time talking to her back.

518.   When idioms coincide with real-life occurrences, for instance: waking up, realising something and simultaneously smelling coffee.
521.   The word 'plinth'.

I began leaving Post-It notes around the house, stuck to various things. On her mirror was:

575.	Piglets.

On the kettle:

654.	Marlon Brando.

And on her bed:

11.	Bed.

Every morning I would open my door and I would see a small stack of yellow squares of paper. I became more inventive, writing on the inside of cereal packets or shoes, carving words into fruit or rearranging the fridge magnets.

201.	Hammocks.

...inside the lid of some mustard.[14]

324.	Nina Simone's voice.

...stencilled onto a baguette.

It was my aim to reach a *thousand*. I wasn't allowed to cheat, which meant:

a.	No repetition.
b.	Things had to be genuinely wonderful and life-affirming.
c.	Not too many material items.

For a few months the list became my sole focus.

761.	Deciding you're not too old to climb trees.

14	In George's production, this entry was written on an actual mustard lid.

823. Skinny dipping.

Then, the week before I left for university:

992. Knowing to jangle keys at the wildlife park if you want the otters to come out.
993. Having dessert as a main course.
994. Hairdressers who listen to what you want.
995. Bubble wrap.
996. Really good oranges.

I started to be bothered by the thought that my Mum no longer loved my Dad. I put the thought out of my mind and returned to the list.

997. Cycling downhill.
998. Aromatic duck pancakes with hoisin sauce.

It's common for the children of suicides to blame themselves. It's natural.

999. Sunlight.

However much you know that you're not to blame, you can't help feeling like you failed them. It's not fair to feel this way. But it's natural.

,

In the first week of university, I posted the list to my Mum, anonymously.[15] When I returned that Christmas I found it on my desk, neatly folded back in its envelope. I still don't know whether or not she had read

---

15 Jonny would often tell the AUDIENCE how he uses this joke as a barometer for how the show was going, sometimes telling them: 'they don't laugh at that in the matinees.'

it. It certainly hadn't seemed to change her outlook.

I put the list between the pages of a favourite book and I forgot about it.

That Christmas was quiet. Difficult.

In the New Year, Dad drove me back to university. He gave me a box of his records. I wanted to ask him why but I knew better than that. We didn't speak. We just listened to the radio.

The NARRATOR sits down next to the person he cast as his DAD.

Music plays – Ella Fitzgerald's 'My Melancholy Baby.' They listen for a moment, then it fades slowly as the NARRATOR speaks.

I was quite shy at university. I didn't socialise. I'd mostly just listen to records in my room. I would even avoid lectures and seminars. But there was one lecture series that I never missed.

It was lead by someone whose books I had read and loved and had inspired me to choose the course in the first place.

Would you mind being my lecturer? It's just because you really look like her.[16]

The NARRATOR selects someone from the audience to be the LECTURER, leads them to the centre of the room and gives them a copy of The Sorrows of Young Werther.

---

16 The LECTURER can be a man or a woman. Jonny would often describe the lecturer first, explaining that they always wore red-rimmed glasses for instance, before asking someone who is dressed exactly how he's just described to take part, saying 'I don't know why, but you really remind me of her...'

This particular lecture series was on the Victorian Novella and built up to this one book, *The Sorrows of Young Werther* by Johann Wolfgang von Goethe.

What she would do is, at the start of the lecture, she would hold the book aloft...

The LECTURER holds up the book.

And then she would leave a long dramatic pause...

...and when she felt she had everybody's undivided attention...

,

...she would give a very accurate and detailed précis of the novel.

The NARRATOR sits in the audience and waits.

,

Eventually, the LECTURER realises they can simply read the plot summary on the back of the book. The summary will be different depending on the copy, but will basically say something like:

LECTURER   Visiting an idyllic German village, Werther, a sensitive young man, meets and falls in love with sweet-natured Lotte. Although he realises that she is to marry Albert, he is unable to subdue his passion and his infatuation torments him to the point of despair. The first great 'confessional' novel, *The Sorrows of Young Werther* draws both on Goethe's own unrequited love for Charlotte Buff and on the death of his friend Karl Wilhelm Jerusalem. The book was an immediate success, and a cult rapidly grew up around it, resulting in numerous imitations as well as violent criticism and suppression on the grounds of its apparent support of suicide.

The NARRATOR puts his hand up.

NARRATOR   Excuse me, I have a question.

LECTURER   Yes?

NARRATOR   Are you saying that a book, that this book, caused people to take their own lives?

LECTURER   Yes.

NARRATOR   And you want *us* to read that book?

LECTURER   Yes.

The NARRATOR thanks the LECTURER and indicates for them to return to their seat.

,

NARRATOR   I left the lecture and went to the library.

In fact I read up on social contagions; obesity, divorce, suicide. We're all subconsciously affected by the behaviour of our peers.

In the month after Marilyn Monroe's death by overdose, the number of suicides in the US increased by twelve percent. Every time suicide is front-page news, every time a celebrity or a character on prime-time television takes their own life there is a spike in the number of suicides.

Suicide is contagious. It's called the 'Werther Effect', named after Goethe's protagonist.

Discovering this fact really scared me. Then it made me angry. I thought about the way suicide was presented in films and on TV, how it was reported in the news.

I found that the Samaritans had published a set of guidelines for how the media can report suicide intelligently. It's astonishing how rarely these guidelines are followed. They're really simple:

The NARRATOR refers to a piece of paper.

Don't provide technical details. Never suggest that a method is quick, easy, painless or certain to result in death.

Avoid dramatic headlines, terms like 'suicide epidemic' or 'hot spot'.

Avoid sensationalist pictures of video. Avoid excessive detail.

Avoid using the word 'commit'. Don't describe deaths by suicide as 'successful'.

Don't publish suicide notes.

Don't publish on the front page.

Don't ignore the complex realities of suicide and its impacts on those left behind.

Include references to support groups, such as the Samaritans.

Don't speculate on the reason. That's crucial.

The NARRATOR puts away the paper.

Don't supply simplistic reasons such as 'he'd lost his job' or 'she'd recently become bankrupt'.

I read the book. *The Sorrows of Young Werther.* It was shit. Well, I didn't connect with it. I'd never been very interested in romance. Or at least, I hadn't been. Until I locked eyes with the only other person who was always in the library.

'At Last' by Etta James begins to play and the NARRATOR locks eyes with an AUDIENCE MEMBER. This is now SAM.[17] The NARRATOR waves, blushingly. The vocal starts and the song continues as the NARRATOR speaks.

For weeks we would sit opposite each other without speaking. Occasionally we'd make eye-contact and then immediately look away as if blinded by the sun.

For the first time in my life I understood the lyrics of pop songs.

And then finally, after weeks, I summoned-up the courage to say hello.

Slowly, bashfully, the NARRATOR walks towards SAM. On his way he asks the person who read out 517 to check his teeth for broccoli, then gives The Sorrows of Young Werther *to someone else.*

Can you just…deal with this?

As he is about to reach SAM, he suddenly turns to the person next to her.

Can I move you?

The NARRATOR gets the person next to SAM (usually their partner) to vacate their seat and move to the other side of the room. This is done very apologetically. Once relocated, the NARRATOR returns to SAM.

Is anyone sitting here?

SAM   Not anymore.

---

17   SAM can be male or female. For the purpose of this draft, it's a woman.

NARRATOR   Oh good.

The NARRATOR sits down in the empty seat.

Hello.

SAM   Hello.

NARRATOR   What's your name?

The AUDIENCE MEMBER says their name.

No, in real life her name was Sam.

What's your name?

SAM   Sam.

NARRATOR   Hi Sam. Nice to meet you. What are you reading?

The NARRATOR addresses the AUDIENCE.

Oh, I forgot, does anyone have a book?
We're in the library so I need a couple of
books.

The NARRATOR indicates The Sorrows of Young
Werther.

Not that one.

*The NARRATOR gets a couple of books from the AUDIENCE
and throws one into SAM's lap.*

What are you reading?

SAM reads the title of the book.[18]

What's it about?

SAM reads the back of the book.

Sounds really good.

---

18   Books that have been contributed by the AUDIENCE have included *God's Gift to
Women*, *The Catcher in the Rye*, *Fifty shades of Grey* and *The Denial of Death*
among many others.

The NARRATOR tells SAM what he's reading and tries to explain how great it is:[19]

> It's really good. In fact, why don't I lend it to you? And I could read *(says title of SAM's book)* and we could meet up and talk about them, perhaps get a coffee sometime or a cup of tea or an or an or an orange juice, maybe, perhaps, if you'd like to, if you think that would be…[20]

SAM agrees.

> I had a date! We began to meet up in the library. We'd swap books and discuss them over coffee. I read things I would never have encountered otherwise. I probably learned more from the books Sam gave me than from any of my course texts.
>
> After several months of reading and meeting and trying not to look at each other, Sam returned a book to me, one of my favourite childhood books, and said:

---

19 Occasionally Jonny would be given the perfect book to start a flirtatious conversation – *Jane Eyre* for instance – and give the book's owner a big thumbs up. Most often though, he'd have a real struggle to make the book he's been given sound exciting. In one performance in New York he was given an enormous hardback history of Manhattan's sewage system. 'It's really…great' he enthused: 'You'd be surprised just how much there is to say about the history of Manhattan's sewage system. If you're going to read one book about the history of Manhattan's sewage system, it really should be this one.' He asked SAM if she had read the book and when she said she hadn't he replied 'No, of course not. No one has.' At one performance in Edinburgh Jonny was given *Nana* by Émile Zola, in French. This prompted him to turn to the person who'd contributed it and say 'aren't you clever?' and then add 'it's funny, for a minute I forgot I could speak French.' He then began to discuss the book with its owner in French, a language he happens to speak fluently. The conversation was cut short by the sign interpreter who was having a tough enough time as it was. During a press night performance he was given a copy of *Macbeth*, giving him a dilemma of whether or not to say the title out loud, given the circumstances. In London he was given a copy of my play *Lungs* which was playing in the same theatre. Aware that I was sitting directly behind him he explained 'his plays are okay I suppose but, for me, they're all about the performance'.

20 Jonny would just keep going here until SAM agreed.

The NARRATOR says the lines and encourages SAM to repeat them back to him.

NARRATOR   <u>Really</u> interesting read.

SAM   <u>Really</u> interesting read.

NARRATOR   There's something <u>really interesting</u> in this book...

SAM   There's something <u>really interesting</u> in this book...

NARRATOR   That I want <u>you</u> to read.

SAM   That I want <u>you</u> to read.

NARRATOR   Now, this confused me because I'd already read the book. *I'd* lent it to *her*. Because I'm an idiot, I didn't work out that it was code until weeks later, when I opened the book and the list dropped out.

I was mortified. I'd never told anyone about my Mum. Ever. As a kid there were times when...I'd have nothing in my lunchbox or I wouldn't have socks on or something and I...I didn't want people to think that because my Mother was...I don't know. And out of context this was just a stupid, childish list. The idea that a list of nice things could combat hardwired depression was embarrassingly naïve.

I got so upset I went to rip it in half...and then I noticed someone else's handwriting.

The NARRATOR says each number. SAM reads all the entries.

1000. When someone lends you books.
1001. When someone actually reads the books you give them.

1002. When you learn something about someone that surprises you but which makes complete sense.
1003. Realising that for the first time in your life someone is occupying your every waking thought, making it hard to eat or sleep or concentrate, and that they feel familiar to you even though they're brand new.
1004. Finding an opportunity to say this in a way which doesn't involve being in the same room at the same time, as we're both shy and terrified of rejection and if I don't say something now, it'll never happen.
1005. Writing about yourself in the Third Person.

I have some advice for anyone who has been contemplating suicide. It's really simple advice. It's this:

Don't do it.

Things get better.

They might not always get brilliant.

The NARRATOR indicates SAM.

But they get better.

,

What I'm about to say might be really hard for some of you to understand, particularly the younger members of the audience. Back then there was no way to communicate with anyone after midnight. No texting or instant messaging, no email or Facebook. This world was called '1998.'

I couldn't do anything but stare at what Sam had written. For about three hours.

Eventually, I just continued the list from where Sam had left off.

1006. Surprises.
1007. The fact that sometimes there is a perfect song to match how you're feeling.

Music begins: 'Move On Up' by Curtis Mayfield. The NARRATOR moves quickly around the room.[21]

1008. Dancing in private.
1009. Dancing in public, fearlessly.
1010. Reading something which articulates exactly how you feel but lacked the words to express yourself.

I wrote late into the night.

1427. Not worrying about how much money you're spending on holiday because all international currency looks like Monopoly money.

I wanted to get to 2000 and I kept writing as the sun came up.

1654. Christopher Walken's voice.
1655. Christopher Walken's hair.

So much to include that my hand cramped up.

1857. Planning a declaration of love.

My morning alarm went but I'd not slept. I passed:

---

21 In George's production, Jonny would use a microphone during this section, and get the AUDIENCE MEMBERS to speak into it too. This was partly so we could have the music loud but also to introduce a microphone that will be used later.

2000. Coffee.

With:

2001. Films that are better than the books
        they're adapted from.

And I kept going.

The NARRATOR does the following entries himself, at speed:

2002. Seeing someone make it onto the train
        just as the doors are closing, making
        eye-contact and sharing in this little
        victory.
2003. This song. Especially the drums on
        this track. The single ends at around
        four minutes but the album version
        continues for another five minutes and
        has the most insane drums. In fact...
2004. Any song with an extended drum
        break involving a full kit, bongos and
        cowbell, have you heard 'I'm a Man'
        by Chicago?
2005. 'I'm a Man' by Chicago.
2006. Vinyl records. I'm not being
        pretentious, the sound quality is
        better, it isn't compressed and it's
        tactile, you get to feel the weight
        of it in your hands. You can't skip
        like with CDs or MP3s, you listen
        through to the entire album. Dad's
        room had records on every surface
        and I loved the gatefold sleeves, the
        artwork, I love reading through the
        acknowledgements and the sleeve
        notes, the story of the making of the
        object.

The next morning I took the list and I ran to the library and Sam and I kissed for the very first time.

From that moment on we spent every second together. I wrote new list entries every day as a gift for Sam.

The NARRATOR continues with the list entries himself:

2389. Badgers.

The NARRATOR puts his hand on someone's shoulder.

2390. People who can't sing but either don't know or don't care.

Pages and pages of it.

4997. Gifts that you actually want and didn't ask for.
4998. Falling asleep as soon as you get on a plane, waking up when you land and feeling like a time-traveller.

Everywhere I looked, everything I thought about...

9993. Dreams of flying.
9994. Friendly cats.
9995. Falling in love.
9996. Sex.
9997. Being cooked for.
9998. Watching someone watching your favourite film.
9999. Staying up all night talking.
10000. Waking up late with someone you love.

The drum-break kicks in.

Now, this is the drum break I was telling you about. I know what you're thinking: it just

sounds like a bunch of drums but wait for it,
you're about to hear...

The NARRATOR waits for it.

...bongos! You are not getting into this in the
way I anticipated. Alright, fine, listen, I'm
going to try to be a little bit more...American
about this. Let's try...everyone put your right
hand in the air.

Everyone raises their right hand.

I'm going to HIGH-FIVE THE ENTIRE
ROOM!

He high-fives as many people as he can.

*Eventually, the NARRATOR signals to the STAGE MANAGER
to stop the record.*

No that was a big mistake. It's actually much
harder than I anticipated.

The NARRATOR is out of breath.

My Mum...

She would do this. Get carried away. Ups
and downs.

,

As a little boy, it was never shyness, or
thoughtfulness. Happiness scared me
because it was usually followed by...

you know.

The NARRATOR looks at SAM.

This was all very new. Feeling like this.

,

Studies have shown that children with depressed mothers have a heightened reactivity to stress. Mothers who are withdrawn leave children to fend for themselves and it actually changes the chemistry of the brain, the fight or flight impulse.

But the real risk as I perceived it...

,

The real risk, that I'd felt my whole life, was that I would one day feel as low as my Mum had and take the same action.

Because alongside the anger and incomprehension is an absolute crystal clear understanding of why someone would no longer want to continue living.

,

I took Sam back home to meet my parents. They were amazing. They were wonderful. They were fantastic. It was awful. It made it seem like I'd exaggerated everything from my childhood. My Dad made lasagne and played Cab Calloway records. My Mum laughed a lot and told a story about breaking a guy's nose on a train in Egypt. We drank a few bottles of wine and sang songs at the kitchen piano.

The NARRATOR produces an electric keyboard and stands with it in the centre of the room. It doesn't have a stand, so for a moment he tries to work out how to play it. Then he recruits two people from the AUDIENCE to hold either end of it while he plays. He thinks about the logistics of the room and speaks to the people holding the keyboard.

Um, because we're in the round, we're just going to do a very slow revolve.

Clockwise, obviously.

The NARRATOR speaks to the room.

Mum would always sing first. She sang Ray Charles…

(Sings.) I'm so blue here without you
it keeps raining more and more. Why can't YOU…

Dad wouldn't normally sing. But he did this night. It was amazing. I'd never seen anything like it. He sang:

(Sings.) That's Life. That's what people say.
Riding High in April, shot down in May.

oh…and:

(Sings.) And now the end is near,
and so I face the final curtain.

Which, for me, was a little too on the nose.

And then, quite spectacularly:

(Sings.) Wake me up before you go-go,
don't leave me hangin' on like a yo-yo.

Which, because he'd clearly never heard it before, actually sounded like:

(Sings, to the tune of 'Fly Me To The Moon')
Wake me up before you go-go,
don't leave me hangin' on like a yo-yo.

Sam sang the last song that night. 'Some Things Last A Long Time' by Daniel Johnston. I'd not heard it before.

The NARRATOR sings a few lines of the song, ending:

> *(Sings.) The things we did, I can't forget.*
> *Some things last a long time. Some things last a long time.*

,

The NARRATOR takes away the piano and his assistants return to their seats.[22]

With Sam's encouragement, the list grew.

123321.   Palindromes.

People asked if they could read it, add to it, photocopy it. The document got scrawled all over with different handwriting in different colours, exclamation marks, underlining, asterisks, footnotes and amendments, drawings and even the odd diagram.

Anything generic or universal (clean sheets, new socks, freshly cut grass, the smell of bacon) had already been included and entries had become more specific:

253263.   The feeling of calm which follows
            the realisation that, although you
            may be in a regrettable situation,
            there's nothing you can do about it.

525924.   Track 7 on every great record.

777777.   The prospect of dressing up as a
            Mexican wrestler.

Not the *action* of dressing up as a Mexican Wrestler, but the *prospect* of it.

Sam and I got married. A year after university. Sam proposed. Got down on one knee. The whole thing.

---

22   This should be done in a way to ensure that the audience don't applaud at this
     point.

It was beautiful, it was…in fact, no, let's just do it.

We were walking in a park near my parents' house. It was raining. I was saying that this is where I used to walk Sherlock Bones when I was a child. I kept walking and I thought she'd stopped to tie a shoelace because when I turned around she was on one knee.

The NARRATOR turns around to look at SAM, who is down on one knee.[23]

She took my hands and said…

SAM   Will you marry me?

NARRATOR   And I said yes.

Let's kiss later.

SAM returns to her seat.

We picked a date. Hired a hall. Caterers. Band.

Everyone was there. Even our old Vet. We didn't invite him, but he came.[24]

Dad did a speech. It was the most wonderful, beautiful speech I'd heard in my entire life.

And you know Dad, he hated public speaking. I said to him, Dad, you really don't have to say anything but he said…

The NARRATOR gets the microphone, takes the DAD by the hand and leads him into the middle of the room.

---

23 In one performance in Edinburgh, the wonderful stand-up Josie Long was chosen to play SAM. At this point, she took a receipt from her pocket, fashioned it into a ring and used it to propose to Jonny. Jonny wore the ring for the rest of the performance.

24 It could be the VET or the LECTURER who crashes the wedding, whichever seems more amusing for the particular performance.

...no I really want to. I really want to take
this opportunity to talk to everyone, so...

The NARRATOR speaks into the microphone.

...Ladies and Gentlemen, in a break from
tradition, please welcome the Father of the
Groom.

*The NARRATOR gives the DAD the microphone, asks him to
wait for a moment, then sits next to SAM and links arms.*

Say what's in your heart Dad.

*The 'DAD' improvises a short speech, after which the
NARRATOR hugs the DAD and lets them return to their seat.*[25]

I remember every word.

After the reception, when most of the guests
had gone home,[26] Mum sat at the piano and
played soul songs.

The snippet of Ray Charles plays – 'Why can't YOU...'

,

After the wedding Sam and I went on
holiday to Whitstable in Kent.[27] We were so
happy. The sun shone every day. We ate the
most incredible seafood.

We moved to London. We got jobs. A car.
A joint bank account. A cat who peed on
everything then ran away. We called her
Margaret Scratcher. We settled into a routine.

---

25 This is probably the most unpredictable moment of the play. Sometimes it's
very brief, sometimes the NARRATOR needs to cut it short. It can be very funny
or very emotional, such as the occasion when the DAD (who turned-out to be
a real-life Rabbi) ended his speech with the words 'Son, you used to always ask
me 'why?' and I never had an answer for you. Well, today I know that you have
found your answer.'

26 Depending on the DAD's speech, this sometimes became 'After the speeches,
once we'd all recovered...'

27 In America this often got a laugh, prompting Jonny to say 'that's not supposed
to be funny. It's just where we went.'

We saw less and less of each other. We were tired. We argued. We argued about money. We argued about whether we wanted to live in the city or the countryside. We argued about whether or not we should start a family.

We had one argument in particular.

Sam suggested that I talk to someone. Professionally.

That made me so angry. I knew what depression was and I knew I was fine.

I had a study at home and I'd sit in there, listening to records and reading the sleeve notes.

The lives of other people have always fascinated me. I always read the liner notes in record sleeves. The trials and traumas behind the music. Tortured geniuses.

Weldon Irvine. Albert Ayler. Ronnie Singer. Donny Hathaway. Amazing musicians. All took their own lives.

I'm so grateful to be ordinary.

Sam told me I was becoming morose. That I was isolating myself. Wallowing.

She encouraged me to carry on with the list, but I found it hard to notice new things.

826978.

,

826978.

,

826978.

'

The list ended, just one hundred and seventy three thousand and twenty two short of a million. It was finished. So I boxed it all up and threw it away.

'

I sat in my study while Sam packed her things. I helped her carry boxes to her car. I stood in our doorway and she looked at me from the car.

That horrible feeling when something is broken and can't ever be fixed. The trapdoor swinging open. Fight or flight or stay as still as you can.

I'd been feeling like that for a long time.

'

I watched her drive away.

'

She left me a note, written in an album sleeve. She knew that when I wanted to think of her I'd look for the Daniel Johnston song she sang at my parent's house and, as always, I'd sit and read through the record sleeve.

Sam's note said that she loved me and that when I was ready we should try again.

But I didn't find the note for seven years.

'

Perhaps Sam had been right. Perhaps I'd been difficult to live with. Difficult to love.

But I couldn't hear it from her. I needed to talk to someone else.

So, the night I found Sam's note, I did one of the oddest things I've ever done.

,

Mrs Patterson?

MRS PATTERSON Yes.

NARRATOR I hope you don't mind me calling you so late, I know you've retired, I know that because I called the school and they gave me your number. I know this is really inappropriate but...I'm an ex-pupil of yours. I was the little boy with the list. Do you remember me?

MRS PATTERSON Yes.

,

NARRATOR You do?

MRS PATTERSON Yes.

,

NARRATOR You used to have a sock puppet, do you remember?

MRS PATTERSON Yes.

NARRATOR A black dog. Which, now I come to think of it is a little ironic. Mostyn, wasn't it?

MRS PATTERSON Yes.

NARRATOR I was always able to talk to Mostyn. This may sound strange, but, would it be possible to talk to Mostyn now?

> *MRS PATTERSON takes off her shoe and her sock once again and puts the sock over her hand.*

SOCK   Hello.

NARRATOR   Hello Mostyn. How're you?

SOCK   I'm fine, how're you?

NARRATOR   Well, I'm talking to a sock dog on the phone, so apparently not great.

,

I'm sad.

I'm really sad Mostyn and I don't know how to change that. And I wanted to speak to you because when I was a little boy you knew me better than anyone.

I wanted to ask you: was I always like this? Do you remember what I was like?

SOCK   Yes.

NARRATOR   Was I happy?

> *The NARRATOR leads the SOCK PUPPET through a brief conversation until a conclusion is reached that allows the NARRATOR to take the next step – either he's always been sad or he was once happy.*

,

Thank you. It means a lot to hear that from you.

I'm sorry I called so late. I won't call you again. Goodnight.

MRS PATTERSON Goodnight.

,

NARRATOR   I did talk to someone.

A group. A support group.

,

Hello everyone.

The NARRATOR indicates for everyone to respond.

AUDIENCE   Hello.

NARRATOR   This is my first session. I've resisted doing
                this.

                I'm –

                you know,

                ,

                British.

                I now realise that it's important to talk about
                things. Particularly the things that are the
                hardest to talk about.

                When I was younger I was much better at
                being happy.

                At feeling joy.

                Being a grown-up, being conscious
                of the problems in the world, about
                the complexities, the tragedies, the
                disappointments…I'm not sure I can ever
                fully allow myself to be joyful. I'm just not
                very good at it. It's helpful to know there are
                other people who feel the same.

                I um –

                I made a list. Everything that's brilliant about
                the world.

                I began making it as a present for my Mum.
                It's kind of a long story.

The list is –

Actually, wait a second, I have it with me...

The NARRATOR exits the stage, then returns with a trolley on which sit several large, heavy, worn boxes.

You see, I threw it away but, unbeknownst to me, my partner at the time...

The NARRATOR looks at SAM.

...got it out of the trash and hid it in the garage under an old tablecloth and then left a note about it in the record sleeve of a Curtis Mayfield record...well, you don't need to know the details.

He opens one of the boxes. It is full of scraps of paper, the list, written on pages of colouring books, on receipts and beer mats, on the backs of envelopes etc. He takes a moment to just look at it. He carefully takes out a stack and looks through it. He reads entries at random and drops them, scattering them on the floor.

Peeling off a sheet of wallpaper in one intact piece.

He reads another.

Mork and Mindy.

He holds up a sleeve from a shirt and reads what's written on it:

My new sleeveless top.

He reads another.

Old people holding hands.

,

He smiles and looks around the room.

If you live a long life and get to the end of it without ever once having felt crushingly depressed, then you probably haven't been paying attention.

,

I wasn't around for the last time. I was in Australia with work and when I got the call I was on the beach. Dad wasn't around either. A neighbour complained about the exhaust fumes and eventually the police cut through the garage door. Hosepipe through the driver-side window.

That surprised me actually, because Mum hated driving.

She had poor circulation and would always complain about her ankles on long journeys. They say that it's a masculine way to choose to die. But I don't know what that means.

There was a pad and pencil on the passenger seat but she hadn't written anything.

I drove Dad to the funeral. We sat in silence. He smoked with the window down. I helped him with his tie.

After the service, meeting my Mum's friends and colleagues, I realised how much the list had changed the way I see the world.

31.   Birdsong.
45.   Hugging.
341.   Alcohol.
577.   Tea and biscuits.
1092.   Conversation.

The list hadn't stopped her. Hadn't saved her. Of course it hadn't.

,

I got a text from Sam.

The NARRATOR gives SAM his phone to read.

SAM   I heard about your Mum.

I'm so sorry.

Give me a call.

Anytime.

I'd love to hear your voice.

Love,

Sam x

Ps. I heard the other day that Beyonce is related to the composer Gustav Mahler. It occurred to me that this is a fact that should be on your list. Truly a brilliant thing.

,

I stayed with Dad for a few months after the funeral. We'd spend the days walking or reading or listening to records. He'd fall asleep in his armchair and I'd sit at his desk and type up the list, starting at the very beginning.

1.   Ice cream.

It was a lot of work. Several weeks of sleepless nights. Once I got to the end I kept going from where I'd left off.

826979.   The fact that Beyonce is Gustav Mahler's eighth cousin, four times removed.[28]

---

28 Jonny would take this entry out of his pocket and give it to the person he'd moved away from SAM, then allow them to return to their seat.

I completed the list.

,

I printed it out and left it in Dad's chair. I drove back to London.

He never mentioned it directly, but when we spoke a few weeks later, he said 'thank you.'

DAD   Thank you.

NARRATOR   And he said 'I love you'.

DAD   I love you.

NARRATOR   I told him that sentimentality didn't suit him.

999997.   The alphabet.

999998.   Inappropriate songs played at emotional moments.

999999.   Completing a task.

The NARRATOR says the final entry.

1000000.   Listening to a record for the first time. Turning it over in your hands, placing it on the deck and putting the needle down, hearing the faint hiss and crackle of the sharp metal point on the wax before the music begins, then sitting and listening while reading through the sleeve notes.

,

'Into Each Life Some Rain Must Fall' by Ella Fitzgerald and the Ink Spots plays.

The NARRATOR shakes hands with or hugs the members of the AUDIENCE who played the principal characters – the VET,

LECTURER, MRS PATTERSON, DAD and SAM, indicating for applause to be directed to them and inviting them to bow.

The NARRATOR then bows and leaves. The list remains scattered around the stage so that the AUDIENCE can look through the box and read the entries.

The music continues to play as they exit.

PEOPLE, PLACES AND THINGS

For my sisters

Acknowledgements

Lots of people helped make this play happen, by reading drafts, helping with research, taking part in read-throughs or by providing childcare while I worked. The names of many of them appear in the production credits. Many others wish to remain anonymous. I'd like to thank the generosity of many who told me their own stories, allowed me to attend meetings and treatment facilities, provided links and books and other resources. Thanks in particular to Neil Brener and the staff of the Priory and everyone at the Freedom Recovery Centre, Catford.

Jeremy Herrin, Henny Finch, Stephen Daly, Liz Eddy, Debbie Farquhar, Sarah Grochala, Samantha Potter and all at Headlong. Rufus Norris, Tessa Ross, Ben Power and Emily McLaughlin and all at the NT and NT Studio. Lyndsey Turner. Robert Icke. Lennox Thomas. Daniel Raggett. Katie Mitchell. Chloe Lamford. Matthew Herbert. Steve Marmion. Nina Steiger. Ally Gipps. Simon McBurney. Beth Macmillan. Simon Vinnicombe. Stephen Daldry. Clare Lizzimore. Jon and NoraLee Sedmak. Becki Willmore. Ella Kearns Concannon. Rachel Taylor, Kirsten Foster, Anthony Mestriner, Helena Clark and Mel Kenyon. Effie Woods and Marlowe Macmillan.

Characters

EMMA

KONSTANTIN

STAGE
MANAGER

CREW
MEMBERS

CAST MEMBERS

UNDERSTUDY

DRESSERS

MEN

PAUL

FOSTER

NURSES

DOCTOR

THERAPIST

MARK

MEREDITH

T

JODI

SHAUN

LAURA

EMMAS

CLUBBERS

YOUNG WOMAN

DRESSERS

WOMAN

PARAMEDICS

DOCTORS

NURSE

MEDICAL STAFF

DAD

MUM

VOICE

ACTRESSES

ACTRESS

The GROUP are ethnically diverse,
of different classes and ages.

A forward slash (/) marks the point of interruption
in overlapping dialogue.

People, Places and Things, a co-production between the National Theatre and Headlong, had its World premiere at the Dorfman Theatre, London on 1 September 2015 with the following cast

EMMA, Denise Gough
PAUL / DAD, Kevin Mcmonagle
DOCTOR / THERAPIST / MUM , Barbara Marten
MARK, Nathaniel Martello-White
FOSTER, Alistair Cope
MEREDITH / ENSEMBLE, Sally George
T / ENSEMBLE, Jacob James Beswick
JODI / ENSEMBLE, Jacqui Dubois
SHAUN / ENSEMBLE, Nari Blair-Mangat
LAURA / ENSEMBLE, Laura Woodward

Director Jeremy Herrin
Set Designer Bunny Christie
Costume Designer Christina Cunningham
Lighting Designer James Farncombe
Music Matthew Herbert
Sound Designer Tom Gibbons
Movement Polly Bennett
Video/Projection Designer Andrzej Goulding
Company Voice Work Jeannette Nelson
Dialect Coach Richard Ryder
Staff Director Holly Race Roughan

ACT ONE

As the lights fade, the sounds of a theatre auditorium increase. Mobile phones, coughing, chattering and general sounds of anticipation. It builds to a cacophony.

Darkness. Chaos.

Suddenly the lights snap up and the sounds cease. We are in the same theatre, but at a different time. A play is in progress, the final act of Chekhov's The Seagull. A Naturalistic, period set of a study which was once a drawing-room. Doors left and right. A French window opens onto a terrace. It is raining.

Evening. One shaded lamp is alight. It is dark. Trees rustle outside and wind howls softly in the chimneys.

EMMA is playing Nina Zarechny. Her hair is wet. She has been crying. She sits on an ottoman in the centre of the stage next to KONSTANTIN GAVRILOVICH TREPLEV. The lights snap up mid-sentence.

KONSTANTIN   for ninety years on this earth. My youth *robbed* from me.

> *EMMA looks around the stage and out into the auditorium. It is as if she's just come-to and is trying to establish where she is.*

> I've cursed you Nina. Ripped up your photographs and letters. But it's no use. I see your face everywhere. I say your name. I kiss the ground you walk on. I'm bound to you forever. And now you're *here.*

> *He waits for EMMA to speak. After a while he decides that she's not going to say her line, so continues.*

> I'm sad. Lonely. *Utterly* alone and cold as if I've been imprisoned underground. And everything I write is so bleak.

KONSTANTIN takes EMMA's hand.

> Nina. Stay here. I beg you. Stay here or let
> me go with you.

*For a moment, EMMA looks into KONSTANTIN's eyes. She looks
down at their interlocked hands.*

,

> Nina?

*Suddenly, EMMA stands and quickly prepares to leave, grabbing
her coat and putting it on.*

> Nina, for God's sake, Nina.

EMMA My carriage is waiting. Don't walk me out.
     Can I have some water?

KONSTANTIN Where will you go?

He pours some water.

EMMA Is Irina Arkadin here?

KONSTANTIN Yes. Uncle was taken ill and we telegraphed
     / for her.

EMMA advances to KONSTANTIN angrily, interrupting him.

EMMA Why did you say you worship the ground I
     walk on? Death. Death is what I deserve.

*EMMA doubles-over. KONSTANTIN doesn't know what to do. He
stands still, holding the water. He looks off into the wings.*

> I'm so tired. I need to sleep. I'm a seagull.
> No that's not right. I'm an actress.

Laughter in the wings. EMMA looks up.

> He's here too isn't he?

EMMA laughs.

Of course. It doesn't matter.

She walks to KONSTANTIN and takes the water from him.

He didn't believe in the stage. He laughed at me. I don't believe in it either. Not now.

As EMMA talks her acting becomes more genuine. She is talking less in character and more as herself. She is sincere, vivid, compelling. She doesn't slur her words.

Not now that I've had real problems. Real things have happened. My heart is broken. I don't know what to do with my hands when I'm onstage. I'm not real. I'm a seagull. No, that's wrong.

The lamp flickers. EMMA notices it. KONSTANTIN doesn't.

You shot a seagull. Do you remember? Earlier in the play?

EMMA laughs.

I mean the *story*, I mean
long ago you shot a

that's wrong too. Not you. What was I saying? I was talking about the *theatre*. I love acting. I'm a real actress. I was a real actress. Will you come and see me when I'm a real actress? I'm different now. And I feel better and better every day. You don't need to worry about me anymore. I have

faith.

EMMA hears something. She is twitchy.

KONSTANTIN   Nina,

EMMA   things don't hurt me so much anymore. I'm not afraid. I'm

The lights fade around her slightly. The Naturalistic sounds fade and for a moment there's something more ominous and subjective. A low rumble. A whine of tinnitus.

,

I'm a

EMMA looks up as if she's been daydreaming and just coming-to. The sounds have returned to normal.

,

She looks around, seemingly unaware of where she is.

KONSTANTIN   Nina?

EMMA's physicality changes. She drops the water without realising it.

Nina?

Er...

EMMA looks into the auditorium. She walks towards the edge of the stage and peers into the darkness at the audience. She moves out of her light. She pulls her wig off. She has very different hair underneath.

Nina?

The lights flicker. Her nose starts bleeding, heavily. She touches the blood and looks at it, fascinated.

Emma?

Emma?

EMMA is about to step off the edge of the stage. A STAGE MANAGER hurries on from the wings and takes EMMA by the arm. Sounds offstage. The scenery starts moving, revealing CREW MEMBERS, props tables, cables and the back wall of the theatre. Costumed CAST MEMBERS of The Seagull watch what's happening,

*including an UNDERSTUDY dressed exactly like EMMA. EMMA
looks at her, not sure what she's seeing. A DRESSER wipes the
blood from EMMA's face. Another helps her into a jacket. EMMA
is uncooperative. The furniture is taken off into the wings.
The lights scroll through various colours. Naturalistic sounds,
including a gunshot, play then begin to repeat rhythmically.
EMMA can see a man in the distance, dancing under a flashing
light. She thinks she's in a nightclub, but she knows that can't
be possible. MEN suddenly surround her. A pill is put onto her
tongue. She takes someone's drink and downs it. She snatches a
phone from someone. She takes someone's cigarette. She pushes
the MEN away, violently. They leave. She is alone, holding the
phone to her ear and trying to light the cigarette. She is in the
reception of a drug and alcohol rehabilitation centre. The dance
music continues faintly, coming from a radio on the reception
desk. There's a row of plastic chairs in front of a window next
to which sit EMMA's bags.*

EMMA   Just this one thing can you please do this one
thing for me please I'm just asking for

*EMMA looks around at her new surroundings, a little surprised
to find herself there. She listens to the voice on the phone and
remembers what she's doing.*

listen to me listen to me okay alright please
this is important to me I'm trying to do
something for once in my life do something
for myself and

don't be like that why do you have to be like
that no, listen please for a second because
right now you're being a complete cunt.

Well I'm sorry you hate that word, that's
really unfortunate because in one syllable it
so perfectly describes your entire personality.

She throws the lighter down and searches in her bag for another.

Look, obviously I called the wrong person.
Obviously you're unable to help me, you
can't give me half an hour to do something
that could save my life.

She stops searching.

Yes it *is* that serious.

I'm not being dramatic. That's such a cunty
thing to say.

I'll stop calling you a cunt when you stop
being a cunt.

Listen,

,

Mum.

,

Mum, please, listen to me for a second.

You're already in my flat, just

She starts searching again.

there's a large, clear-plastic box in the
hallway on the

like a big, plastic

box
it's see-through, it's
I don't know how else to describe it.

Yeah, that's just unread post. Tip it out.
I don't know, the floor. It's bills Mum. I'll
deal with it when I get home.

Okay now fill the box with anything that
looks

you know,

medical or

yes, any alcohol, of course yes, and anything
that looks like drugs or

She finds a small clear plastic bag of powder. She looks around.

okay.

,

*Aware of her surroundings, she quickly pours out the powder
onto the seat of a chair and makes a few lines with a fingernail.*

On the coffee table in the living room,
there's a wooden box. You see it? That's the
one. Don't look inside, just chuck it.

Yes it's the one Dad got me. I know that but

that's not what I've used it for.

She holds the phone away from her and snorts the powder.

*For a moment, the lights in the room glow brighter, the music on
the radio slows down and all other sounds cease, then everything
speeds up to catch up to reality.*

She puts the phone back to her ear.

Just
will you please just chuck it out?

She turns up the radio a little and moves slightly to the music.

Okay, and in the kitchen,

you found all that? Great.

Yep. Yep. Yep. Yep. Yep. Yep.

She cracks her knuckles and rolls her head around her shoulders.
She stretches the muscles in her face.

> And the cupboard under the sink? No on the
> left of
>
> okay good.

She rummages in her bag again.

> And the oven?
>
> Okay open the oven.
>
> Because I don't use it for
>
> Mum, I don't cook.

She finds her lighter.

> Put it in the box with the rest of it.

A loud crash nearby. Shouting. EMMA *looks in the direction of the*
sound but can't see anything. She lights the cigarette.

> And then the bathroom, but, Mum, listen
>
> I want you to just
>
> ,
>
> don't be shocked okay?

EMMA *sits down on one of the plastic chairs. She listens to her*
mother.

> ,

She puts the phone on the seat next to her and rubs her eyes
with both hands.

She listens to the rain. She twists around in the seat and looks
out of the window.

She looks at one of her hands, checking for tremors. She makes a fist then relaxes it again.

She stretches out her legs. She moves her jaw.

,

She picks the phone up and continues to listen.

,

That's why I'm here Mum.

I am.

I am.

I'm trying to get myself well.

She rubs her nostrils and takes another drag on her cigarette.

,

No I'm not smoking.

,

Mum, I really need you to

Another crash. A light begins to flash above reception. A tone sounds each time it alights.

,

please.

More sounds, things being overturned. Shouting.

,

Yeah.

Yeah.

Okay.

,

Mum, / thank you.

The doors to the clinic burst open and a man, PAUL, rushes into the room. He is shirtless. He has the words 'THE END' written on his torso. His eyes are wide. One of his hands is bleeding heavily, dripping blood. He speaks directly to EMMA. EMMA stays still.

PAUL   They're trying to take it all out from us drain our blood and use it for gold this is gold and they're scared of its power and they're right they're right they're right they should be scared. They should be TERRIFIED.

EMMA   I've got to go Mum.

NURSES from the clinic rush in and approach PAUL.

NURSE 1   Mr Waverley.

NURSE 2   Mr Waverley let's go back inside alright?

PAUL   WE ARE LOVE WE ARE GOD WE ARE POWER AND LIFE AND WE WILL NEVER SURRENDER!

FOSTER has entered. He has long hair and wears a bandana. He wears a different uniform to the NURSES. There is blood on FOSTER's shirt.

FOSTER   *(To EMMA.)* You can't smoke in here.

EMMA   Oh. What?

FOSTER   You can't smoke in here.

NURSE 2   *(To PAUL.)* Mr Waverley,

NURSE 1   Paul, will you please

PAUL climbs up onto the reception desk and throws and kicks whatever is in his path onto the floor. He throws pens at the NURSES. PAUL continues to shout as FOSTER talks to EMMA. NURSES try to persuade PAUL to climb down from the desk.

PAUL			
THESE PEOPLE ARE	FOSTER	it's a medical building, this is a medical	
SHADOWS,	EMMA	yes of course.	
THEY'RE SKELETONS AND	FOSTER	you can smoke outside.	
THEY'RE SUCKING	EMMA	It's raining.	
OUR BLOOD. I HAVE LOCKED EYES WITH	FOSTER	I don't know what to tell you, it's a medical building, this is part of a medical / building, you can't	
GOD I HAVE TOUCHED THE EYES OF GOD I	EMMA	yes, I know, I understand that, it's just	
HAVE LICKED GOD'S EYEBALLS.	FOSTER	you can take it outside or put it out, those are your options.	

Members of the GROUP have entered the room to watch the chaos. One of the NURSES talks into a handset.

NURSE 1   Doctor please come to reception. Doctor to reception please.

PAUL	Listen. I'm sharing a truth with you.	EMMA	Do you have an ashtray?
	This is an act of LOVE, don't you understand? The	FOSTER	There isn't an ashtray no, it's a medical building so
	world has to	EMMA	right.
	change and it can start here it can	FOSTER	I'm not being petty.
	start this minute!	EMMA	No.
	With us! I can see what we need to do.	FOSTER	There have to be rules or things descend into chaos.

The DOCTOR enters hurriedly. She has been eating lunch. She prepares a needle. PAUL walks towards EMMA, looking directly at her.

PAUL

You can see it too. Can't you? It should all be torn to pieces.

The walls are losing definition. Everyone in the room seems to be moving in slow motion. PAUL and EMMA are the only people moving at normal speed. PAUL speaks to EMMA with a surprisingly conversational matter-of-factness.

Things need to change but they won't.
There'll be so much death, one after another
and then many at once. It'll be such a loud
party.

The DOCTOR administers an injection. PAUL stays staring at EMMA and smiles. The room catches up to normal speed and PAUL loses a little of his clarity.

They're going to ask for everything but
you've got nothing to begin with. Nothing.

NURSES support him as he slumps back into a waiting wheelchair.

Never

surrender.

He loses consciousness.

DOCTOR   EVERYONE BACK INSIDE PLEASE.

NURSES usher GROUP members back into the clinic.

FOSTER   Checking in or picking up?

PAUL is taken back into the clinic. FOSTER stops the alarm.

EMMA   Is he okay?

FOSTER   Are you checking in?

FOSTER changes the radio station. Choral music plays.

EMMA   I'm

FOSTER   if you'd like to finish your cigarette outside
                         I'll check you in once you've

EMMA   oh, sorry.

FOSTER   Do you have anyone with you?

*EMMA shakes her head. The word 'EXIT' lights up above the front
door. EMMA looks at it.*

EMMA   Actually, sorry. I think. Yeah. I'm going to
                         just go outside for a second.

EMMA gathers all her belongings.

FOSTER   You can leave your bags.

EMMA   Yeah, no I'll just
                         I'm going to just

FOSTER   how about we check you in first and / then
                         you can

EMMA   is there a lot to do?

FOSTER holds up a clipboard.

FOSTER	Just a few questions.
EMMA	Like
FOSTER	like what's your name?

,

The questions do get harder so you may want to

EMMA	I'd like to
FOSTER	anonymity.
EMMA	Something like that.
FOSTER	The privacy policy is all on the back of the form, it's important that you read and sign that too. But your recovery depends on you being completely truthful while you're here. Do you understand that?

,

So what name shall I put on the form?

,

EMMA	Nina.
FOSTER	Right. Nice to meet you Nina.

The forms are all quite self-explanatory. I'll need a bunch of signatures. And I'll need your phone and if you've got a laptop, iPad, any electronic devices, you'll have to hand / those in.

EMMA	I need my phone.
FOSTER	Yeah, no. It's policy. It's like the policy about smoking.

EMMA looks at the cigarette in her hand.

EMMA   I thought I put that out.

FOSTER   You didn't.

EMMA   Right. Sorry.

              ,

              The thing is that this is my last cigarette and
              once it's out I'm

*FOSTER takes the cigarette from EMMA and drops it into a cup
of coffee.*

FOSTER   we'll keep your devices safe for you and once
              you've / finished your

EMMA   I'm waiting to hear about this thing, I need
              my phone because there's a thing / I'm

FOSTER   tell me Nina, when did you last use?

              ,

EMMA   I

FOSTER   blunt, I know, but

EMMA   er

FOSTER   more than a week or less?

The 'EXIT' light flickers.

              ,

              In the last 72 hours?

              The last 24?

              ,

              Are you high right now?

              ,

EMMA studies him. FOSTER appears to be a different person than he was a moment ago. EMMA can't be sure, the clothes and bandana are the same.

Can you tell me what you've taken?

EMMA   I just needed something to get me here.

FOSTER   It's important to be accurate so we know
              how to treat you. And it won't help you to
              lie. You're going to have a full medical and
              history taken so you may as well start being
              honest now.

EMMA   I drank a bit and smoked some weed.

FOSTER   What alcohol did you drink and how much?

EMMA   Some wine. Red wine. Rioja. Quite an
              expensive one.

FOSTER   Okay.

EMMA   And gin. I was anxious about coming here so
              I just wanted to take the edge off.

FOSTER   Nina, I'm not judging, I just need to get as /
              accurate a

EMMA   I took a couple of beta-blockers and some
              ibuprofen too.

FOSTER is writing all of this down. EMMA tries to read what's being written.

FOSTER   Right.

EMMA   And some speed just to balance me out. Get
              me motivated.

FOSTER   And how long ago did you take the speed?

              ,

EMMA   Oh, I don't know.

She is chewing her lips.

        Ages.

        ,

FOSTER   Is that everything from the last 24 hours?

        ,

        Nina?

EMMA   Like a half a gram of coke.

        And a multivitamin.

FOSTER   Any prescriptions?

        ,

EMMA   For anxiety. Valium. Benzos and Ativan.

FOSTER   And you smoke.

EMMA   Until just now.

FOSTER   Right.

EMMA   Is that important?

FOSTER   There's a checklist, I'm just

EMMA   trying to fill your bingo card.

FOSTER   Right. *(Not smiling.)* That's funny.

        ,

        How did you get here today Nina?

EMMA   I drove.

FOSTER looks at EMMA.

        ,

        It's fine. I'm a really good driver.

And I'm okay really. Overall. It's not a problem, my using. I just want to get a tune up. I'm not completely in control of it anymore. I've had some problems at work because of it and some blackouts and I think I tried to kill myself so I'm just a bit

FOSTER   blackouts?

EMMA   Yeah.

FOSTER makes some notes. He continues to write without looking up.

,

I'm actually quite healthy. I know I'm not giving that impression. I go to the gym. Sometimes.

FOSTER appears to be a different person again, perhaps a woman.

FOSTER   Is there a contact I can have, a partner or

EMMA   no.

FOSTER   Family member or

,

we won't contact them unless there's an emergency.

,

Work colleague?

EMMA   Mum.

My Mum.

The lights flicker again. Only EMMA seems to notice it.

,

FOSTER   Just pop her details on the form. Then I'll
          take you through for your medical.

FOSTER hands EMMA the form.

EMMA   You won't contact her / unless

FOSTER   unless there's an emergency.

EMMA looks at the form. FOSTER takes her bags.

          I'll let them know you're ready.

          ,

FOSTER pauses at the door and looks back at EMMA.

          Don't go anywhere.

          ,

FOSTER leaves.

EMMA considers writing on the form but doesn't.

          She sighs.

She talks to herself.

EMMA   *Whoever you are, I have always depended on the
          kindness of strangers.*

*EMMA looks at the door to the outside world. The EXIT light seems
to have grown impossibly large.*

*She approaches the doorway. Lights in the room start to fade.
She is lit by the light from outside. The choral music from the
radio seems to be coming from all around her.*

*NURSES approach EMMA and take the form, her phone, her coat.
They take her shoes and help her into a pale blue medical gown.
They attach a blood-pressure cuff to EMMA's arm. One shines a
torch in EMMA's eyes and mouth.*

FOSTER returns, takes EMMA's coat, bags and mobile phone, then closes the door to the outside world. The choral music ceases. Electric lights snap on.

DOCTOR   Nina?

EMMA doesn't look up.

                 Nina?

Still no response.

                 Excuse me, hello.

                 ,

EMMA looks around. She is in the DOCTOR's consultation room.

EMMA   Sorry. Yes, that's / me.

                 Well the good news is that this looks
                 perfectly normal.

The D O C T O R is looking at the contents of a small, clear plastic box.

EMMA   What is that?

DOCTOR   Your stool sample.

EMMA   Not mine.

DOCTOR   Oh. Really?

                 ,

The DOCTOR looks at the contents, picks it up, sniffs it, then takes a bite of it. EMMA stares.

                 ,

The DOCTOR looks up.

                 Falafel. It's falafel.

EMMA remains very still.

                 I'm making a joke. I didn't finish lunch.

,

The DOCTOR takes the form from one of the NURSES and reads it. She makes a couple of notes. EMMA watches her.

	Seriously though, you may have to do a stool sample. Has she done a UDA?
EMMA	What's that?
DOCTOR	Urine.
NURSE	Not yet Doctor.
EMMA	Could I have some / water?
DOCTOR	Your name is 'Nina.'
EMMA	Yes. Why are you saying / it like
DOCTOR	and you're an alcoholic and drug addict.
EMMA	Fucking hell.
DOCTOR	Aren't you?
EMMA	I'm
DOCTOR	why else would you be here?
NURSE	*(To DOCTOR.)* 160 over 110.
DOCTOR	Your recovery can't start until you admit you have a problem.
EMMA	This was a mistake.
DOCTOR	You're *not* an alcoholic and drug addict?
EMMA	I'm not saying I'm anything, I just need a
	I don't know.
	I just want to get clean, get my certificate and go back to / work.
DOCTOR	Certificate?

EMMA   A piece of paper or a signed whatever, something that says I can work. That I'm not a risk.

DOCTOR   Once you complete the programme / we can

EMMA   how long will that take?

DOCTOR   It varies. First I'll need to see your results and take a history and / psychological examination.

EMMA   Isn't there a way we could just speed this along?

The DOCTOR is consulting the form.

DOCTOR   Benzodiazepine, Lorazepam.

EMMA   Valium, yeah. For anxiety. It's a prescription.

DOCTOR   And do you use beyond your prescription?

,

EMMA   I have a few GPs. And I get some online and from a few people / I know.

DOCTOR   Has your use of pills impacted on you and those around you? Work? Relationships? Family?

,

EMMA   I was

I was at work and I

I was confused about where I was. Who I was.

DOCTOR   Dissociation.

EMMA   I guess so. You look like my mother.

DOCTOR	That's projection. Assigning familial attributes onto an authority figure.
EMMA	No, you really fucking look like her.

The DOCTOR has taken EMMA's hands and is holding them out, looking for tremors.

DOCTOR	Detoxing from benzos takes about ten days.
EMMA	Ten / days?
DOCTOR	You'll start tonight, and tomorrow morning you can begin with Group.
EMMA	I don't need that, I just need the first thing.
DOCTOR	Nina, the Group *is* the programme. The truth is that it doesn't take long to get everything out of your body. It's the behaviour, the psychology that is the important thing to address. We can't do that until we've dealt with the physical symptoms. Then it's twenty-eight days of therapy. Ideally it'll be closer to ninety.
EMMA	Ninety? No, that's not possible.
DOCTOR	Tell me Nina, how do you think this story ends?
EMMA	What story?
DOCTOR	You. Your life. How does it play out, do you think, if you don't prioritise getting well?
EMMA	I'm not ill, I'm

The DOCTOR consults the form.

DOCTOR	blackouts.
EMMA	A few, yeah.

A NURSE checks EMMA's pulse.

DOCTOR   Memory loss?

EMMA   Sometimes I think. It's like time travel or a
             skipping CD. One minute I'll be talking to
             someone, the next I'll be walking in the road.
             Could I have some water please?

NURSE   You have water.

EMMA   No I

*EMMA sees that she's holding a plastic cup of water. It wasn't
there a moment ago.*

             oh.

She drinks the water.

NURSE   *(To DOCTOR.)* 130.

*The DOCTOR stands very close to EMMA. EMMA is unnerved by this
but tries not to show it. A NURSE prepares to take a blood test.*

DOCTOR   Look at me.

She does.

             I know you don't I?

EMMA avoids eye-contact.

EMMA   I've just got one of those faces.

DOCTOR   What's your occupation?

EMMA   Is that one of the questions?

DOCTOR   It is.

EMMA   Is it important?

DOCTOR   Is it a secret?

             How are you with needles?

EMMA   Excuse m – *ouch.*

A NURSE has put a needle into EMMA's arm and begins to take blood. EMMA winces.

A hiss of blood in EMMA's head. Lights begin to fade. The DOCTOR shines a torch into one of EMMA's eyes.

DOCTOR   Do you often pass out?

The lights in the room flicker.

EMMA   I suppose so. I wake up places.

DOCTOR   Do you feel like you might pass out now?

EMMA   A little, yes.

The room is losing detail somehow, the walls are moving further away or dissolving into a pixelated fuzz.

DOCTOR   It says here 'suicide attempt'.

EMMA   Not a successful one.

DOCTOR   Evidently.

EMMA   That's me. Never seeing anything through. Violin lessons. Diets. Suicide attempts. I never finish what I start.

DOCTOR   If you're trying to be funny can you let me know because it's not immediately obvious.

NURSE   Hold this.

The NURSE places EMMA's thumb so that she's holding a small ball of cotton wool where the needle was. EMMA looks at her blood in the tube. The DOCTOR's voice increasingly sounds like it's underwater.

DOCTOR   Memory loss?

EMMA   Didn't you just ask me that?

DOCTOR   Nina, I'd like to hear you say that you need my help. I feel uncomfortable giving you help if you haven't asked for it.

EMMA   I've been managing just fine.

DOCTOR   When I look at your blood results am I going
               to see that you're just fine or am I going to
               see something else?

               If you don't want help then why are you
               here?

EMMA   I'm not sure if I am.

DOCTOR   I'm sorry?

A sense of things falling.

EMMA   I said I don't know if I am.

               '

               Here.

*The lights blackout. Chaotic sounds, like a thousand television
channels playing simultaneously, all rising in pitch.*

After barely a second the lights snap up again and the sounds stop.

*EMMA is surprised and scared to find herself on the floor,
surrounded by NURSES.*

DOCTOR   *(To NURSES.)* Give her some space please.

EMMA   Get off me.

DOCTOR   Stand back.

EMMA   GET THE FUCK OFF ME.

EMMA pushes the NURSES away.

DOCTOR   Leave us please. It's okay.

*The NURSES leave the room. The DOCTOR refills EMMA's water
cup. Her voice no longer sounds like it's underwater. The detail
of the room has returned. EMMA concentrates on controlling her
breath. The drawers of a filing cabinet breathe in and out with
her. Gradually this will stop and the room will stabilise.*

Do you know where you are Nina?

,

EMMA   Who's Nina?

,

DOCTOR   Do you need to be sick?

            It might help.

EMMA   I shouldn't be here.

DOCTOR   It's pretty obvious that you should.

            You came here for a reason. That was a good
            impulse.

EMMA looks at her hands. She's shaking.

The DOCTOR refills EMMA's water.

            Your addiction will fight any progress. It's a
            parasite and it will fight for its own survival
            until you're dead. But progress is possible. I
            just need to hear you say that you are willing
            and motivated to make changes.

EMMA   *'I cast you out, unclean spirit!'*

            You know. From The Exorcist.
            'Your mother sucks cocks in hell!'

DOCTOR   I haven't seen it.

EMMA   Oh. Really?

DOCTOR   Are you willing and / motivated to

EMMA   you've never seen The Exorcist?

DOCTOR   I can't help you unless / you

EMMA   my Mum has gone to my flat and she's
            boxed up everything. Bottles. Pills.
            Everything.

DOCTOR   That's good. That's a very clear commitment
                to getting well.

EMMA   There was blood on the bathroom walls.
                She'll have seen that. Not my blood. Not all
                of it anyway. Needles aren't my thing. Lucky
                for me.

                She's probably still there now, some
                marigolds on, scrubbing away.

                ,

                I know that the next time I drink or use

                That'll be the end. I'll be dead.

                I'm not sure if I knew that until now, until I
                just literally just said it. But it's true.

                It's going to kill me.

She rubs her eyes.

                Yes.

                I need help.

                Please help me.

The DOCTOR speaks into a handset.

DOCTOR   Could Foster come to medical please? Foster
                to medical please.

The DOCTOR writes on a prescription pad.

                Withdrawal from benzodiazepines can be
                physically and emotionally very tough. You'll
                likely hallucinate and your body will be put
                under a lot of stress.

*The DOCTOR places some pills into a small paper cup. EMMA
hears the rattle.*

I'm going to give you some medication
that will stabilise you and reduce your risk
of seizure, and some benzodiazepine at a
reduced dosage. Now, I understand that
you've come here to get off drugs, not to take
more so you may be reluctant to

*The DOCTOR places the pills on the table. EMMA immediately
takes them, throwing them back and swigging down the water.*

right. Good. Okay.

FOSTER enters.

FOSTER   Hi, did you

DOCTOR   wait a moment please Foster.

(To EMMA.) We'll be monitoring you, checking
in regularly. You'll have, in your room, there
are cords and buzzers for when you need
help.

Don't be afraid to ask for it.

,

The DOCTOR nods to FOSTER.

FOSTER   Come with me.

Lights fade around them.

*EMMA walks to the window and watches as the sun sets. FOSTER
turns on a bedside lamp. They are in a bedroom. There is a
bathroom and a single bed. FOSTER puts EMMA's bags on the bed
and EMMA takes out some clothes.*

You're lucky. Everyone else is sharing but

*EMMA changes out of the medical robe and into comfortable
clothes. FOSTER turns his back to her.*

you're an odd number.

367

FOSTER looks out of the window.

Snowing.

If you want to ask me anything let me know. I'm an old hand at this.

Hat? Is it old hat or old hand?

EMMA   It smells like disinfectant.

FOSTER   If madam would prefer a room which smells of vomit and diarrhoea I'm sure she that can / be accommodated.

EMMA   I'm just saying that / it's

FOSTER   this is a medical building, it's not / a hotel.

EMMA   This will be fine.

FOSTER   Did the Doctor ask about your suicide attempt?

EMMA   Excuse me?

FOSTER   It's one of the psych questions. If you're thinking of or planning to kill yourself. You said you'd tried to

EMMA   right.

FOSTER   This bit can get pretty tough. I don't want to come in and find you bled out in the bathroom or something. That sort of clean up. The paper work. It's just a massive headache for me that I don't need.

,

Nah, you'll be fine.

Best thing about detox is, once you've been through it once you'd do anything to not have to go through it again. Here.

FOSTER gives EMMA a big book.

Some reading material you may find useful.

EMMA   Not a fucking Bible.

FOSTER   Not exactly.

And you didn't fill out the form. You were
going to give me that contact info.

For your Mum.

              ,

EMMA   Yeah. Right. I will.

Tomorrow.

FOSTER   Make sure you do.

FOSTER turns to leave. EMMA looks at the book.

EMMA   Foster, is it?

He stops.

FOSTER   Yeah.

EMMA   I'm

I'm a little bit

              ,

FOSTER   scared?

EMMA nods.

              ,

Do you want to see a picture of my dog?

*EMMA doesn't respond. FOSTER takes a mobile phone from his
pocket and loads up a photo.*

She's a mongrel. Mostly English Mastiff.
Refuge dog. Used for fighting and left for

dead. She, look, her ear isn't all there and she's blind in her right eye. The kennel was going to put her down, so I took her home with me. She's impossible to house train. Destroyed almost everything I own. She's bitten my right ankle, both my calves, my knee, my elbow, my hand here here and here and my shoulder. Her name's Eleanor. I love that dog.

,

EMMA   How come you're allowed a phone?

FOSTER   I work here.

EMMA   Can I borrow it?

,

FOSTER puts the phone away.

,

FOSTER   There's a buzzer next to the bed and a cord in the bathroom. We'll check in on you and make sure you don't choke on your own vomit or hit your head if you start fitting.

              Did you take the meds?

She nods.

              It's much better with the meds.

,

              Hang in there.

              This is the easy part.

,

FOSTER leaves.

EMMA looks around. She itches her arms.

She sits on the bed. She opens the book and starts reading.

She looks up and watches the snow outside.

She watches another EMMA get out of the bed and start to unpack, clutching her stomach as it cramps. EMMA watches as another EMMA gets out of the bed and starts to pace around the room, itching her arms. She sees another EMMA get out of the bed and fill a glass of water from the sink in the bathroom then drink it quickly. She is shaking and smashes the glass in the sink.

A rumble, increasing in volume and pitch.

Another EMMA appears and vomits into the toilet. Another EMMA sits on the floor, holding her legs to her body. She reaches up to the light switch and turns it on and off rhythmically. EMMA walks around the room, looking at the other EMMAs who do not notice her or each other.

The pacing EMMA is sweating and breathing heavily. Another EMMA is shivering with cold.

Time is passing, the sun rising and falling, faster and faster, days turning to night, nights turning to day. The sounds of the outside world increase, the hush of late night traffic in the darkness, the chaos of the busy city in the daylight. The rumble is getting louder and louder.

FOSTER enters the room, bringing food on a tray.

FOSTER   Good morning. It's time to meet the Group.

EMMA   I'm not ready.

A NURSE comes in to take the food tray away. Another brings in more food and FOSTER takes it away.

EMMA sits on the bed. Snow falls onto her. The EMMAs continue to move around the room, each one privately struggling with the physical effects of withdrawal.

A THERAPIST enters. The THERAPIST is played by the same actress who plays the DOCTOR.

THERAPIST   Hello I'm Lydia. I'm one of the therapists here.

EMMA   No, you're the Doctor, you look like my Mum.

One of the EMMAs starts to have a seizure. STAFF rush in to attend to her.

THERAPIST   I understand you don't feel ready to join the Group.

In the bathroom, a NURSE helps to clean another EMMA after she's wet herself.

Isolation is the first step towards relapse.

Another EMMA enters the room and drags the desk chair to below the light fitting. She ties a belt around her neck and stands on the chair. NURSES rush in and help her down.

The work is done *in* Group, *by* the Group.

EMMA   Mum,

EMMA approaches the THERAPIST but she's vanished. She watches her UNDERSTUDY, in costume, walk across the room holding a dead seagull, then climb out of the window.

FOSTER enters.

FOSTER   you have to take part in the Group. I'm afraid we're pretty strict about this. You can't just pick and choose what to take part in. You have to do everything.

PAUL is in the darkness.

PAUL   They want everything but you've got nothing to begin with.

The room is now full of EMMAs all dressed identically. Both PAUL and FOSTER have disappeared. The DOCTOR is there.

DOCTOR   I'm going to ask you a few questions to get a
                sense of historical context for your using.

EMMA   It doesn't work. It doesn't work like that.

*The movements of the EMMAs have become faster and faster, all
except EMMA who has slowly moved back to the bed and started
to read the book. She rips pages out of it, one after the other.
FOSTER appears again.*

FOSTER   Please understand that if you refuse to take
                part in the Group you will be required to
                leave treatment. We're going to send you
                home. I'll have to call your mother. Alright?

EMMA   No.

EMMA gets into bed. Her eyes are wide open.

                No.

It begins to snow across the whole room.

                No.

*Time continues to pass, night turning to day turning to night so
fast it becomes a strobe.*

One EMMA is laughing. Another is screaming.

The sound is deafening.

The sounds suddenly stop. Birdsong. Traffic.

Morning. EMMA wakes. She looks around. She is alone.

*FOSTER enters. He looks different. Perhaps he's grown a beard or
maybe he's just wearing a different bandana. Days have passed.
FOSTER opens the curtains. Sunlight fills the room.*

*EMMA's head hurts. The light is too bright. The sounds are too
loud.*

FOSTER   Good morning. Well, afternoon. Technically.

She pulls back the covers. She puts her feet on the floor. There is something fundamentally different about her appearance, as if another actress is now playing her.

EMMA   What day is it?

She stands. She holds the big book.

FOSTER   How are you feeling?

EMMA   Like the worst is over.

FOSTER laughs. He gives her a cup of coffee then tidies the room with the brisk confidence of someone who does this a lot.

FOSTER   Well, what will it be? Will you speak to the therapist and join the Group or am I going to have Security throw you out into the street?

EMMA has taken out some make up and is applying some to her face.

What are you doing?

EMMA   Nothing, I'm
            getting ready.

FOSTER   You don't have to do that here. I mean, you can, but

EMMA is self-conscious. She continues to apply the make up.

three things:

One: Over the next few days you're going to cry at things you wouldn't ordinarily cry at and it won't be easy to stop. This is normal.

Two: From this moment on, you're going to drink more coffee than you should. You won't even notice you're doing it. You'll just always have a cup in your hand. You have to watch that because it messes with sleep and you're going to need to sleep more than before.

Three:

FOSTER turns his attention to EMMA.

You have to be completely truthful or the process won't work. There's no judgement in here. Every one of us is here for the same reason and we're all very good at lying. We're also good at spotting liars.

EMMA   This is great coffee.

FOSTER   Prime example. It's terrible coffee.

,

Are you ready to begin?

EMMA   No.

DOCTOR   Let's start with your name shall we?

EMMA is in the DOCTOR's consultation room.

Your real name.

,

EMMA looks at FOSTER.

EMMA   Emma.

DOCTOR   Emma. Good.

How are you feeling?

EMMA   Like my insides have been scrubbed with bleach.

DOCTOR   Right.

Vivid.

	Emma, before you join the Group I need to get some historical context for your using.
EMMA	That A led to B and therefore C.
DOCTOR	Exactly.
EMMA	Beginning, middle, end.
DOCTOR	Isn't that how life works?
EMMA	No.
DOCTOR	How does life work?

,

EMMA	You have a lot of certificates. It's impressive. I've not got that.
DOCTOR	You didn't go to university?
EMMA	I went to loads. Just not for long. Never got that scroll.
DOCTOR	I can't give you a letter for work Emma. Not until you've completed the programme.
EMMA	The twenty-eight days.
DOCTOR	At least.
EMMA	Thing is, I came here to get everything out of my system and now I have, nearly, and I really feel like I'm ready to get back out into / the real world.
DOCTOR	You've addressed the chemical hooks but not the central cause of your addiction.
EMMA	Which is
DOCTOR	trauma.

,

You've done the first stage, you / may as well

EMMA   I can leave when I want, right?

DOCTOR   Absolutely, / but

EMMA   great, thanks. This has been fun. I've
            changed. I'll never use again, Brownie's
            honour. Bye.

FOSTER   Emma you really / should

DOCTOR   you can leave us now thanks Foster.

            ,

FOSTER leaves.

            Sit down.

EMMA   You even *sound* like my mother.

EMMA drops the heavy book onto the desk.

            I don't know if that's your copy or Foster's
            but I've made some corrections.

DOCTOR   Corrections?

*The DOCTOR opens the book. It is full of scribbled notes, pages
turned-down and torn out, asterisks in the margins etc.*

EMMA   Amendments. Notes and things. Have you
            actually read this thing?

DOCTOR   Emma, the programme works for a lot of /
            people.

EMMA   Except you don't know that. Nobody does.
            It's all anonymous, there's nothing evidence-
            based it's just / anecdotal, so

DOCTOR   Emma, you asked for my / help.

EMMA   If it's vital to my recovery that I come to
            believe in a power / greater than me

DOCTOR   Emma, if you let me

EMMA   to turn my will and my life over to God and
              have Him remove my defects of character,

DOCTOR   will you let me just

EMMA   if this all depends on me having a spiritual
              awakening then we might all just be wasting
              our time.

DOCTOR   We're not.

EMMA   I think we might be.

DOCTOR   You're worried about the steps.

EMMA   I'm worried that a trained medical
              professional with this many certificates can
              also wear a crucifix.

DOCTOR   I don't believe the scientific method
              disproves the / existence of

EMMA   such a boring conversation of course it does
              of course it fucking does I really need you
              to be cleverer than this. I really need you
              to at least match me intellectually because
              otherwise I'm going to leave and if I leave I
              don't know if

              ,

              I'm not powerless. I'm not helpless. I don't
              believe addiction is a disease and I'm scared
              and angered by the suggestion that from now
              on it's either eternal abstinence or binge to
              death. I can't surrender to a higher power
              because there isn't one. There just isn't. And
              you, as someone who lives in the twenty-first
              century should know that.

DOCTOR   Emma,

EMMA   I wake up in wet sheets. In places I don't
              recognise. With bruises I can't account for.

Men I don't know. I've stolen from people. I've slept on the streets. I'm in trouble. I know that. But this book, this *process* can't help me. You can't help me.

DOCTOR   I see a lot of clever people in here. People who drink and use because they just can't stop their big brains from thinking thinking thinking. Does that sound / familiar?

EMMA   You want me to conceptualise a universe in which I am the sole agent of my destiny and at the same time acknowledge my absolute powerlessness. It's a fatal contradiction and I won't start building foundations on a flawed premise.

DOCTOR   That's not a fair / characterisation of

EMMA   there is no *meaning* to anything. There are no beginnings, middles and ends.

DOCTOR   Emma,

EMMA   I am not the product of the decisions I've made or the things that have happened to me. I will not be reduced to that.

DOCTOR   I'm not / suggesting

EMMA   my brother had a brain haemorrhage while reading Pinocchio to a group of five year olds. Mark. He was two years younger than me and never touched drugs or alcohol. He ran fucking *marathons*. For *charity*. I should have died a thousand times but it was him who

,

if I tell you I was sexually abused or the child of alcoholics, if I tell you I returned from back-to-back tours of Iraq and started to self-

379

medicate wouldn't that all just be a massive simplification of the complexity of just being a human fucking person?

DOCTOR   Were you?

EMMA   Was I what?

DOCTOR   Sexually abused.

EMMA   That's / not

DOCTOR   because we'll also have to do a full sexual / history.

EMMA   You're not listening to what I'm

,

EMMA sighs.

I first got drunk with my brother when I was eleven and he was ten. I stole three bottles of Communion wine and when I vomited it looked like blood. Is this the kind of thing you want to hear?

DOCTOR   Is it the truth?

EMMA   No. I never had a brother.

And he didn't die in front of children. He died in his car. Or he was stillborn maybe. Or he grew up and died of old age.

The DOCTOR clicks her pen closed and puts it down on the form.

DOCTOR   Do you lie to protect yourself or your addiction?

EMMA   It's not lying. It's admitting there's no truth to begin with. Have you read Foucault?

DOCTOR   Not lately.

EMMA   Or Derrida? Baudrillard? Barthes?

DOCTOR   You're an addict because of Post-Modernism?

EMMA   I can't base my survival on slogans and
        abstractions and vagueness. I'm not someone
        who can do Pilates on a beach and mistake
        relaxation for spirituality. I spent a year in
        the Far East but I didn't find enlightenment,
        I found slums and sex tourism.

        I chose this place because it's ugly and
        grey and in the middle of a car park and
        I can look out on traffic and homeless
        people and remind myself that the world
        is just purposeless chaos. I need something
        definitive. I need to be fixed.

DOCTOR   It doesn't work like that. It's a long-term, /
        daily

EMMA   I don't do long-term.

DOCTOR   You're going to learn. Because the strategies
        you've been using just aren't working. I hear
        all your concerns about the programme. I've
        heard them all before. But right now it's the
        best we've got. You think you've worked it
        all out, great, you're still dying. Intellectually
        inferior as I may be, I'm trying to save your
        life. Now, sit down.

                ,

EMMA sits.

                ,

        The Twelve Steps outline the process of
        recovery as experienced by its earliest
        members and, yes, they were about
        accepting God. But here we use a modified
        version with religiously neutral wording.

	Have you heard the expression 'powerless over nouns'?
EMMA	Nouns? As in
DOCTOR	people, places and things.
EMMA	You mean like *Facebook*?
DOCTOR	Excuse me?
EMMA	On Facebook the search box / says
DOCTOR	I'm not on Facebook.
EMMA	No.
	No nor am I really. I have a profile but I hardly ever
DOCTOR	it's a rewrite of Step One of Twelve. Instead of declaring ourselves powerless over alcohol or drugs we admit that we are powerless over people, places and things. People who make us want to relapse, places we associate with using and things that reactivate old behaviour. Does this make sense to you?

,

EMMA	Yes.
DOCTOR	When you're in recovery,
EMMA	back in the real world.
DOCTOR	You'll need to find a way to handle being in those places. With those people.
EMMA	And those things.

,

I find reality pretty difficult.

I find the business of getting out of bed and getting on with the day really *hard*. I find picking up my phone to be a mammoth fucking struggle. The number on my inbox. The friends who won't see me anymore. The food pictures and porn videos, the bombings and beheadings, the moral ambivalence you have to have to just be able to carry on with your day. I find the knowledge that we're all just atoms and one day we'll stop and be dirt in the ground, I find that overwhelmingly

disappointing.

And I wish I could feel otherwise. I wish I could be like you. Or my mother. To feel that some things are predetermined and meaningful and that we're somewhere on a track between the start and finish lines. But I can't because I care about what's true, what's actually, verifiably *true*. You're able to forfeit rationality for a comforting untruth so how are you supposed to help me? You're looking at the world through such a tight filter you're barely living in it. You're barely alive.

DOCTOR   You talk about your mother a lot.

EMMA   Drugs and alcohol have *never* let me down. They have always *loved* me. There are substances I can put into my bloodstream that make the world *perfect*. That is the only absolute truth in the universe.

I'm being difficult because you want to take it away from me. So

sorry.

DOCTOR   If we don't bond with people, particularly parents, we seek a connection elsewhere. Drugs. Alcohol.

EMMA   God.

            Mark, my brother, he believed in God.
            He wasn't as bright as me. He didn't really
            stretch himself. He once told me that he
            believed the entire universe was happening
            in his imagination and that when he died
            everything would be snuffed out. But then he
            died and everything carried on, so

            that's that hypothesis disproved.

DOCTOR   I can't force you to stay. I can't force you to
            be truthful. I can just tell you that the process
            only works if you are honest. With yourself,
            with me and with others. Denial. Denial is
            what kills you.

EMMA   I'm not good in groups.

DOCTOR   I can believe that.

            You've already come so far Emma. Don't let
            that be for nothing.

The DOCTOR stands by the door.

            I'd like you to see how the programme
            works in practise. Meet the Group and my
            colleague, Lydia.

EMMA   Who's Lydia?

*A GROUP of people sit down in a circle of chairs. The DOCTOR
exits. EMMA is in the Group Therapy room. The THERAPIST
enters and holds out her hand for EMMA to shake. It is the same
actress who played the DOCTOR but her clothing and appearance
is different. Perhaps she is barefoot and has let her hair down.*

THERAPIST   Hi. I'm Lydia, I'm one of the therapists here.

EMMA   God, you all look like my mother.

THERAPIST   Why don't you introduce yourself?

EMMA stands at the edge of the room. She looks at the room full of people. The GROUP looks at her.

EMMA   Er, okay. Hello everyone. I'm

She looks at the THERAPIST.

                        Emma.

GROUP   Hello Emma.

THERAPIST   Take a seat.

EMMA   I'm alright here.

THERAPIST   Emma, we're all in recovery. You can say
                        whatever you like here.

EMMA   You're not in recovery.

She points at FOSTER.

                        He's not in recovery.

FOSTER   Seven years.

THERAPIST   Twenty-one.

A little smattering of applause from the GROUP.

EMMA   You're kidding.

THERAPIST   We're all here for the same reason.

EMMA looks around the room.

EMMA   Look, no offense to anyone or to the *process*
                        but I'm sort of private.

THERAPIST   Gotcha.

EMMA   Just want to keep my head down and do my
                        time.

THERAPIST   You're a lone wolf.

EMMA   Exactly.

THERAPIST   Who else here is a lone wolf?

Everyone in the GROUP puts their hands up.

Take a seat Emma.

,

EMMA sits with the GROUP.

Why don't you tell us about yourself?

EMMA   Seriously? I have to just jump straight in?

THERAPIST   This is a safe space. Tell us your story.

The reception bell sounds. FOSTER exits.

EMMA   Alright, fine, fuck it. Where should I start?

,

I suppose it all started when I was much younger and met this guy. I bet that's how a few of these stories start, right ladies?

She's trying to be funny but is failing.

Anyway. I was in a relationship with this guy. Norwegian guy. Older. Writer. He was really talented but never really lived up to it because, well, he was an alcoholic.

Some nods of recognition and sounds of encouragement from the GROUP.

Anyway. That ended. Predictably. And I met someone else. A much more solid, reliable, nice guy. George. An academic. I now know, I think I knew at the time really, that I wasn't in love with him. We got married.

She is absent-mindedly playing with her ring finger. There is no ring.

Anyway. We had some money troubles.
George went for a professorship at

MARK, a member of the GROUP, has his hand up.

MARK	excuse me, sorry,
THERAPIST	let her talk, Mark.
MARK	Okay but
THERAPIST	Mark.
EMMA	Anyway, things were sort of fine, in a way, but, small world, an old school friend, Thea, started seeing my ex. The writer.
MARK	Okay, sorry, but this is
THERAPIST	please, / Mark.
EMMA	Is he allowed to just interrupt like / that?
THERAPIST	Go ahead Emma.

,

EMMA	Well. So, things came to a head when the manuscript of my ex's new work just went missing.

MARK stands.

MARK   Alright, enough, / this is stupid, this is

A frisson of activity in the GROUP.

THERAPIST   Mark, sit down and / let her speak.

EMMA   Yeah, sit down and let me finish *Mark.*

Suddenly, the door opens and PAUL enters, urgently. He is much less wild than before. He is followed by FOSTER.

PAUL   I'd like to say something to the / Group please.

FOSTER   Paul, don't do this, come on.

Everyone stays still and looks at PAUL.

PAUL   I'd just like to speak briefly to the Group / if
                I may.

THERAPIST   I'm sorry Paul, but you have to leave / now.

PAUL   I will I promise, but, please, please let me
                just / say a few words.

PAUL takes a piece of paper from his pocket and unfolds it.

THERAPIST   Your treatment has been terminated, you
                can't / be in here.

PAUL reads from the paper.

PAUL   I want to apologise to you all with my whole
                heart.

FOSTER puts his hand on PAUL's arm.

FOSTER   Paul, please.

THERAPIST   It's okay.

                Go ahead Paul.

                ,

PAUL clears his throat and prepares himself.

PAUL   I know that my behaviour here was stupid
                and dangerous. Not only to myself but, also,
                as a trigger for others' relapse. I smuggled in
                some substances. Ketamine. It was a breach
                of my agreement and resulted in my ejection.
                But

He lowers the paper.

                I don't like begging. I was making progress
                here. I was doing well. Please.

He kneels down.

THERAPIST   Paul.

PAUL   Please give me a second chance.

THERAPIST   Paul,

He reads from the paper again.

PAUL   I believe I have extenuating circumstances. I wouldn't have used if what happened

if what happened
hadn't happened. I just really wanted it all to stop.

EMMA turns to the person next to her.

EMMA   What happened?

The person ignores her.

THERAPIST   Emma it's best that we don't talk amongst ourselves, if you have a question you can / ask the

EMMA   what circumstances? What happened?

An awkward silence. A couple of people look around the room or shift in their seats.

,

PAUL   Robert.
My partner,

fiancé

of eighteen years.

Dead.
Heroin.

We didn't do needles. I don't know where he got it.

I can't go home again. It's not real. I don't want to die. I want it all to stop. I've got these voices and they're scaring me. I just want it to

stop.

EMMA   You should stay.

THERAPIST   Emma.

EMMA   He should.

THERAPIST   Emma there are strict rules / about

EMMA   fuck that. He'll die. Or kill someone.

PAUL   I don't / think I'd

THERAPIST   this has to be a drug-free / environment,

FOSTER   Paul can come back / once he has

EMMA puts her hand in the air.

EMMA   who here thinks he should stay?

THERAPIST   Emma, this isn't a democracy, / you can't just

EMMA   you wanted me to join the Group well I have, I'm in the sacred circle of truth and this guy seems like one of our people. Now who thinks he should stay and get well and who thinks he should be sent to his death?

FOSTER   That's unfair / wording.

EMMA   That's the reality of the fucking situation. Put your hands up if you want him gone.

Some hands go up.

And who wants to save his life?

More hands go up. A majority.

EMMA turns triumphantly to the THERAPIST.

THERAPIST   Emma, I'm sorry but that's simply not how /
we work.

PAUL walks towards EMMA.

EMMA   It's ridiculous, he's

PAUL spits in EMMA's *face.*

MARK   no!

MARK gets between PAUL *and* EMMA. *The* GROUP *move out of
their seats, either away or towards the fracas.* FOSTER *radios
for* SECURITY.

PAUL   This isn't safari.
It's not character
building. Don't
scrabble in the dirt
with us poor cunts
then put on smart
shoes.

FOSTER   Security please
come to Group.
Security to Group,
thank you.

MARK   You're talking shit mate.

THERAPIST   Thank you Mark, / if everyone could

PAUL   little princess fuck off to Goa. Fuck off up a
yoga mountain with magic / crystals.

EMMA   You don't / know me.

PAUL   Fuck off to paradise you / prim prig.

THERAPIST   Okay that's it. Enough.

EMMA   No, he's alright. What else do you want to
say Paul?

THERAPIST   Emma.

PAUL   I don't owe you. I'm not in your debt.

EMMA   Thank you for making that clear. I don't
                         want to be your friend. I just want to get
                         well and go home. Yes, I could have gone
                         somewhere else but I chose not to. I don't
                         think I'm better than anyone. I think we're
                         all the same. I'm sorry your fiancé died. My
                         brother died too. The week before I came
                         here. Pills. I found him in the stairwell of
                         our building curled into a ball. He'd cried
                         blood. I wish I'd died instead. I wish I'd died
                         without having to see him dead. We're all the
                         same.

                         ,

THERAPIST   Paul, you understand you can't simply re-join
                         the Group.

                         ,

PAUL looks around.

PAUL   Fuck this. Fuck all of this. It's all bullshit.

PAUL laughs.

                         It's all just bullshit. None of this is real. When
                         you're sitting here tonight being all serious,
                         think of me out there. I'll be having the night
                         of my life.

PAUL leaves the room.

FOSTER follows him.

*The GROUP talk amongst themselves. The THERAPIST attempts
an upbeat tone.*

THERAPIST   Alright, let's all take five for some tea and
                         biscuits shall we?

The GROUP leaves the room. The THERAPIST speaks to EMMA.

I have every right and inclination to eject you from treatment. First you refuse to join Group, then you attempt to / demolish it from within.

EMMA   He attacked me!

THERAPIST   Believe me when I tell you I've seen it all before. I can't be shocked and I won't be undermined.

EMMA   Then eject me. I'm happy to go, just give me / my letter.

THERAPIST   You're not going anywhere. You're going to sit there, calm down and when the Group returns you're going to apologise, then you're going to sit, listen and learn something.

The THERAPIST leaves the room.

,

This has all been witnessed by MARK, who begins clapping, sarcastically.

EMMA looks up to see him sitting opposite her in the circle of chairs. It's just the two of them in the room.

MARK   Bravo.

              Quite a performance.

EMMA is wiping her face.

EMMA   You know, it's rude to interrupt people when they're telling their life story.

MARK   I do know that, yes. But that wasn't your life story. It's the plot of Hedda Gabler.

,

              How far were you going to go with it? I mean, she fucking dies in the end.

EMMA   Don't we all.

MARK   Not me. I'm immortal. I've taken hits that
              would kill an elephant.

MARK offers EMMA a cigarette without getting up.

EMMA   I quit.

MARK   First time huh? Yeah, I quit everything my
              first time. But you got to take it easy.

EMMA sits down opposite MARK.

              First couple of times I went through
              treatment the *guilt* I felt. The *weight* of it.
              Came out thinking 'I've failed so badly
              at life.' Went straight to my dealer both
              times. Took enough to snuff it. First time,
              I chickened out and called an ambulance.
              Second time I went down by the canal.
              Stupid. Some good fucking Samaritan jogged
              by and happened to be medically fucking
              trained for fuck's sake.

EMMA   What was the high like?

MARK laughs.

MARK   Yeah, that's the question. Take enough to kill
              you must be a great high. You *are* in trouble.

EMMA   Was it?

                      ,

MARK lights a cigarette.

              You can't smoke in here it's a / medical
              building.

MARK   Medical building yeah.

He smokes.

Did Foster warn you about the coffee? You'll find you'll need much more coffee and then you won't sleep and that's dangerous because you shouldn't get too tired. Or hungry. Angry. Lonely. Horny. Too anything, really. Keep the right size is what they say. *We* say. Keep perspective. *We're addicts because we have a toxic combination of low self-esteem and grandiosity.*

EMMA   If I need advice on how to fail at recovery I'll come to you.

MARK   You're mean.

You're a mean woman.

EMMA   I'm trying to change.

MARK   You're in the right place.

Although no major changes in the first year is what they say. Don't move house. Don't change jobs. Don't start new relationships.

,

So you're an actress?

EMMA   No.

MARK   Really.

EMMA   Really. I'm not an actress. I'm a seagull.

,

MARK   Right. Yeah. I don't know that reference.

When I first came here I thought this place would be full of actresses and singers. But it's just, you know,

normal people. You done any telly?

395

EMMA   Can we not talk about it actually? This is
              supposed to be a bubble away from reality.

MARK   Right.
              I agree with you.
              Although you're completely wrong.

              This is as real as it gets.

MARK holds out the packet to her again.

              Go on. Treat yourself.

              ,

EMMA stands, walks across the circle and takes a cigarette. MARK lights it for her. MARK remains seated. EMMA stands above him. They both smoke.

EMMA exhales and watches the smoke in the air. She looks at the cigarette between her fingers.

              ,

EMMA   People who aren't addicted to anything
              are really missing out, you know? To have
              something that can make you feel complete
              and loved and satisfied and to be able to
              actually *get it*. It's not unrequited, it *loves you*
              back.

              ,

              So the therapist's an addict too?

MARK   It's so smart to get a job here. I'm thinking of
              applying for one. I'd never have to leave.

              ,

EMMA   Do you want to come to my room later?

              ,

MARK laughs.

EMMA laughs too.

> ,

MARK   You're a nightmare.

> ,

The Group doesn't work unless we all
contribute. Everyone is vulnerable. If
you mess around in here you jeopardise
everyone's recovery. Right now you're a
human hand grenade. Tell the truth about
who you are or I will.

> ,

EMMA   I told you the truth. I'm a seagull.

*The GROUP re-enter the room, with polystyrene cups of tea and
coffee. EMMA and MARK stub out their cigarettes.*

THERAPIST   Alright. Good.

The GROUP return to their seats.

We were hearing from Emma.

EMMA   I'm done.

THERAPIST   Was there nothing you wanted to add?

> ,

EMMA   Yes.

I'm
very
very
sorry.
For undermining the process just now.
This is all very new to me.

THERAPIST   Would anyone like to comment on what
happened?

,

No? Okay. Would anyone like to practise?

EMMA	Practise what?
FOSTER	One of the ways we prepare for life in recovery is to practise certain interactions, important conversations,
EMMA	what, like, *role-play*?
THERAPIST	Would you like to practise Emma?
EMMA	God no.

MARK stands, very eager.

MARK	I will.
THERAPIST	Alright. Where are we?
MARK	In my boss's office. Couple of months from now. If all goes well.
THERAPIST	What time is it?
MARK	First thing. 7 A.M.

He points at EMMA.

You're my boss.

EMMA	What?
THERAPIST	Go on Emma.
EMMA	I have to pretend to be his boss?
THERAPIST	It's an exercise.
MARK	Chester. He's fat and bald.
EMMA	Then get *him* to do it.

EMMA points at someone in the GROUP who matches the description.

MARK   I just feel you'll be good at this sort of thing.

EMMA   I'd rather not.

THERAPIST   You don't have to look like the person.

FOSTER   Go on Emma.

                ,

She stands.

MARK   Ask me what Chester is like.

EMMA   Why?

THERAPIST   It's how we play the game.

                ,

EMMA   *(Through gritted-teeth.)* What's Chester like?

MARK   He's a fucking idiot.

FOSTER   Feelings are not facts Mark.

                Has someone been smoking in here?

MARK   He lies. He deludes himself and thinks he
                can get away with it.

EMMA   Is that right?

THERAPIST   How about some observations that are less
                judgemental?

MARK   He's got twin girls in their thirties. A
                grandchild I think. Scottish. Glasgow maybe.

EMMA   You want me to do an accent?

MARK/ THERAPIST/ FOSTER	No.
MARK	He values loyalty. Hard work. He smokes cigars. He shakes your hand too hard. He makes eye contact. He goes to strip clubs. He will die in this office. I've let him down a lot and he's always looked out for me.
THERAPIST	And you're going to practise your first day back. Okay?
MARK	Yes.
THERAPIST	Emma?
	,
EMMA	Yes.
THERAPIST	Alright, in three,
	two,
	one,

The lights suddenly change. It's a different day. MARK is sitting, another member of the GROUP, MEREDITH, is standing on the other side of the circle.

MEREDITH	hello, I'm Meredith and I'm a heroin addict.
GROUP	Hello Meredith.

The GROUP look at EMMA who remains standing in the middle of the circle, confused by the change of time.

,

THERAPIST	Would you like to say something Emma?

EMMA looks around at the GROUP, bewildered and a little scared.

,

EMMA   No.

    EMMA moves to sit down.

MEREDITH   Will you help me practise?

EMMA   No. Sorry.

FOSTER   Emma, if someone / asks you to

EMMA   I'm just feeling a bit spaced-out / and I

MEREDITH   I was just like you.

EMMA   That sounds like projection.

THERAPIST   Emma.

        ,

    EMMA returns to the middle.

EMMA   Go on then, Ghost of Junky Future, let's do
              this.

MEREDITH   Last year I fell onto a glass table and /

    EMMA smirks.

EMMA   you sound like an insurance advert.

MEREDITH   Do you know what diamorphine is?

EMMA   Sorry, what's the role play here?

MEREDITH   It's the medical name for heroin. Did you
              know doctors give you heroin? Because I
              didn't.

EMMA   This is on the NHS, yeah?

MEREDITH   Twenty years clean, being a new person,
              driving my husband's kids to school, making
              packed lunches, and the whole time it was
              just *waiting* for me. That feeling. It loved me.

THERAPIST   What would you like to practise Meredith?

MEREDITH   *(To EMMA.)* You're my stepdaughter. You're
            fourteen. You're very brave and very angry.
            You took a needle out of my arm and hid
            it from your dad, cleaned me up before the
            ambulance arrived. Put the sheets in the
            washing machine. I need to practise how to
            have a normal conversation with you now.

EMMA   What do I say?

FOSTER   Just listen.

MEREDITH nods at the THERAPIST.

THERAPIST   Three,

            two,

            one,

*Another light change. It's evening. The weather is different.
LAURA is standing. MEREDITH is seated, EMMA is still standing
in the centre of the circle.*

LAURA   I'm Laura. I'm an alcoholic.

GROUP   Hello Laura.

LAURA   *(To EMMA.)* You're my sister.

EMMA   No.

FOSTER   Emma, the exercise is / about *active listening.*

EMMA   Pick someone else.

SHAUN   / So disrespectful.

JODI   Just stand / there and listen.

THERAPIST   It's alright, everyone's at different stages, let's
            allow Emma to / find her own

LAURA   we're in your kitchen. You'll have your back
            to me, doing the washing up. I'll offer to
            dry but you'll say 'leave that'. You had a kid
            three years ago and I still haven't met him.

This will be the first time. Assuming you'll ever see me again.

EMMA   What did you do?

THERAPIST   Emma, you don't directly / ask what

LAURA   I stole from you and I got high at your wedding.

EMMA   You sound fun.

LAURA   You started me drinking, then cut me out when you got your life together.

EMMA   Okay. '*Sorry*'. Are we done?

THERAPIST/
FOSTER   No.

LAURA   I think about everything that's happened I just want to die. Then I have days where I think *look how far you've come*. I'm alive. It's a miracle. I'm a fucking *miracle*.

Some support from the GROUP.

I want to tell you that we're the same. That you're a miracle too.

Another day. LAURA is sitting and SHAUN is standing.

SHAUN   Yes, hi, hello. I'm Shaun.

GROUP   Hello Shaun.

EMMA is looking at LAURA, disoriented.

SHAUN   I'm a cocaine addict. Mostly.

EMMA looks at SHAUN who speaks to her.

We've never met face-to-face, but it's important because I ruined your life.

FOSTER   Emma, are you alright?

403

EMMA   Where are we?

SHAUN   Somewhere public. Neutral. A Starbucks or
              something.

FOSTER   Emma, you don't / have to

EMMA   who am I?

SHAUN   You're the CEO of the company I
              bankrupted.

EMMA   Right. Then you should pay for the coffees.

SHAUN   I want you to *see* me. To be people in a room,
              not names on a screen. And I need to say
              that everything you believe in is wrong and
              will kill you. I thought I was in control. Pills
              and powders to keep me awake. To help
              me exercise. Have sex. Sleep. I'd look at
              trading charts and see the inner workings of
              the universe. Patterns everywhere. Lottery
              numbers. Registration plates. Flocking birds.
              None of it's real. You're not a God. There are
              no patterns. No meaning. There's just chaos.

*A different day. SHAUN is sitting, JODI is standing in front of her
chair. EMMA stays in the centre of the circle.*

JODI   Hi. Jodi. Alcoholic.

GROUP   Hello Jodi.

JODI   Addict too. Prescription pills.

EMMA   Come on then, let's practise.

JODI   Excuse me?

EMMA   You were going to choose me, right? Where
              are we? Who do you want me to be?

FOSTER   Jodi, you don't have / to

JODI   *(To EMMA.)* you're my husband. You're
              impatient. You don't listen. You think you
              know everything.

EMMA   Got it.

JODI   I need to tell you we can't be together
              anymore. That I never really drank until I
              got pregnant. That I stockpile. Painkillers.
              Sleeping pills. Go without and then

              I don't want to die. I don't think that's what
              I'm trying to do. But everything's gone so
              wrong. I want to be all brand new but

              look at me.

              Either I lose my son, my home, my family,
              my *life* even,

              or I stop drinking. To most people that
              sounds like an easy choice. But it's not.

JODI is finding this difficult. EMMA is too.

              Sorry.

THERAPIST   You don't have to apologise. Not to us.

FOSTER   Where are we Jodi?

JODI   Not face-to-face. On the phone I think.

EMMA   Should I mime or

THERAPIST   not on the phone Jodi. These important,
              immediate conversations should all happen
              here. With support from us.

JODI   Right.
              Okay. So, we're
              here.

              (To EMMA.) You're my husband and you're
              standing there. And

FOSTER puts his hand up.

Foster's Foster. And he's there.

And here we go.

Another day.

T	Yeah, hi everyone. T. Like the letter. Addict.
GROUP	Hello T.
T	Addicted to pretty much anything, honestly. What you got?

Quiet laughter from some of the GROUP.

Born an addict. Addict in the womb. Methadone. I'm not blaming Mum,

THERAPIST	it's alright T, it's context.
EMMA	Don't make me your mother for God's sake.
T	I weren't gonna.
EMMA	Thank fuck.
T	You're Marcus, my care worker.
EMMA	Pick someone else. / Please.
T	I ain't seen you since I was fifteen. I stabbed you in the hand with a broken bottle.
EMMA	Let me just sit this / one out, yeah?
T	There's a lot to fill you in on. Did the 'rent' thing. Robbed some people. Climbed in windows. Cash in hand, straight on gear. I thought I was alright but I was just *surviving.* Dog without an owner. I found out recently, I sort of want to tell you because I haven't told anyone in my life outside, I found out I'm HIV positive.

FOSTER	Where are we T?
T	Playground near Thorpe Road, my first placement. I'm wearing an ironed shirt. Want it to feel official somehow. Want to show you that I'm good. That you don't have to worry, if you have been.
EMMA	What am I like?
T	You used to pull this face like you were listening to me.

I think maybe, right now I'm realising, I think that maybe you *actually were listening to me.* That you did
do
care
what happens to me.
I think maybe I don't need to say nothing. I can just

be there. Alive. Clean. Not so angry or

that'll all mean something without me having to say.

You looked at me like I'm a real person and I wouldn't still be here, wouldn't have made the effort if it weren't for that, so

I'm sorry for what I done to your hand.

(To THERAPIST.) Is that okay?

THERAPIST	Would you like to say something Emma?

,

EMMA shakes her head.

Is there anything else you'd like to say T?

T   Uh

                     yeah there is.

                     I made a list.

He takes out a piece of paper.

                     Pubs. Clubs.

                     All the places I can't go no more.

                     Gigs. Festivals.

JODI   Parks.

T   Funfairs.

MEREDITH   Restaurants. Beaches.

JODI   Birthdays. Christmas.

T   Brick Lane. Soho. Hoxton. Camberwell.

JODI   Chemists. Asda.

SHAUN   Stamford Bridge. Terminal 5.

LAURA   New Year.

MEREDITH   Weddings.

SHAUN   Stag dos. Christmas parties.

LAURA   The Wellington. The Printworks.

T   Friday nights. / Saturday nights.

SHAUN   Saturday nights.

JODI   / Sundays.

LAURA   Sundays.

MEREDITH   Monday mornings.

JODI   Winter.

MEREDITH   Summer.

T	My boys.
JODI	My friends.
SHAUN	Colleagues.
LAURA	My sister's house.
T	If I'm around these people, if I walk in these places, that's me a dead body.
JODI	*(Laughing.)* Where are we supposed to go? What am I supposed to do?
T	I'll be under house arrest. How am I supposed to be in my house, *sober*? Watching daytime TV, *sober*?
LAURA	Going on a date *sober*. Having sex with someone for the first time *while sober*. How does anyone do that? At what point do I tell them the *truth*? Anyone sensible would run a mile. I would. I'd run. I can't be around people like me. *(To GROUP.)* No offence.
	But if you haven't been through it how can you possibly understand?
THERAPIST	Do you want to say something today Emma?
EMMA	No.
LAURA	Life is just so boring. I've got to find a way to enjoy that.

Another day. MARK is standing. EMMA is still in the centre of the room.

| MARK | *(To EMMA.)* You're my sister. You could be any woman in my life, really. It's the same thing I need to say. |
| | Amends. That's the hardest and most rewarding part of this whole thing. You put it out there with no hope of getting anything |

back. Like a prayer I guess. I mean, *Amends*.
The word has got 'Amen' in it.

I used to have a temper. Still do, it's just
different now.

MARK can't look at EMMA while he says the following.

You'd poured a bottle of Smirnoff down
the sink. Vodka to me was like spinach to
Popeye. I broke your jaw and stamped on
your leg, broke your ankle.

You forgave me. Let me stay that Christmas.
I stole your kid's new bike from under the
tree. Flogged it Christmas Eve. My Gran.
She raised me.

*He's finding this hard, but finds it cathartic to speak directly
to EMMA.*

Cancer.

He takes a breath in and lets it out, trying to keep his composure.

I took her pain relief. I'd hear her calling out.
Trying to scream. And I'd be like 'sorry Nan.
There's nothing left. They must have made a
mistake again.' Now she's dead so how do I
amend for that?

I didn't really plan what to say. Sorry. I just
felt like sharing so I stood up and started
talking. I used to go days without talking to
anyone. But this. Here. Now. Listening and
being listened to. Being *seen*. It's saving my
life I think.

He looks at EMMA.

You're this girl I went home with one time.
Beautiful. Really wasted. You didn't know
what planet you were on. I should have put

you in a taxi. Been a gentleman. You had
little scars all over her legs and arms. You
were barely awake during. I didn't learn
your name until after when the police said it.
Joanna. When I woke up you were cold. Blue
lips. I'm going to Hell for that. For not being
a good person when you needed one. For
being the opposite. I heard this expression
in a meeting: *I was a scream in search of a
mouth.* I don't know what it means exactly
but that's me, before. A scream in search
of a mouth. In prison they get you to make
your bed every day. Like here. Anyway, I
made my bed this morning. Without having
to remember to do it. I just got up and did it.
I never used to do that. Take care of myself.
And now I'm doing things without thinking.
Good things. I don't know. It's little but I
thought it was worth mentioning.

He sits down. EMMA remains the only person standing.

THERAPIST   Thank you Mark.

                 '

                 Emma.

                 Anything you'd like to share with the Group
                 today?

                 '

*EMMA looks around the GROUP. She is drained from listening
to everyone's stories.*

She sits down in her chair and looks at the floor.

                 Still nothing?

                 This is your fifth week with us.

FOSTER   We're only as sick as our secrets Emma.

EMMA	Fuck off Foster.
THERAPIST	Alright. Well,
	anything pressing for anyone before we finish?
MARK	Yes.
	Emma's refusal to engage with the process is compromising everyone's recovery.
EMMA	Fuck off Mark.
MARK	I'm helping you Emma.

EMMA gestures 'fuck off.'

	We recover as a Group. We need this to be a safe place to share and she's just sitting there looking at us like we're material.
EMMA	Fuck. Off.
SHAUN	Material for what?
EMMA	Shut up Mark.
THERAPIST	Alright, well, thank you Mark. Is anyone else frustrated by Emma's lack of engagement?

Everyone in the GROUP puts their hands up.

,

EMMA	Fuck this.

The GROUP disperses.

EMMA is in her room, angrily packing her things into a bag. MARK appears.

MARK	Knock knock.
EMMA	Fuck off.

She continues to pack.

MARK	I really am trying to help.
	If you can't say it then you can't get well.
	Hello. I'm Emma and I'm an alcoholic and drug addict.
EMMA	Look, I've served my time, I'm out.
MARK	Time?
EMMA	Doctor said a minimum twenty-eight days.
MARK	So you waited out the clock?

She continues to pack.

,

If your progress here can be jeopardised by me being a cunt then you truly are a lost cause.

She continues to pack.

Hello. I'm Emma. I'm an alcoholic and drug addict.

Hi, how you doing? I'm an alchy and a pill head.

EMMA	You're right. You're a cunt.
MARK	I might also be your best friend in the world.
EMMA	You don't know anything about me.
MARK	I've seen you.
	It took me a while to work it out but
	I saw you in that Shakespeare where you got your hands cut off.

She stops packing.

413

I spent a lot of time in theatres above pubs.
It's less suspicious to drink alone if you're in
an audience.

,

EMMA   Yeah. I used to think that too.

,

She sits.

With a play you get instructions. Stage
directions. Dialogue. Someone clothes you.
Tells you where to be and when. You get
to live the most intense moments of a life
over and over again, with all the boring
bits left out. And you get to *practi*se For
weeks. And you're *applauded.* Then you get
changed. Leave through stage door. Bus
home. Back to real life. All the boring stuff
left in. Waiting. Temping. Answering phones
and serving canapés. Nothing permanent.
Can't plan. Can't get a mortgage or pay for
a car. Audition comes in. Try to look right.
Sit in a room surrounded by people who
look just like you, all after the same part.
Never hear back. Or if you get the part it'll
be sitting around in rehearsal and backstage
making less than you did temping. Make
these friendships with people, a little family,
fall in love onstage and off and then it's over
and you don't see them again. You try not to
take it personally when people who aren't as
good as you get the parts. When you go from
being the sexy ingénue to the tired mother
of three.

But you keep going because sometimes, if
you're really lucky, you get to be onstage
and say things that are absolutely true, even

if they're made-up. You get to do things that
feel more real to you, more authentic, more
meaningful than anything in your own life.
You get to speak *poetry*, words you would
never think to say but which become yours
as you speak them.

When he shall die
take him and cut him out in little stars,
and he will make the face of heaven so fine
that all the world will be in love with night,
and pay no worship to the garish sun.

,

It feels like Lydia wants me to acknowledge
some buried trauma but there isn't any. I
played Antigone and every night my heart
broke about her dead brother. Then my own
brother died and I didn't feel anything. I
missed the funeral because I had a matinee.
I'm not avoiding talking to the Group
because I've got something to hide. It's the
opposite. If I'm not in character I'm not
sure I'm really there. I'm already dead. I'm
nothing. I want live a hundred lives and be
everywhere and fight against the infinitesimal
time we have on this planet.

Acting gives me the same thing I get from
drugs and alcohol. Good parts are just harder
to come by.

,

I really

I really miss my brother.

'Piece of my Heart' by Janis Joplin can be heard from another
room.

Is that music?

MARK   My graduation party.

EMMA   You're leaving?

MARK   Tomorrow, first thing.

            ,

EMMA   Good.

MARK   Orange squash and karaoke.

EMMA   You're kidding.

MARK   Can I ask you something?

            Is your name really Emma?

            ,

            I'm leaving so you may as well tell me.

            ,

EMMA   Emma is my stage name. There was already
            someone with my real name.

            ,

            My real name is Sarah.

MARK   Sarah.

EMMA   This isn't even my real voice. I lost my
            accent at drama school. I naturally talk

EMMA speaks with an accent.

            like this.

            ,

            Don't tell anyone.

            Please.

,

MARK stands. He's disappointed. Angry.

What? What did I say?

MARK   Is your brother dead?

,

Did you even have a brother?

EMMA   Mark,

MARK   did you?

,

If you come to the party I won't stop you.
But if you try to sing I will.

EMMA laughs. MARK isn't joking.

It may be stupid but it's important. A lot of
people here are trying really hard to make
themselves well. They're being honest to
a group of strangers. They're taking risks.
They're turning themselves inside out and
not sitting on the side-lines. You don't get to
do karaoke unless you're part of the Group.
You want to join the party, join the party.

EMMA   Are you fucking serious?

MARK stands in the doorway.

MARK   Hello, I'm Sarah. I'm Sarah and I'm an
alcoholic and drug addict. I'm a liar and
I'm going to fuck this up and break all your
hearts by dropping dead on a bathroom floor
because I'm too fucking interested in staring
into the blank void of my own personality.
I'm Sarah. Possibly. Who really knows? I'm
Sarah and I'm brilliant at being other people
and totally useless at being myself. I'm Sarah.

,

He leaves. EMMA listens to the music. It gets louder.

A small stage has been constructed.

FOSTER is singing.

The song finishes, polite applause and hugs for FOSTER. General chatter as the DOCTOR taps the microphone.

DOCTOR   Thank you Foster.

EMMA watches from the edge of the room.

The song list is going around, if you'd like to get up here and sing then put your name on the sheet.

Someone hands EMMA a cup of orange squash.

Tonight we say goodbye and good luck to a valued member of the Group. Mark.

General sounds of support and pats on the back for MARK. The DOCTOR gives MARK a scroll, tied with a ribbon.

I'd like to raise a non-alcoholic toast.

The GROUP put their cups in the air. All except EMMA.

This isn't your first graduation. I hope it's your last. Please understand what I mean when I say I hope I never see you again.

FOSTER   Don't come back.

The GROUP cheer and drink their squash.

EMMA takes the microphone.

EMMA   Janis Joplin died of a heroin overdose.

Quite an ironic choice of song there Foster.

God, is this what parties are like without alcohol?

She's trying to be funny but it's not working.

> No, but seriously, I want to say a few things.

DOCTOR   Emma, this isn't / the best

EMMA talks into the microphone.

EMMA   it's Sarah actually. My name is Sarah. I'm sorry I've not been honest with you about that. Or anything, really. Truth is difficult when you lie for a living. But here goes.

> Hello I'm Sarah.

The GROUP give her their attention. For a moment, she doesn't know what she's going to say next.

> I'm not going to say that I'm an addict and an alcoholic.
>
> I'm not going to say I'm powerless or surrender.

FOSTER   Surrender isn't / defeat, it's

EMMA   I won't join your tribe. I don't belong to you. I can't surround myself with people who think the same as me because that's / madness.

MEREDITH   This isn't / the time or place.

EMMA   I'm sharing a *truth* with you. You all talk as if *you're* the problem but the problem isn't you, the problem is EVERYTHING ELSE. Self-medicating is the only way to survive in a world / that is *broken.*

SHAUN   Someone pull the plug.

LAURA   Fuck you / '*Sarah*'.

LAURA leaves the room.

EMMA   It took my brother eight hours to die.
        Where's the meaning in that? If there's a
        higher power then strike me down. / *Come ye
        spirits that tend on mortal thoughts.*

The DOCTOR takes the microphone.

DOCTOR Okay Sarah, that's enough.

T   Let her / speak.

JODI   This isn't about you. This is about Mark.

MARK   It's okay Jodi, / she needs to do this.

Some of the GROUP have left the room. EMMA calls after them.

EMMA   I'd like to believe that my problems are
        meaningful. But they're not. There are
        people dying of *thirst.* People living in
        war zones and here we are thinking about
        ourselves. As if we can solve everything
        by confronting our own defects. We're
        not *defective.* It's the world that's fucked.
        Shouldn't we *feel good* for all those who can't?
        Don't we owe it to them to say *'fuck this, let's
        drink'?*

MARK   Sarah,

EMMA   if I deny myself *choice* then what am I? I want
        to *live.* I want to live *vividly* and make huge,
        spectacular, heroic mistakes.

Some of the GROUP are vocalising their agreement with EMMA.

        Because what else is there? This? Shame and
        boredom and orange fucking squash? Let's
        have a *real* drink.

        One drink just to know that the world won't
        end.

FOSTER throws a cup of squash in EMMA's face. She continues undeterred.

> Don't you remember how *good* it feels? Can't you just taste it? The weight of it all just melting away?

FOSTER exits. MARK and the THERAPIST look back towards EMMA as they leave. She continues, alone.

> The whole universe in one room. Your body hot with joy and certainty and love love love love love.

Pounding music. Lights flash. EMMA is confused to find herself in a nightclub. The EMMAs dance around her. One of them puts a pill on her tongue. EMMA takes someone's drink and downs it.

YOUNG WOMAN   You're so gorgeous.

EMMA   Thanks, I'm just trying to say a few things.

YOUNG WOMAN   Amazing! I love everything you do.

EMMA   That's so nice! I'm having such a great time!

The room is moving, warping, tilting with the thumping bass. The lights of the club flash red and blue, the emergency light from an ambulance. DRESSERS dress EMMA as Marie Antoinette. The sound of a truck approaching, sounding its horn. The spotlight is the light from the truck's headlights. It glares into EMMA's eyes.

> Am I driving right now?

The screech of brakes. A moment of impact. Sparks, or perhaps golden ticker tape, fall from the ceiling. EMMA is given a bouquet of flowers. A WOMAN holds out a clipboard.

WOMAN   Will you sign this?

EMMA   What I'm trying to say is
what I need to say is

PARAMEDICS cut EMMA out of her clothes and dress her in a hospital gown. A NURSE takes the flowers.

NURSE you need to get back in bed. It's dangerous for you to be walking around, do you understand?

EMMA But I'm in the middle of something.

PARAMEDICS put an oxygen mask on EMMA's face. She fights them off.

PARAMEDIC 1 Can you hear me?

PARAMEDIC 2 We're going to have to pump your stomach. Okay?

DOCTORS and NURSES surround her, attaching monitoring apparatus. EMMA pulls off the oxygen mask.

EMMA Thank you. Thank you so much!

MEDICAL STAFF rush around the room.

What I'm trying to say is

The music and all other sounds increase. This is all happening very fast. The EMMAs continue to dance. EMMA's nose begins to bleed heavily. The music is euphoric. Everyone except EMMA leaves the stage. She pulls off the hospital gown.

all I'm trying to say is

Lights flicker on and the music stops abruptly. Horrible artificial light, the light that ends the party, that makes skin look grey and eyes look bloodshot. She looks to where the GROUP had been standing but she is alone.

is that there's a bar right outside.

She looks around. She can see us, sitting, watching her.

We could just go for one drink. Yes?

Now. Together.

EMMA looks around.

> Let's all just have a drink. Yes?

> Yes?

The lights cut out. Silence.

,

The music begins again. Lights up on the audience.

,

Interval.

ACT TWO

The music from the end of ACT ONE has been playing in the auditorium and the foyer throughout the interval. It rises in volume as the lights fade, then cuts out as:

Electric lights flicker on. The reception at the rehabilitation centre. Night. The music continues playing, faintly from the radio. MARK has just turned on the lights. He is dressed in the same uniform FOSTER wore in ACT ONE.

EMMA is lying across the chairs in reception. The hood of her jacket covers her face.

MARK   Can I help you?

,

MARK approaches EMMA.

                Checking in or picking up?

,

                Hello?

EMMA sits up. She mumbles.

EMMA   I need help.

MARK   What did you say?

She takes off her hood. She is very badly bruised.

EMMA   I said I need help.

MARK recognises her.

MARK   Holy shit.

EMMA   Will you please / help me?

MARK speaks into a handset.

MARK   Doctor to reception please, Doctor to
                reception.

The DOCTOR's consultation room. Night. A desk lamp is on. The DOCTOR sits behind her desk. EMMA sits opposite. She looks very tired. She is bruised and bleeding.

MARK is with them, standing by the door with EMMA's bags.

EMMA   You changed your hair.

                ,

                My name is Sarah. My name is Sarah and
                I'm an alcoholic and drug addict. My life is
                unmanageable. I am willing and motivated
                to change. I need help. I surrender. I
                surrender. I surrender.

                ,

DOCTOR   Sarah, do you know what went wrong last
                time?

                ,

                You tried to control everything. Every part
                of the process. That didn't work so you hit
                the self-destruct button. Addicts control
                everything. They fear chaos. They think
                they're the broken centre of the universe.

                You have to have faith that things aren't
                going to fall apart. Trust the process Sarah.
                Let go.

EMMA   How?

                How do I do that?

                I'm not being difficult or controlling, I really
                want to know.

                I want to try.

                ,

The DOCTOR writes on a prescription pad and puts some pills in a little paper cup.

No.

DOCTOR Take them.

EMMA I came here to get off drugs, not to / take more.

DOCTOR I understand that. But

EMMA I don't want medication. I want to feel it. I need it to be *irrevocable*.

DOCTOR It's completely natural to want to have the most vivid experience because that's what you're used to, that's what you feel you deserve and that's what will make you feel more connected with your recovery. I get that. But going cold turkey is dangerous. It can kill you. There'll be time for guilt and punishment and connection later.

This is the easy part. Don't be stupid.

Take the pills.

The DOCTOR gives EMMA the cup of pills.

Go to your room.

,

EMMA You really do sound like my mother.

The room.

EMMA looks at the meds. She goes into the bathroom. She drops the pills into the toilet. She flushes the chain.

MARK puts EMMA's bags on the bed.

MARK You know the drill right? Need me to go over anything?

EMMA   I can't believe you actually got a job here.

MARK smiles.

MARK   Living the dream.

EMMA   What happened to Foster?

            ,

MARK   Oh, yeah, shit, you don't know.

            Stupid bastard. His um

            his dog died. Went under a motorbike. And
            Foster just

            he took it badly.

EMMA   Relapsed?

MARK   He was really low and they changed his
            antidepressants. The new meds sort of

            knocked him off balance.

            We don't know if he meant to do it.

EMMA   Dead?

            ,

            Shit.

MARK   Yeah.

            Oh, listen, I need you to complete the forms.
            Next of kin. Your Mum? And we'll need to
            arrange for her to visit. Both your parents.

EMMA   No.

MARK   It's important those conversations take place
            here and are mediated / by a

EMMA   I don't want them here. I need them to see
            me back home. Not as a patient.

I know you'll think that's a bad idea.

MARK   It *is* a bad idea. Sarah listen,

A knock on the door. PAUL enters. He looks very different to how he did in ACT ONE.

PAUL   I heard you were here.

He enters the room and walks quickly over to EMMA. She steps back and braces herself. He is going to embrace her but senses that this might be inappropriate.

Welcome back.

,

I'm sorry I wronged you.

It was the bleakest, darkest time in my life. But out of that darkness came a great light and the love of Jesus Christ. He came to me when I most needed him and he spoke to me and told me what I had to do.

,

MARK   Tell her what Jesus told you to do.

PAUL   He told me to drink. He told me to drink until I drowned. He told me to put heroin in my veins and join him in heaven. That Robert and I would be together. That it would be blissful. That he would turn the poison into love in my veins.

EMMA   Okay.

PAUL   And I listened. And I followed him. And he brought me into his church. And I felt something break. And I felt his love. And I know the poison is love and that he is testing me. And I can overcome it.

He smiles at MARK.

We can all overcome it.

He holds EMMA's and MARK's hands in his.

He sent you here. Bless you for your kindness. And bless you Lord. We are three sinners. You watch our paths. You author them. You have given us the gift of desperation.

God, grant me the serenity to accept the things I cannot change,
the courage to change the things I can,
and the wisdom to know the difference.

PAUL/MARK   Amen.

,

PAUL looks at EMMA.

PAUL   You have to say Amen.

EMMA   Why?

MARK   It's like pressing 'Send' on an email.

,

EMMA   Amen.

PAUL grins at them, then leaves.

,

So I see Paul's back.

MARK   Yeah.

They smile at each other. They become aware of being alone together.

,

Right, then. I'll leave you / to it.

EMMA	Mark,
MARK	you're going to be alright. We'll be / monitoring you.
EMMA	My first acting job was a corporate / for this London-based
MARK	I'm not supposed to be alone with you in here. The rules are / pretty strict about
EMMA	I feel like I owe you. Like I owe you
	I don't know,
	a true story.
	,
MARK	What's a 'corporate'?
EMMA	Like a tradeshow thing. Not a play / or a
MARK	right.
EMMA	Advertising, basically. A hall full of little stages. Repeating a terrible monologue to a handful of bored businessmen.

She delivers a bit of the speech, mockingly.

> *Why bring the past into the present? We stand*
> *resolutely in the present, arms wide, looking*
> *towards the future!*

MARK laughs with her.

> I am now!
> You are now!
> We are now!
>
> What a thing it is to be alive! What

She watches as, unseen by MARK, an identically-dressed EMMA
enters slowly, places a chair down and stands behind it.

MARK   are you okay?

EMMA tries to ignore the EMMA.

EMMA   I had to stand in a spotlight and make this
              horrible, generic speech sound *meaningful.*

*Another EMMA enters the room, places a chair down and stands
behind it. There is an ominous rumble, gradually increasing in
volume and pitch.*

              I got a hundred pounds for the day and
              thought I'd hit the big time. Mark, my
              brother, helped me learn my lines.

*Another EMMA. EMMA is trying to concentrate. She grips the
edge of the bed.*

MARK   Sarah,

EMMA   *in a world that sets limits, that says you shouldn't
              try, that says you'll fail...in a world that says 'no',
              'Quixotic' says 'yes'.*

Another EMMA. Gradually, a circle of chairs is being formed.

MARK   Quixotic?

EMMA   Like Don Quixote.

MARK   What, Road Runner?

EMMA   That's Wile E Coyote.

MARK   That's the company name?

EMMA   It means romantic, chivalrous. Visionary.
              Are all your references cartoons? Seriously,
              read a book.

Another EMMA.

              At 'Quixotic' we don't believe in boundaries
              or limitations.

              We believe in the pioneer.

We believe in

in the

The room continues to fill with EMMAs.

MARK   Sarah,

EMMA   sometimes, when you audition, they ask for a classical or a modern speech. And I'd use it as my modern.

EMMA winces. Simultaneously, all the EMMAs stop moving and wince in pain.

My thinking was that if I could make this bullshit marketing speak work, if I can make this list of abstract nouns sound *meaningful* then they'd see how good an actress I am.

EMMA is struggling through, clearly in pain. She is surrounded by a circle of EMMAs.

MARK   Sarah, you don't / owe me

EMMA   Mark learned it before I did. I had to repeat and repeat and repeat. He'd quote it to me. I have a text from him on my phone saying: *what a thing it is to be alive. What a thing it is to swim in the sea. To look up at the*

She winces again. All the EMMAs wince then, one-by-one, start to fall down.

and it's gone. He's gone. I can't get remember it. I can't get through it on my own. I can't. I can't. I can't.

The low, rumbling sound is starting to shake the walls. EMMA cries out in pain and collapses.

MARK   Sarah,

did you take your medication?

One by one, the EMMAs begin to stand.

> Sarah can you hear me?

The lights are changing. MARK's voice sounds increasingly like it's under water. He moves to where she just was and addresses one of the other EMMAs, who has collapsed and has lost consciousness.

> Sarah?

> Sarah?

EMMA watches MARK tend to the unconscious EMMA, she has stepped outside herself.

> Look at me.

> Sarah?

He leaves the room.

EMMA walks around, looking at the other EMMAs. She is no longer in the bedroom. The light is eerie, unreal. The sound has ceased. Her movements around the room echo as if in a dream.

She sees that there is an unoccupied chair. She crosses the room and stands in front of it, completing the circle.

A moment. Then the EMMAs leave.

The sun rises. EMMA looks around. She's in the Group Therapy room before anyone else. MARK enters.

MARK   You're early.

EMMA   I'd like to practise.

The GROUP enter the room and take their seats. EMMA speaks to the THERAPIST.

> I'd like to practise.

THERAPIST   Go ahead Sarah.

EMMA stands in the centre, looking around the room at the members of the GROUP.

EMMA   You're my father.

She takes PAUL's hands, stands him and leads him across the room.

              You're hovering in the doorway. Which is
              sort of

              here.

She places him.

THERAPIST   Where are we?

EMMA   This is my old bedroom at my parent's
              house. It's like a museum to my childhood
              self. The bed is here.

She pulls some chairs in a line to make the bed.

              The door is there. There's all this stuff
              piled up everywhere because they use it for
              storage now.

She looks at MARK.

              You're my brother.

THERAPIST   Sarah, we're practising for the future, not re-
              enacting

EMMA   you're my brother. You're Mark. You died
              almost two years ago. Your bedroom is next
              to this one. When we were kids you used to
              hear me crying sometimes and you'd come
              in and we'd sit on the bed in silence and
              you'd hold my hand until I stopped and then
              you'd go back to your room and I'll always
              love you for that even though you're gone,
              even when I'm gone those moments were,
              are, will be *meaningful.*

              All I need you to do is sit with me and hold
              my hand without speaking okay?

MARK nods and takes her hand.

,

She looks at the THERAPIST.

You're my mother.

THERAPIST   I don't participate in / the

EMMA   you won't have to do much. Trust me.

THERAPIST   Sarah, really, it doesn't

The GROUP encourage her, cheerfully.

okay fine but

EMMA   you're standing over there.

EMMA points and the THERAPIST moves to the spot.

I've called you in. You hate being in here.
You want to be watching your programmes.

PAUL   What am I like?

EMMA   You're uncomfortable being in here. You
hate any kind of confrontation or emotional
display. You feel you never really got to
know me because I had different interests to
you and that made no sense. You're insecure
about your intellect because you know that
your wife and daughter are cleverer than you
are. You loved Mark because you understood
him. You've been unable to help me, and
you're angry that what you hoped my life
would be like is not at all what it has been.
You've been downstairs using the kitchen
table for your genealogy charts. You've been
doing this for at least ten years. We've not
eaten at that table for a decade. You don't
want to talk about my problems and you
don't want to talk about Mark's death.

She looks at the THERAPIST.

Mum, you're frustrated with me. You had hardship in your life and you never abused drugs and alcohol. You can drink wine and re-cork the bottle for another day. You don't know why I can't do the same. Your father died when you were five, your mother when you were eleven. You were moved around a lot and you triumphed in spite of everything. You have a doctorate. Lots of framed qualifications. You created an international fund to provide support for children in times of crisis. You used to play piano but you haven't for years. You think acting is a fun hobby and isn't worthy of your child. You've never approved of a single boyfriend or career choice and you've never said anything to stop me.

I've just got home.

She and MARK sit on the 'bed'.

,

Okay. Yeah, okay.

,

THERAPIST   Three,

two,

one,

,

EMMA   Mum, Dad, this shouldn't take long. I want to talk you through what has been happening with me, to let you know where I'm at now and to apologise for my behaviour.

But I don't want to do it in that order. I want to apologise first.

She looks at the THERAPIST to see if that's okay. The THERAPIST nods.

> I've been a pretty terrible daughter over the years.
>
> I've been unhappy and self-destructive. I've self-medicated with drugs and alcohol which has made me more insular and self-absorbed. I've made some terrible decisions and I've taken you for granted. I've broken promises. Many many times. I've stolen from you. I've said some
>
> I've said things that I regret and that I wish I could take back. Someone would've interrupted me by now.

THERAPIST   To say what?

EMMA   To disagree with me. To get defensive or

THERAPIST   don't pre-empt. You may be surprised how people react when you give them absolute honesty. They may welcome it.

EMMA   I'd be really fucking surprised.

> ,
>
> I wasn't there for either of you when Mark
>
> when Mark died. I disappeared and it must have put even more stress on you and that was selfish and unthinking. I'm not asking for forgiveness. I'm acknowledging that I was wrong and that I wish I could take it back. I miss him.

She's finding this very difficult, but cathartic.

> I miss him.
>
> I know you do too.

,

> I know that over the years I've scared you.
> Disappointed you.
>
> Wow this is really hard.

PAUL wants to go to her but doesn't. MARK takes EMMA's hand in both of his and rests his forehead on her shoulder.

,

> I want you to know that I've worked really
> hard at getting better. And I'm starting to
> find peace. And it's an on-going process.
> Because I've scared myself. I've disappointed
> myself. And the hardest part is taking myself
> seriously enough to do it. Feeling that my
> happiness is worth fighting for. My life. And
> I'm doing it for you two as much as anything.
> And for Mark.
>
> And it should have been me. Not him. I
> know that. Everyone's been waiting for it. It's
> not fair. And I can't forgive myself / for it.

PAUL   It's not your fault.

EMMA   I'm not

PAUL   Mark's death was not your fault.

EMMA   It's not fair.

PAUL   We love you. We always love you. We'll do
        anything you need.

,

EMMA is trying not to cry.

EMMA   Thank you.

        He'd never say that.

	But thank you.
PAUL	It's alright darling.
EMMA	He wouldn't say that either.
PAUL	Oh.
EMMA	He'd say 'uh huh. Well'.
	Like that.
	,
PAUL	Uh huh.
	Well.
	,
THERAPIST	And what would your mother say?
	,
EMMA	Who the fuck knows?
	,
THERAPIST	How do you feel?
	,

EMMA looks at the THERAPIST.

EMMA	Who are you being?
	,
THERAPIST	Me.
	,
EMMA	I feel like
	,
	I feel like I spent my life surrounded by people trying to make me miserable. And

I'm slowly realising that every last one of them was probably just trying to help me. They probably just

loved me.

,

THERAPIST   You're doing great Sarah.

,

EMMA looks up at the THERAPIST.

EMMA   Thank you.

The GROUP take their chairs away.

The room.

MARK is there, holding a piece of paper.

At 'Quixotic' we don't believe in boundaries or limitations.

We believe in the pioneer.

We believe in the

,

yes?

MARK   Visionary.

EMMA   Visionary visionary visionary.

However impulsive or impractical.

We say '*yes.*' We say that life is

,

MARK   for the living.

EMMA   Don't help me.

MARK hands the paper back to EMMA. He knows it word-for-word.

MARK   We look at the world with *joy*.

                    With *love*.

                    We look at the world with wonder.

                    ,

EMMA   It's so totally meaningless isn't it?

MARK   Not to me. I'm a sucker for a vague slogan. Adverts. Politicians. AA.

                    Wage a war on an abstract noun, I'm right behind you.

                    And not to be all Dalai Lama or John Lennon about it but that's what it's all about. *Love*. It sounds dumb,

EMMA   yep.

MARK   But it's true. You said it yourself. The hardest thing is to love yourself. To be kind to yourself. After everything.

                    ,

EMMA   *Quixotic Limited.* They're probably the only people who'll hire me now.

MARK   What? Go back to doing tradeshows?

EMMA   Why do you think I'm trying to learn it?

                    Do you have any cigarettes?

MARK   You can't smoke in here.

EMMA laughs.

EMMA   Right.

                    Wait, are you serious?

MARK	It's a medical building so
EMMA	right, of course, yeah.
MARK	You had it yet?
EMMA	What?
MARK	Your spiritual awakening.
	You can't leave without having your spiritual awakening. It's, like, in the rules.
EMMA	I don't think that'll happen for me.
MARK	Don't be so sure. If God's going to appear anywhere it'll be here. He may be coming for someone else, but I'll get in on it. One day I'll be mopping up after a messy stomach pump and there he'll be. Smiling down. And he'll say: 'well done, that's it. Go out into the world and don't harm yourself or others. Go visit Sarah. She's doing a play above a pub.'
EMMA	God watches my plays?
MARK	He prefers the more fringy stuff.
EMMA	I thought you were an atheist.
MARK	I'm open to possibilities. I'd welcome fucking Poseidon if that's who shows up.

They smile.

'

EMMA	I already have my higher power. And she very much exists.
MARK	Don't bank your recovery on other people.
EMMA	Last time I spoke to her she was clearing out my flat. Putting everything bad into a big plastic box. All the bottles and bags of

	powder. Pots of pills. My stash of weed. All piled in this box.
MARK	Sounds like a great box.
EMMA	I can't stop thinking about it.
	,
MARK	I've got nobody to do that for me.
	It's wonderful.
EMMA	She'd be the one getting the phone call. The police at the door. 3 A.M.
MARK	That'd be my ex-wife.
EMMA	Do they wake you up do you think or do they wait for morning?
	Did Foster have anyone?
MARK	Just his dog I think.
	And us.

MARK and EMMA look at each other.

	,
EMMA	I need to hear her say that she's proud of me. I know that sounds stupid.
MARK	It *is* stupid.
EMMA	Or not even proud. I just want her to see that I've changed. If I hear it from *her*
	then I think I'll be able to put things to an end.
MARK	surrendered.
EMMA	I don't know. Maybe.
	No.

443

I came to a realisation. Paul said it once.

This is all bullshit. None of it's real.

When I'm on stage I know it's all pretend.
I'm not the person I'm pretending to be.
Everyone else knows that. But somehow it
doesn't matter. We all just sort of

decide

that it's real.

It's the same with the programme. With
everything, really. Language. Politics. Money.
Religion. Law. At some level we all know it's
all bullshit. A magical group delusion.

MARK   Right, yeah, no you've lost me.

EMMA   Wile E Coyote only ever falls when he looks
            down. He runs off the cliff and just keeps
            running in mid-air. It's only when he looks
            down and sees that he should be falling that
            gravity kicks in.

            That's my spiritual awakening.

            Don't look down.

MARK   Don't look down.

            ,

EMMA   I'm not ready.

MARK   None of us are.

EMMA   But you get to stay.

MARK   Maybe. Funding's always a bit

EMMA   yeah, of course.

MARK moves to leave but then stops in the doorway.

MARK   I hope he does show up tonight.

EMMA   Who?

                ,

MARK   God.

He flicks the light off. EMMA is lit by the bedside lamp and the streetlight coming through the window.

,

Slowly, EMMA looks up at the ceiling.

,

She kneels.

,

EMMA   Come on then.

                Show yourself.

                I'm ready if you are.

,

Silence. Stillness.

                Yeah. That's what I thought.

,

Morning breaks. The Group Therapy room. EMMA begins to stack the chairs.

DOCTOR   Here.

The DOCTOR hands EMMA a book.

EMMA   What's this?

DOCTOR   Foucault.

                I made a few corrections.

It's all very interesting but I'm not sure if it's particularly applicable to

life.

And I watched The Exorcist.

'Your mother sucks cocks in hell!'

EMMA laughs. She opens the book and finds an envelope inside.

EMMA   What's this?

DOCTOR   A letter from me saying that, in my opinion, you're not a risk to future employers.

,

EMMA   What am I going to do?

DOCTOR   Go to meetings. Ninety meetings / in ninety

EMMA   in ninety days. I will. But I mean

EMMA looks at the paper.

what am I supposed to do now? With my life. How do I go back to normal? How do I walk out on stage after this? If I ever go into an audition again it'll be like climbing fucking Everest.

I thought I might train as a therapist. Like Lydia. Then I thought: maybe I just want to *play the part* of a therapist.

First day of rehearsal is always the same. You sit in a circle of chairs, just like in Group. You introduce yourself one by one, just like in Group. You say, *hello I'm whoever and I'm playing the role of whatever.* There's something about that situation I can't quite

I just can't separate the two circles of chairs. If you see what I mean.

DOCTOR   Don't overthink it.

EMMA   I want to continue to be honest.

,

DOCTOR   Do I still look like your mother?

,

EMMA smiles at the DOCTOR. She smiles back.

,

Happy graduation.

,

EMMA   Thank you.

The GROUP assemble in the room. The DOCTOR is now the THERAPIST.

THERAPIST   Today we say goodbye to someone who has been a challenging, inspiring and important member of the Group.

Sarah, we're proud of you. I'm proud of you. Of the work you've done here. I want you to be proud of that work too and to understand that it doesn't stop here. But you only have to do one day at a time.

General sounds of support from the GROUP.

We wish you success, happiness and peace. And please understand what I mean when I say I hope I never see you again.

PAUL   Don't come back.

Don't come back.

EMMA smiles and embraces PAUL.

The GROUP gathers around EMMA and begin to chant. She shakes hands with some and embraces others.

GROUP   Don't come back.

Don't come back.

Don't come back.

Don't come back.

Don't come back.

EMMA is handed her coat which she puts on.

EMMA picks up her bags. She stands in the doorway and looks back at the GROUP.

She shakes hands with the THERAPIST.

MARK hugs her as the GROUP disperses. He gives her a scroll, tied with a ribbon.

MARK   Don't look down.

He leaves.

EMMA stands alone with in the doorway of her childhood room. It has been preserved as she left it as a teenager. Different times and tastes collide. There are fluffy toys and teddy bears, piles of books and stacks of cassette tapes. There is a Nirvana poster. The room has also been used for storage, it is cluttered with boxes of photographs, books etc.

There is something more 'real' about this room, more detail somehow.

Her DAD enters, carrying her bags.

DAD   This it?

EMMA   Sorry?

DAD   Everything? This everything?

EMMA   Yes.

DAD	Travelling light.
EMMA	Yes.
DAD	Uh huh. Well.
EMMA	Would you get Mum?
DAD	Get her?
EMMA	Would you bring her up here?
DAD	Now?
EMMA	Yes.

,

DAD   Um,

uh huh, okay.

,

He smiles at her.

Glad you're home.

She smiles back, sadly. He leaves.

EMMA looks around. She picks up a copy of today's newspaper from her pillow. She looks at the front page.

She mutters to herself.

EMMA   In a world that sets limits, that says you shouldn't try, that you will fail, in a world that says 'no', 'Quixotic' says 'yes'.

,

She puts down the paper. She picks up a cuddly toy.

Her DAD returns.

DAD	She's just coming.
EMMA	I can't believe you kept all these things Dad.

She looks at the toy in her hands.

> I probably won't have kids now. Probably for the best. With Mark dead that's the end of the line isn't it? That story's done. You'll be able to finish your family tree.
>
> The end of history.
>
> ,

DAD   Uh huh.

EMMA   Dad, shit, sorry that

             I didn't mean it to sound like

EMMA's MUM enters. It is the same actress who played the DOCTOR/ THERAPIST. Her DAD continues to loiter by the door.

MUM   you wanted me?

EMMA   Yes. Right. Okay.
             So,

EMMA sits down on the bed.

> this shouldn't take long. I want to
> I wanted to talk with you both and

MUM   here it comes.

EMMA   It's not
             please, I just want the chance

MUM   don't say we haven't given you / chances.

EMMA   I'm not I'm

MUM   you steal from us, you go missing, we thought / you were dead.

DAD   Let her speak.

MUM   I will not be made the villain in this.

EMMA   I know I've been a pretty terrible daughter /
                over the years.

MUM   Have we ever said that? I've never said that.

EMMA   Will you please

                this is hard for

                I'd just

                ,

                I've been unhappy and self-destructive. I've
                self-medicated with drugs and alcohol which
                has made me more insular and self-absorbed.
                I've made some terrible decisions and I've
                taken you for granted. I've said things that
                I regret and that I wish I could take back. I
                wasn't there for either of you when

                I wasn't there when Mark died.

                I was wrong and I wish I could take it back.

                I want you to know I've worked really hard
                at getting better. And I'm starting to find
                peace. And it's an on-going process. Because
                I've scared myself. I've disappointed myself.
                And I'm doing it for you two as much as
                anything. And for Mark. And it should have
                been / me.

DAD   Alright enough.

He speaks calmly.

                Look, whatever you're into now,

                all of this is just words. You're saying you'll
                be less selfish and then talking about yourself
                even more. I can't listen to it. The number
                of times we've tried to help you. Tried to
                save your life. The energy it's taken. The

451

sleeplessness. The money. Every time the phone rang or the doorbell we thought it would be the police. We neglected Mark. He should still be here. You're right. It should be you. It should be you that we buried. At least we'd know you were out of trouble.

We grieved for you long ago. So, thank you for your little speech but it doesn't mean anything. We've heard it before. The damage in this family is not going to be fixed by a pretty story.

Get a job. Keep the job. Call us once in a while. Just to chat. Not to borrow money or to ask for help. Because you're interested in us. Get out of yourself.

I'm sorry. There's a lot been unsaid for a long time.

,

EMMA   I love you Dad. Thank you.

,

DAD   I love you too darling. It's just really hard.

EMMA   I'm going to try to make it easier.

,

DAD   I've got

I'm in the middle of something.

I'll order us a take out later yes?

EMMA   Yeah.

DAD   Uh huh. Right.

Well.

,

He leaves.

EMMA clenches her fist, as if squeezing an invisible hand.

She looks at her MUM.

,

EMMA   He's right.

MUM   Yes, he is.

              You staying the night?

EMMA   I was thinking I'd stay for a while actually.

,

MUM   It's your home.

EMMA feels a sudden wave of emotion and tries hard not to show it.

,

EMMA   I've worked really hard Mum.

,

              I've taken myself apart and put myself back
              together.

              If you could see what I went through

              I think you'd be proud of me.

,

EMMA doesn't get the response she wants. She smiles to herself, sadly and takes a deep breath in and out.

              They tell you, in rehab they tell you: avoid
              people who make you want to relapse. Places
              you associate with using and objects that
              might be a trigger.

People, places and things. That's basically,
you know,

everything.

As long as you steer clear of people, places
and things you'll be fine.

,

Some places, some people, are more
dangerous to be around than others.

MUM   And you want to hibernate here until you
feel safe to face them.

EMMA   No, no that's not

,

EMMA looks to her MUM.

this is the place Mum. This is the most
dangerous place I can be. This town. This
house. All this *stuff.*

You.

You are the biggest threat to me relapsing.

If I can be with you, here, at a time when
I'm defenceless and vulnerable, if I can get
through this then I'll know, *definitively*, that
I'm okay. Forever.

,

Are you going to say something Mum?

Dad obviously needed to.

I'm saying some pretty horrible things.

Why are you smiling?

,

MUM	Who are you being?

Her MUM is unemotional, matter-of-fact.

EMMA	What?
MUM	I know you sweetheart. You think I can't see when you're lying.
EMMA	I'm not lying.
MUM	That time I caught you smoking and you sat right there and / swore blind, tears rolling down your cheeks
EMMA	I was a kid! I was just a *kid* Mum.
MUM	And you only smoked to pretend you were interesting. Because, unlike Mark, you never had a personality of your own.
EMMA	Don't say that.
MUM	You think you're this chameleon, living hundreds of lives but you're always just you. Full of certainty when you discover something but you never see it through and this will be no different.
EMMA	That's not true.
MUM	We've still got your violin somewhere.
EMMA	I can't believe / you'd still hold that against me.
MUM	Insisted on having a good one and then quit lessons within half a year. Tennis gear the same. Pets. Moved school three times. Quit university four times. Evening classes. Fad diets. Exercise crazes. Just once I would like to have seen you graduate.
EMMA	I did.

MUM   You'll just have to excuse us if we / see this
       latest lifestyle decision within the context of a
       thousand abandoned projects.

EMMA   I do excuse you. Lifestyle decision?

MUM   It doesn't suit you darling. The self-righteous,
       pleasure-denying role. It's boring. If you
       want honesty, real, no bullshit, gloves-off
       truthfulness sweetheart, drink and drugs were
       the only things that made you any fun.

       And now you want closure or whatever they
       call it in this new cult of yours, you want to
       say sorry and for that to heal wounds and
       make us a happy clappy family and that's
       just not going to happen. The family is
       broken. Forever.

EMMA   I'm trying my best Mum.

       I really am.

MUM   Okay good. Just don't expect a fucking
       trophy for trying your best. That's the bare
       minimum you should be doing.

       ,

EMMA takes her MUM's hand. Her MUM doesn't resist.

       ,

       Approaching forty and back living with your
       parents.

EMMA   I'm not approaching forty.

MUM   Sweetheart, the one person you can't fool
       about your age is the person whose body you
       came out of.

       ,

EMMA smiles. Her MUM lets go of EMMA's hand, and walks to the door.

	I changed the bedding.
EMMA	Thank you.
MUM	Towels are in / the
EMMA	yeah.
MUM	I brought the things over from your flat.
EMMA	What things?
MUM	I picked up the things you asked me to.
	Boxed it all up and brought it here.
	,
EMMA	It's *here*?
MUM	Yes.
EMMA	Where?
MUM	Under the bed.

,

EMMA reaches under the bed and pulls out a large clear plastic box full of pills, bottles of alcohol and various drug paraphernalia.

EMMA	Holy shit.
MUM	Look what you were doing to yourself.

EMMA pushes the box across the floor away from her. She stares at it.

EMMA	Why would you bring this here?
MUM	What was I supposed to do? Every time I've tried to intervene you've punished me. You broke my fingers when I flushed those pills.
EMMA	I broke your fingers?

457

MUM	Why do you think I don't play piano anymore?
EMMA	Mum,
MUM	you want to get rid of this stuff go ahead. If you want to use it then take it and go. But don't come back to us if you do. We've had too much Lucy.

,

Her MUM stops in the doorway and turns back.

It's a new Chinese take-away that's opened on the corner. He's been waiting for a reason to try it out.

,

EMMA	Mum, please don't leave me with

Her MUM leaves.

,

EMMA walks to the door.

She closes the door.

She leans against it and looks at the box on the floor.

She rubs her face, runs her fingers through her hair.

She walks back to the box and takes the lid off it. She is breathing heavily.

She takes her phone out and calls a number.

hi yes hello

I was given your number by

yes hi, that's me.

I was hoping there might be a meeting this evening and maybe

> great, yes I've got a pen.

She finds a pen, a fluffy-ended child's pen, and writes an address on her hand.

> Thank you. Thank you.

She hangs up the phone. She tries to steady her breath.

,

She puts a jacket on. She heads for the door but stops.

,

She slowly turns back to the box.

She mutters her lines to herself.

> Why choose 'Quixotic'?
>
> In a world that sets limits, that says you shouldn't try, that you will fail, in a world that says 'no', we say 'yes'.
>
> We say 'yes'.

She approaches the box.

> We don't believe in 'no'.
>
> 'No'. 'No'. 'No'. 'No'.

EMMA kneels down by the box.

> Why choose 'Quixotic'?
>
> why why why why?

She tries not to cry. She stretches her face and tries to grin.

> In a world that sets limits, that says you shouldn't try, that you will fail, in a world that says 'no', we say 'yes'.
>
> We don't believe in 'no'.

,

459

She speaks with more volume, more confidence.

> We don't believe in boundaries or
> limitations.

> We believe in the pioneer.
> We believe in the visionary.
> However impulsive or impractical.

> We say 'yes'.

Gradually, the lights in the room are falling and a spotlight is emerging on EMMA.

> We say that life is for the living.
> We look at the world with *joy.*

> With *love.*

> We look at the world with wonder.

EMMA gradually speaks more naturally, more sincerely. She really means what she says.

> Why bring the past into the present?
> We stand resolutely in the present,
> arms wide,
> looking towards the future.

> I am now.
> You are now.
> We are now.

EMMA stands up into the tight, bright spotlight. The rest of the stage is in darkness. She is compelling, moving, in her element.

> What a thing it is to be alive.
> What a thing it is to swim in the sea.
> To look up at the wide clear sky.
> To feel the sun on your skin.
> To climb a mountain or just a flight of stairs.
> To eat a donut.

> To love and be loved.
> What a thing it is.
>
> I am now.
>
> You are now.
>
> We are now.
>
> This is the beginning.
>
> ,

She squints into the darkness.

> ,

> Was that okay? I could go again on that if
> you'd like. I can do better.
>
> ,

> Hello?

A man's VOICE from the darkness, amplified.

VOICE   Thank you.

> ,

EMMA   Right.

She looks around. She is no longer in her bedroom, she is now standing on a bare stage. At the back of the stage is a queue of ACTRESSES, all the same age and demographic as EMMA. Some of them are stretching their facial muscles or shaking their limbs loose, some of them hold pieces of paper and silently practise their lines.

> Yes, okay.
>
> ,

She smiles into the darkness.

> ,

Thank you for seeing me.

,

*EMMA leaves the spotlight, passing the ACTRESSES as she goes.
She leaves the stage.*

*Another ACTRESS, perhaps the UNDERSTUDY, enters the spotlight.
She steadies her breath and begins.*

ACTRESS   Why

Blackout, cutting the ACTRESS off mid-sentence.

END